Psychoanalysis and Projective Methods in Personality Assessment

Psychoanalysis and Projective Methods in Personality Assessment

The French School

Benoît Verdon & Catherine Azoulay (Eds.)

hogrefe

Library of Congress Cataloging in Publication information for the print version of this book is available via the Library of Congress Marc Database under the LC Control Number [2019945788]

Library and Archives Canada Cataloguing in Publication
Title: Psychoanalysis and projective methods in personality assessment : the French school / Benoît Verdon & Catherine Azoulay (eds.).

Names: Verdon, Benoît, editor. | Azoulay, Catherine, editor.
Description: Includes bibliographical references.

Identifiers: Canadiana (print) 20190156023 | Canadiana (ebook) 20190156031 | ISBN 9780889375574 (softcover) | ISBN 9781616765576 (PDF) | ISBN 9781613345573 (EPUB)
Subjects: LCSH: Projective techniques. | LCSH: Rorschach Test. | LCSH: Thematic Apperception Test.

Classification: LCC BF698.7 .P79 2019 | DDC 155.2/84—dc23

www.hogrefe.com

PUBLISHING OFFICES
USA: Hogrefe Publishing Corporation, 7 Bulfinch Place, Suite 202, Boston, MA 02114
Phone (866) 823-4726, Fax (617) 354-6875; E-mail customerservice@hogrefe.com
EUROPE: Hogrefe Publishing GmbH, Merkelstr. 3, 37085 Göttingen, Germany
Phone +49 551 99950-0, Fax +49 551 99950-111; E-mail publishing@hogrefe.com
SALES & DISTRIBUTION
USA: Hogrefe Publishing, Customer Services Department,
30 Amberwood Parkway, Ashland, OH 44805
Phone (800) 228-3749, Fax (419) 281-6883; E-mail customerservice@hogrefe.com
UK: Hogrefe Publishing, c/o Marston Book Services Ltd., 160 Eastern Ave., Milton Park, Abingdon, OX14 4SB, UK
Phone +44 1235 465577, Fax +44 1235 465556; E-mail direct.orders@marston.co.uk
EUROPE: Hogrefe Publishing, Merkelstr. 3, 37085 Göttingen, Germany
Phone +49 551 99950-0, Fax +49 551 99950-111; E-mail publishing@hogrefe.com
OTHER OFFICES
CANADA: Hogrefe Publishing, 660 Eglinton Ave. East, Suite 119-514, Toronto, Ontario, M4G 2K2
SWITZERLAND: Hogrefe Publishing, Länggass-Strasse 76, 3012 Bern

Printed and bound in the Czech Republic

ISBN 978-0-88937-557-4 (print) • ISBN 978-0-61676-557-6 (PDF) • ISBN 978-0-61334-557-3 (EPUB)
http://doi.org/10.1027/00557-000

Contents

About the Editors

Benoît Verdon, PhD, is a clinical psychologist, psychoanalyst, professor of clinical psychology and psychopathology at the Université de Paris, assistant director of the research laboratory Psychologie Clinique, Psychopathologie, Psychanalyse (PCPP; Clinical Psychology, Psychopathology, and Psychoanalysis), and past president of the French Language Society of the Rorschach and Projective Methods. Verdon is also a past publication director of the journal *Psychologie clinique et projective*. He is also leader of the young adult and adult program of the university diploma in projective psychology (DUPP) and member-at-large of the Board of the International Society of the Rorschach and Projective Methods. E-mail: benoit.verdon@parisdescartes.fr

Catherine Azoulay, PhD, is a clinical psychologist, psychoanalyst, professor of clinical psychology and psychopathology at the Université de Paris, and a member of the PCPP. She is also a past editor-in-chief of the journal *Psychologie clinique et projective* and past copresident of the International Network of Research: Projective Methods and Psychoanalysis. Further, she is director of the university diploma program in projective psychology and director of the Projective Psychology Seminar in Paris. E-mail: catherine.b.azoulay@gmail.com

About the Authors

Marie-Frédérique Bacqué, PhD, is a professor of clinical psychopathology at the University of Strasbourg, France, and head of the research unit Subjectivity, Social Ties, and Modernity (SuLiSoM). She is the editor-in-chief of *Psycho-Oncologie* and *Études sur la Mort* as well as author or editor of thirteen books, some of which were translated into German, Greek, and Japanese. She is a trained psychoanalyst and member of the Fédération Européenne de Psychanalyse (FEDEPSY). E-mail: bacque@unistra.fr

Monika Boekholt, PhD, is a clinical psychologist and was a professor of clinical psychology and psychopathology at University Paris 13. She was editor-in-chief of the first four issues of the journal *Psychologie et projective*, published in 1995 and 1996.

Catherine Chabert, PhD, is professor emeritus at the Université de Paris and a member of the research laboratory PCPP. She is also a trainer–analyst (APF, French Psychoanalytic Association, International Psychoanalytical Association) and series editor of the works *Psychoanalysis and Psychopathology* and *Psychopathology and Projective Methods* (published by Dunod Editions). She also supervises book series (with Jacques André) in the Petite Bibliothèque de Psychanalyse (Small Library of Psychoanalysis), published by Presses Universitaires de France. She has been vice-president of the French Language Society of the Rorschach and Projective Methods and is now honorary president. E-mail: catherine@chabert.org

Jean-Yves Chagnon, PhD, is a professor of clinical psychology and psychopathology at University Paris 13 and editor-in-chief of the journal *Psychologie clinique et projective*. He used to be copresident of the International Network of Research: Projective Methods and Psychoanalysis. E-mail: chagnon@univ-paris13.fr

Michèle Emmanuelli, PhD, is a clinical psychologist and psychoanalyst at the Société Psychanalytique de Paris (IPA) and is professor emeritus of clinical psychology and psychopathology at the Université de Paris and a member of the research laboratory PCPP. She is a former president of the French Language Society of the Rorschach and Projective Methods. E-mail: michele.emmanuelli@wanadoo.fr

Estelle Louët, PhD, is a clinical psychologist and psychoanalyst in the Department of Child and Adolescent Psychiatry at the Pitié-Salpétrière Hospital in Paris (APHP). She is also an associate professor of clinical psychology and psychopathology in the research laboratory PCPP of the Université de Paris. E-mail: estelle-louet@parisdescartes.fr

Françoise Neau, PhD, is a clinical psychologist and psychoanalyst, and a professor of clinical psychology and psychopathology at the research laboratory PCPP of the Université de Paris. E-mail: fr.neau@free.fr

Marie-Christine Pheulpin, PhD, is a clinical psychologist and psychoanalyst. She is an assistant professor at University Paris 13 and qualified to supervise research in clinical psychology and psychopathology. E-mail: mcpheulpin@yahoo.fr

Pascal Roman, PhD, is a psychologist and psychotherapist with an analytical orientation, and a full professor of clinical psychology, psychopathology, and psychoanalysis at Lausanne University in Switzerland. He used to be general secretary of the International Society of the Rorschach and Projective Methods (ISR); he is now a member-at-large of the ISR Board as well as president of the French Language Society of the Rorschach and Projective Methods. He is also publication director of the journal *Psychologie clinique et projective*. E-mail: pascal.roman@unil.ch

Claude de Tychey, PhD, is professor emeritus of clinical psychology and was director of the GR3P (Clinical and Projective Psychopathological Research Group, Prevention Research Axis) at the Interpsy Laboratory of the University of Lorraine, France. He used to be vice-president of the French Language Society of the Rorschach and Projective Methods and member-at-large of the Board of the International Society of the Rorschach and Projective Methods. E-mail: claude.de-tychey@univ-lorraine.fr

Sarah Vibert, PhD, is a clinical psychologist, an assistant professor of clinical psychology and psychopathology at the Université de Paris, and a member of the research laboratory PCPP. E-mail: sarahvibert@yahoo.fr

Catherine Weismann-Arcache, PhD, is a clinical psychologist, assistant professor, and thesis director of clinical psychology and psychopathology at the University of Rouen, France. E-mail: c.weismann-arcache@wanadoo.fr

Preface

Benoît Verdon & Catherine Azoulay

We have designed this book with the idea of providing our colleagues around the world with access to the work of the projective clinicians and researchers of the *French School* (also called the Paris School), which until now has been published almost exclusively in French. Although several articles have been published in various English-language journals, such as *Rorschachiana*, this is the first time that a book of this scale has been fully published in English.

The rapid expansion of the French School is closely linked to the creation of the Groupement Français du Rorschach (French Group of Rorschach; https://www.societerorschach.org/historique/) in March 1950, under the patronage of a number of distinguished personalities from the worlds of psychology, medicine, and philosophy, such as Profs. Henri Baruk, Jean Dechaume, Jean Delay, Paul Fraisse, Georges Heuyer, Maurice Merleau-Ponty, Henri Piéron, and Henri Wallon. This first society was chaired by Daniel Lagache (1903–1972), a highly regarded French psychoanalyst, who particularly stressed the fact that the psychoanalytic interpretation of the Rorschach and projective methods cannot be reduced to a symbolic interpretation of the unconscious through the contents of the responses, and that formal aspects of tests must also be qualitatively analyzed. Since then, the French School has been consistent in this methodological interpretation of the Rorschach that values a system of coding, comparing the collected data with general population norms, and developing clinical hypotheses that are put into practice through a rigorously codified qualitative analysis, articulated together with the analysis of the protocol text. Vica Shentoub and Rosine Debray, clinical psychologists and lecturers in psychology at the Université René Descartes in Paris (now the Université de Paris), applied this approach to the Thematic Apperception Test (TAT) by developing the TAT scoring grid, the first version of which dates from 1958. This present work provides insight into the French School analysis approach and for greater clarity, a method for interpreting the Rorschach and the TAT (Appendix 1), as well as the latent solicitations of the TAT Picture Cards (Appendix 2) and the current TAT Scoring Grid (Appendix 3).

In keeping with the views of Daniel Lagache, Didier Anzieu (1923–1999) was interested in regression and projection in projective tests, as well as convergences and divergences between psychoanalytical practice and projective testing, which he called the *projective situation*. Moreover, he initiated the Projective Techniques in Education program at French universities. In 1964, he worked with Nina Rausch de Traubenberg (1920–2013), giving her the mission to create the Certificate of Projective Techniques (today: diploma in projective psychology, DUPP) at the Sorbonne, which was a great success, with 800 students enrolling each year in the 1970s and 1980s.

With her rich experience of international exchanges, Rausch de Traubenberg, a clinical psychologist at the Hôpital de la Salpêtrière in Paris, then a professor of psychology at the René Descartes University, gave real momentum to research on projective methods and published widely. For over 30 years, supported by a team of psychologists and researchers who were as passionate as she was, Rausch de Traubenberg was a leading figure in projective psychology in France. Among her innumerable works, her book *La Pratique du Rorschach* (The Practice of the Rorschach Test) is now in its ninth edition with Presses Universitaires de France, and her elaborations on the Rorschach Test, between perception and fantasy and the grids of self-representation and affective dynamics, are still in publication.

Nina Rausch de Traubenberg was always careful to pay tribute to Roy Schafer and his work, most of which was compiled in his book *Psychoanalytic Interpretation in Rorschach Testing,* published in 1954 in New York by Grune and Stratton. She considered him to be her greatest inspiration, although she regularly made reference to other American psychologists, such as David Rapaport, Bruno Klopfer, Ernest Schachtel, and David Shapiro, whom she considered to be the other important pioneers in the field. Rausch de Traubenberg was president of the International Society of the Rorschach and Projective Methods (ISR) from 1987 to 1990 and executive editor of the *Bulletin du Rorschach et des Méthodes Projectives* for many years (which became the journal *Psychologie Clinique et Projective* in 1995). She also organized, with great success, the ISR congress in Paris in July 1990.

Concurrently with Rausch de Traubenberg for the Rorschach, Vica Shentoub and Rosine Debray developed a theory of the TAT process as well as a methodology for its interpretation. Practitioners had progressively abandoned this personality test, which was developed by Henry A. Murray in the US in 1935, because the direct interpretation of the contents of the discourse had not proven to be convincing. Building on various American authors such as Leopold Bellak, Roy Schafer, and Robert Holt, Vica Shentoub and Rosine Debray differentiated and identified manifest contents and latent solicitations in 18 cards (out of the 31 cards initially proposed by Murray) and revealed the primacy of the analysis of the form of discourse, from which they developed a grid for the analysis of discourse processes: *how they spoke about themselves* relativizes *what was said.*

The scoring grid for the processes of elaboration of discourse was thus designed to note the mental mechanisms that are close to defense mechanisms and that are expressed through the discourse within the TAT narratives. By showing the clinical relevance, this methodological tool rapidly became the equivalent of the Rorschach psychogram: the quantitative dimension of the collection of processes on the scoring grid involving a qualitative interpretation according to the defensive weight of the mechanisms that are mobilized. With the theoretical and clinical developments over the last 50 years, many modifications have been made to the TAT scoring grid. It is now in its eighth version (presented in Appendix 3).

In the 1980s and 1990s, another generation of psychologists of the French School worked toward testing the projective methods in the context of narcissistic and borderline mental functioning. On the other side of the Atlantic, the works of Otto Kernberg and Heinz Kohut, and – related to the Rorschach – those of S. Fischer and S. E. Cleveland, and Paul and Howard Lerner have joined those of French authors such as André Green, Jean Bergeret, and Didier Anzieu to generate a wave of fruitful advances that have mainly been conducted by Catherine Chabert, Françoise Brelet-Foulard, Monika Boekholt, and Marianne Baudin in Paris, and by Claude de Tychey in Nancy.

In line with the work of Profs. Rausch de Traubenberg and Anzieu, Catherine Chabert has firmly supported the continuation and improvement of the projective methodology based on the psychoanalytic theory. By emphasizing that projective methods per se are atheoretical and that the theory which the psychologist decides to use provides depth to their interpretation, she has accurately demonstrated how projective psychology can be put to the service of psychoanalysis and vice versa. Chabert has made it possible for the combined interpretation of the Rorschach and TAT to take on its full meaning in light of their complementarity, to the point where we cannot now consider studying mental functioning without using both tools together.

The following is a reminder of the foundational principles of the analysis and interpretation of projective methods according to the psychoanalytic viewpoint of the French School:

- The Rorschach Test, because of its nonfigurative nature, which is structured around an axis, gives indications of the participants' body image and the quality of their identity and narcissistic construction. The TAT, with figurative cards which depict human scenes (animal scenes in the Children's Apperception Test; CAT-A), tests the representations of relationships as well as the various conflicts that are related to interiorized objects.
- According to the perception–reality/projection–fantasy dialectics, the TAT cards contain manifest contents and latent solicitations, the latter calling the subject to his/her own mental scene, thereby mobilizing psychic problematics.
- The mental scene comprises agencies (id–ego–superego) and systems (unconscious–preconscious–conscious) that allow the person to express their conflicts, anxieties, and defenses. Projective tests represent a projection surface and a container for the mental movements that are projected.
- Mental conflict is inherent in the mental life of humans. It shapes all mental activities from birth to death, and it may be destructuring. Projective tests reveal those internal conflicts and the level of their structuration, but they also reveal the forces that are present to cope with them.
- Interpretation is founded on the psychoanalytic theoretical corpus and psychopathology, based on the Freudian conception of the continuity between normal and pathological.

Finally, it should be noted that the French School extends well beyond the Parisian universities (i.e., the universities Paris 13, Paris Nanterre, and Université de Paris [for example Paris Descartes and Paris Diderot]), since it covers numerous teams of teachers, researchers, and practitioners, including, not to mention many others, Claude de Tychey, Joëlle Lighezzolo-Alnot, and Nadine Demogeot in Nancy; Magali Ravit, Anne Brun, and François-David Camps in Lyon; Catherine Weismann-Arcache and Teresa Rebelo in Rouen; Marie-Frédérique Bacqué, Mélanie Jacquot, and Céline Racin in Strasbourg; Geneviève Bréchon and Olivier Rouvre in Tours; Dimitra Laimou in Amiens; Delphine Bonnichon in Angers; and Almudena Sanahuja and Rose-Angélique Belot in Besançon. Indeed, it should also be noted that the French School also extends well beyond the French universities, since it covers numerous teams of teachers and researchers, including, to mention only a few, Alex Lefebvre and Simon Flemal in Belgium; Pascal Roman, Olivier Revaz, Vincent Quartier, and Christine Frederick-Libon in Switzerland; Tevfika Ikiz, Irem Erdem Atak, Bengi Düsgör, Neslihan Zabçi, and Elîf Yavuz Sever in Turkey; Maria Abigail de Souza, Deise de Amparo, Alvaro José Lélé, Valeria Barberi, Latife Yazigi, Anna Elisa Villemor-Amaral, Sonia Regina Pasian, Leila Tardivo, and Erika Okino in Brazil; Makhmoud Benkhelifa, Sadjia Makhlouf-Bentounes, Nadia Cheradi, Nacir Benhalla, Fatima Zohra Boualagua, Fatiha Ayad, and Zahra Djadouni in Algeria; Tiziana Sola, Salvatore Settineri, Carmela Mento, and Luca Bruno in Italy; Silvia Fregonese, Hilda Alonso, and Helena Ana Lunazzi in Argentina; and many others in Portugal, Greece, Lebanon, Canada, Togo, Cameroon, Japan, etc.

The publication of this book in English also provides an opportunity to valorize and support the numerous works of teachers and researchers of the French School, while also paying tribute to our American and French masters, as well as to those who have sometimes traveled long distances to train or update their knowledge at our universities.

The book is organized in two main sections: Section 1 focuses on theory and methods, with two contributions outlining the theoretical concerns that govern the clinical use of projective tools, and three other chapters that reflect on the dynamism of the methods from the perspective of continuity between past and present. Section 2 explores clinical applications and case studies from all stages of life, from early childhood, childhood, adolescence, to adulthood and aging, as well as at times of psychopathology or somatic decompensation.

All of the authors in this book are involved in the teaching and transmission of the projective methodology from a psychoanalytic perspective, and actively participate or have participated in scientific progress and in the production of knowledge in this field. Each in their own manner, whether young or old, has maintained the dynamism of the French School and ensured its continuity.

Ten out of the 14 contributions to the book are from the journal *Psychologie clinique et projective*, Issue 20 in 2014, which focused on the theme *Aux fondements psychanalytiques des méthodes projectives* (psychoanalytic foundations of projective methods), paying tribute to Nina Rausch de Traubenberg and Rosine

Debray who both died in 2013. They are reproduced with the kind permission of Erès Editions. The chapter "Dynamics of the TAT Process: Psychoanalytical and Psychopathological Perspectives" is an article that was collectively written by the team of the University Paris Descartes (today: Université de Paris) and published in Volume 35 (2014) of *Rorschachiana*. It is reproduced with the kind permission of Hogrefe Publishing, as is the article "Changing While Remaining the Same: Self-Representation Confronted With Aging," which was published in Volume 33 of *Rorschachiana* in 2011. The chapter by Estelle Louët, "From Bipolar Disorder to Melancholia and Mania: The Contribution of Projective Tests in the Study of Manic Depressive Disorder in a 16-Year-Old Girl," was initially published in a book edited by Catherine Chabert and Catherine Azoulay titled *12 Études en Clinique Projective: Approche Psychanalytique* (Twelve Case Studies in Projective Psychology: A Psychoanalytical Approach) published by Dunod in 2011, and reprinted here with the kind permission of Dunod Editions. The chapter "Traumatic Traces and Projective Figures of Catastrophes of Symbolization" by Pascal Roman is published with the kind permission of the journal *Bulletin de psychologie*.

We hope this book will touch English readers from all backgrounds and initiate new and fruitful exchanges.

Part 1
Theory & Methods

1

Projective Methods in Clinical Psychopathology

Developments, Confirmations, and Contradictions – A Tribute to Nina Rausch de Traubenberg and Rosine Debray

Catherine Chabert

The community of clinical psychologists – and not just that of clinicians who use projective techniques – recognizes the fundamental contributions of the work of Nina Rausch de Traubenberg. When I say "work," not only do I evoke her research works and publications, but I also refer to her clinical activities within a renowned child psychiatry department at the Pitié-Salpêtrière Hospital in Paris and to her essential role in initial and continuing university education for students at the Institut de Psychologie of the University Paris 5 (now the Université de Paris). Her reputation, which extends well beyond the borders of the Francophone parts of Europe, is also based on her work with the same zeal, courage, and dedication, within the Société du Rorschach et des Méthodes Projectives de Langue Française and the International Society of the Rorschach and Projective Methods. Her Rorschach-focused work helped firmly establish psychoanalytic references in projective methodology, at an early stage. Yet, less known, perhaps, is the essential role she played in taking thematic projective tests into account, and in thematic projective test training.

Furthermore, it is to Nina Rausch de Traubenberg that we owe the openness of projective clinical practice to thematic tests, particularly to the TAT. Her acute clinical skills and her qualities as a researcher quickly led her to solicit the assistance of Vica Shentoub in the development of the Certificate of Projective Techniques, almost from its inception. Her well-known stature and generosity were needed to anticipate the challenges to, and lay the foundations of, clinical practice and projective psychopathology from dynamic perspectives, in every sense of the word: meaning *dynamic,* because she was moving forward; dynamic because she supported movement, change, and mobility; dynamic because she promoted the psychoanalytic interpretation of projective methods in France; and finally, dynamic because from very early on, Rausch de Traubenberg understood the extent to which the Rorschach Test, far from being challenged in its validity and relevance by other projective methods, could rather be enhanced, enriched, and refined by a co-mingling.

Although initially, due to the characteristics of clinical practice at the time, Rorschach and TAT protocols were seldom proposed to the same individuals – because of the almost exclusive use of TAT in research – Rausch de Traubenberg supported and encouraged my proposals to combine both tests, not only in the training of clinicians, but also in clinical practice itself. Her intelligence and sensitivity thus allowed her to support new studies focusing on both tests, even though – and this was admirable – she herself always considered the enhancement of the Rorschach to be her personal research priority and, with her exemplary modesty, she often stated that she "did not really understand TAT"!

Much greater and even more remarkable was her merit in giving exceptional freedom to her younger colleagues. Without this openness and enthusiasm, the French School would never have become what it is. It is with pride and gratitude that I follow in her footsteps. As luck would have it, in the same year, Rausch de Traubenberg introduced me to Rorschach and Rosine Debray to TAT! I therefore went from the one to the other in my training in projective methodology, and this experience has remained very vivid in my mind.

Rosine Debray was already an experienced psychoanalyst when she joined Vica Shentoub for further research into the TAT. From this fruitful collaboration, a meticulous analysis of the TAT material was developed in terms of manifest and latent content; and it was Dr. Debray who rigorously and convincingly developed the structural reference of the TAT cards to the Oedipus complex. With the same enthusiasm, she supported the initial modifications of the TAT protocol scoring grid developed by Vica Shentoub, by involving all projective psychology teachers at the Institut de Psychologie. We were fortunate to be invited so early, so quickly to engage in clinical research with such an innovative and entrepreneurial spirit; especially since, in these working meetings, both clinical practice experience and knowledge of theory were needed to make progress.

In an attempt to show the impact of this double legacy, I have chosen to focus on some contributions of projective methods to the establishment of diagnoses, in the dynamic sense of the term. Those contributions are essential in terms of the psychiatric approach, and I am purposely mentioning them first, because I have not forgotten that Prof. Rausch de Traubenberg and Prof. Debray, each working in her own field, fought for and defended the major role of clinical and projective psychology in establishing diagnoses and thus in the therapeutic project. They both showed how the tools of clinical psychologists were essential, not only because of the depth and richness of their contributions to clinical practice and psychopathology, but also because they promoted the independence of psychologists and their uniqueness in the field of psychiatry.

Differential Diagnosis: Psychopathology and Projective Methods

Differential Diagnosis, Complexity or Heterogeneity of Mental Functioning

The apparently classical notion of differential diagnosis is now a subject of original work in clinical psychopathology, because psychiatric classifications deviate from the study of personality organization by focusing mainly on symptomatic behavior, which is a categorization that remains random or even secondary. Paradoxically, it is clinical psychopathology that plays an essential role in this respect, and over time, it is indicative of possibilities that are increasingly subtle and relevant, thanks to the refinement of the investigation methods. Among these methods, projective tests are undoubtedly at the forefront. This is an important observation: Projective methodology is becoming increasingly effective in the fields of clinical practice and psychopathology research, sometimes opening new perspectives through the detection of mental components or configurations that are not always grasped in the initial interviews.

Therefore, there is a consensus today that those current clinical developments, whether in psychiatry, psychopathology, or psychoanalysis, inevitably confront the issue of diagnosis in the broadest sense of the term: This is actually about understanding the functioning modalities available to a person and the range of mental behaviors that enable them to live, to consider with them – if necessary because of their suffering – therapeutic remedies that may develop their potential for change. Diversification of therapeutic methods and the refinement of care techniques have become necessary precisely as a result of an increasingly subtle differentiation of the psychopathological models. Treatments are now individualized and singled out according to the diversity and originality of a specific mental functioning.

The psychoanalytic interpretation of projective tests, essentially the Rorschach and TAT, has helped to significantly promote their use, both as investigation and assessment tools in a diagnostic approach, and as a metapsychological tool for research in clinical psychology and psychopathology. Today, I even support the view that projective methods also serve psychoanalysis! In a projective testing situation, the patient must *associate* and *speak about* material that is certainly ambiguous, but in which the perceptive and latent characteristics of the patient's responses involve a reactivation of a field of sensorial and representational experiences that are reflected in the formulation of those responses. The discourse of the patient is part of a system that mobilizes the emergence of unconscious representations in the associative expression that is made possible by a reduced vigilance and by the test that calls upon fantasy; yet, at the same time, a material reality, the closest to perception, must be taken into account, the impressions and modifications of which should be fundamentally respected by the patient.

Therefore, we are dealing here with a dual issue that is essential to the fate of every human being – that is, on one hand, the recognition of the internal world as a part of the continuous sense of existence or the permanence of identity, and on the other hand, the awareness of the external world as a part of the investment in the relational field, which enhances the potential for change that is mobilized by different choices of objects, that are made by the patient.

Yet, any attempt to define, with an extreme condensation, the issues that are inherent in the very processes of life, is immediately confronted by the need for reorganization that is imposed first by childhood development, then by the changes that are determined by adolescence and early adulthood, by maturity and then by aging. The passage of time entails the mobilization of mechanisms that are responsible, at the same time, for both change and continuity in the modalities of self-representation and in representations that underlie the relationship with others. Without systematically reiterating all aspects involved in these processes of change, we can point to two key lines: One outlines the regular reactivation of separation issues, putting to the test the capacity both to elaborate loss and to maintain a stable subjective identity, and the other is part of the instinctual dialectic and its impact in the formation of sexual identifications and object choices, and thereby part of their integration into conflictuality systems of which the vitality ensures mental elaboration through the labor of thought.

The Rorschach and TAT provide quite interesting and relevant interpretations of these issues: Rausch de Traubenberg developed her work on self-representation based on the Rorschach about which she stressed from the outset that it considerably calls upon the projection of body images, notably in the identification of an initial topography as the basis of the spatial organization. From the perspectives identified by Shentoub and Debray, we consider that the TAT material triggers the creation of narratives about conflicting systems that are dramatized through the characters featured, and it puts to the test the quality of temporality. Yet, the sense of identity and alterity is part of the link between space and time, a link that is necessary between an inside and outside, a before and after.

Such identity and relational questioning could begin in the study of the mental functioning and its avatars or its psychopathological vagaries. The principle of continuity between normal and pathological that is in a way the organizing principle in psychoanalytic theory (through the effect of clinical experience) has been widely validated both by the psychoanalytic method and psychopathology: All projective studies on persons with good mental health and ailing patients lead to considerably nuanced qualifications of the conventional classifications, whether psychological (choice of the "normal") or psychiatric (focus on morbidity).

Projective clinical practice is now engaged in a dialectic approach that leaves room for original articulations and spares the unpredictable part in research on mental functioning. A thorough work thus aims to specify – in the most suitable or subtle manner – the unique quality of the different mental components in a person. The identification of certain signs does not, ipso facto, imply the existence of a range that is necessarily related to it. Rupture and discontinuity and at times the heterogeneous association of various signs must be understood in their heterogeneity even if they prove discordant. However, coherence and convention in seeking a common theory led to a dynamic contribution of various projective tests: Indeed, far too often, apart from cases where psychological tests prove to be congruent, inconsistent data are dismissed without any real elaborative reflection.

Diagnostic assessment is more relevant when based on multiple clinical data, by developing a reorganization of the information that was obtained through different psychological investigation procedures: anamnestic data matching, interviews, cognitive tests, projective tests and so on, but also by interprojective matching, notably by using the Rorschach with a thematic test such as the TAT.

The inconsistencies that are sometimes exposed through the matching of protocols from both tests stimulate necessary questions and indicate in fact different facets, different aspects of mental functioning, unveiling what has hitherto remained hidden or obscured by either test. The gap between the Rorschach and TAT reflects the need for a mental dialectic that further distances us from rigid and somewhat simplistic patterns of formal and categorical nosography, revealing the movements of the human psyche through the expression of its internal dynamics. One might even consider that the gap between the two tests particularly raises awareness of the discontinuity of mental functioning and of its possible heterogeneities, which emerge after the Rorschach or TAT protocol. This observation illustrates one of the major convictions of Freud that was particularly addressed in 1930, in his book *Civilization and Its Discontents,* about the "variegation" of the human mental functioning that must be recognized, accepted, and defended by all means: This is a keystone as it enables the admission of the coexistence of conscious and unconscious processes, the coexistence of opposite instinctual pairs, and the coexistence of agencies that are ruled by the conflicts (Freud, 1930/2001). It then comes as no surprise that within specific psychopathological configurations, we may discover seemingly contradictory and unrelated conducts that reveal a class of functioning that is sometimes surprisingly diverse. The modulations that are provided by the Rorschach or the TAT cards are valuable in this respect, as they may electively mobilize various modalities of conflict management.

The Rorschach: From Self-Representation to Narcissism

The Rorschach can be considered as an identity test, a test of limits allowing the assessment of the solidity of individuation processes and of the constitution of sufficient boundaries between inside and outside. It is in this context that we use it in the first place: The Rorschach is particularly sensitive to the disintegration of self-representation, but at the same time, this sensitivity is also found when it comes to look for signs of construction, the quest for structuring references, holding contour lines of anaclisis, as significant elements of a struggle that is undertaken by the person to conquer or recover both precarious and lost individuality and identity. The Rorschach thus requires a narcissistic focus that, in a way, is called for by the characteristics of the material, as the symmetry that is organized around the vertical axis draws the projection of body representations. However, this narcissistic constraint is regularly put to the test by the change of stimulus: Bilateral configurations are all formal supports that enable the figuration of relational representations; the impact of the chromatic cards may lead to an emotional or instinctual reactivation, the relational dimension of which is flagrant.

Within psychoanalytic psychopathology, borderline functioning constitutes a vast field that brings together quite heterogeneous mental modalities; also for projective clinical practice, it has unfolded in such a thorough and subtle manner that it enables us to distinguish two major configurations that are contrasting and complementary at the same time: narcissistic functioning and borderline functioning that we call depressive. One of the differentiating elements is precisely the question of boundaries, not only between inside and outside and between internal and external reality, but also between ego and object, which provide a particularly relevant diagnostic insight. When the boundaries are firmly protected by narcissistic personalities, they prove to be porous, evanescent, and unstable in the borderline functioning. Echoing these characteristics, the modalities of object relations match to some extent the modalities of self-representation: distance, autarky, refusal of passivity and dependence (apparently), massive enhancement of ego-cathexis in narcissistic personalities, closeness that touches upon mixing lack of autonomy, anaclitic dependence, excessive passivity, and massive enhancement of object cathexis (apparently).

As regards the *narcissistic* factors in the Rorschach that are specific to self-representation and the boundaries between inside and outside, a noteworthy difference supports this distinction: When narcissistic defenses are significantly invested (perhaps overinvested), their most remarkable features first appear in the relentless protection of their boundaries (high F% and F+%, "skin" responses, etc.) while in borderline functioning, envelopes are porous, such as the "strainer" *moi-peau* (ego-skin) that was described by Didier Anzieu (1985). While in narcissistic personalities, the inside–outside distinction is outrageously overemphasized it withers and becomes blurred in borderline functioning.

Clinical correspondences are likely to appear in the vagaries of narcissistic protections – for instance, through the major investment of "skins" that clothing reflects, or even in the particularly smooth nature of a discourse that remains at the periphery and that is used as a protective shield to avoid at most any exchange between inside and outside.

Another narcissistic feature appears at the Rorschach in representations of relationships: overinvestment of symmetry, refusal of instinctual interaction in favor of mirroring, and reflections that maintain mirror images and fight against all signs of difference. Clinically, mirror-like positions appear massively in the dynamics of transference: The asymmetry inherent in the therapeutic situation is circumvented by way of idealization, especially in the early stages of treatment. Elsewhere, the escalation of the qualification that is necessary for being recognized and the overinvestment in being watched that are noticeable in the Rorschach appear very clearly in the characteristics of the discourse during sessions, which is molded by positive or negative judgments that are marked with overvalorization or contempt, or even by the visual control that is held by the patient during face-to-face treatment.

The TAT: From Representations of Relationships to Mental Conflict

The TAT seems to provide more relational solicitations through the very nature of the proposed images. Despite its evident ambiguity, the material is perceptively built. The response required by the instructions should mobilize an effort to think to build a narrative around an imaginary scenario: It is therefore a matter of resorting to a binding activity, especially in the arrangement of instinctual conflicts. Shentoub and Debray have clearly shown the iterative reference of the TAT to the oedipal conflict, which, from the outset, puts identificatory processes to the test. Forsaken for a while, the Oedipus complex is yet again being put to the test by psychoanalysts. However, it is precisely the plurality of oedipal forms that has long been apparent in the TAT: In this respect, it might even be considered that the projective method anticipates or announces certain movements in analytical thinking! Since the work of Shentoub and Debray, we have been trained to look for the nuclear complex valence that is either structuring or not, on one hand, and on the other hand, we seek to analyze its role and function in each person.

Furthermore, we also know the effects of this material in the reactivation of depressive and narcissistic issues: The works of Françoise Brelet-Foulard, in particular, have initiated a subtle analysis of these functionings, and the French School has developed these research directions considerably over the last 20 years. The TAT material solicits the production of discourses that are very close to those that are defined in clinical interviews or in mental treatments. The careful discourse analysis that has been developed for the TAT provides a remarkable listening opportunity during a session. Although psychoanalysts do not engage in the detailed and comprehensive analysis that is recommended for the TAT protocols, the projective experience certainly provides an extremely formative function for associative activities. Consequently, the clinician will appreciate the major defensive armatures as well as the very subtle or even volatile signs that could even be missed by the attentive and competent listener. Of course, I am particularly thinking of the nonconflicting dimension of narratives but, beyond that, of all of the processes that are mobilized by the fight against instinctual emergence.

We can therefore apply the two major sets of questions that are raised by the Rorschach and the TAT, to clinical interviews; this is a key question at the outset of preliminary interviews, but it is also regularly raised over the course of the treatment, and it arises more specifically in the dynamics of transference: Within the dynamics of psychic functioning, does the narcissistic centeredness leave room for instinctual investment in objects? Does the relational mobilization help maintain sufficient narcissistic cathexes to ensure the boundaries and the limits with others?

Consequently, each projective protocol, but also each subjective discourse, helps identify not one but several issues, thus pointing to the coexistence of different levels of conflicts and to their more or less successful articulation. It is then a matter of assessing to what extent this coexistence, and mainly this integration, is made possible by the flexibility, the openness, and the plurality of mental conducts (and thus of defense mechanisms), since the effectiveness of the binding processes allows for the management of a conflictuality that is expressed in terms of representations and affects that can be conveyed, unless faced with excessive heterogeneity as a result of the prevalence of unbinding processes that threaten the continuity of narcissistic and object cathexes, or faced with a rigid, monolithic, and closed mode of functioning with limited potential for change.

What actually seems important to grasp is reflected in the analysis of the dialectic of the instinctual expression and, particularly of its conflictuality through narcissistic and object confrontations. Studying the connections between conflicting drives and the narcissistic mechanisms of regulation is indeed a pivotal point in the interpretation of the projective protocols, but also, even of mental functioning, as it appears in "direct" clinical practice.

A Clinical Example: Obsessional Neurosis and Narcissistic Functioning

To illustrate the point that studying the connections between conflicting drives and the narcissistic mechanisms of regulation is indeed a pivotal point in the interpretation of the projective protocols, I would like now to present a specific situation that may raise the issue of differential diagnosis between narcissistic personality and obsessional neurosis. In this situation, it seems necessary to identify the elements that may appear to be contradictions or confirmations, first between clinical observations and projective data, and then, possibly, between the Rorschach and the TAT.

Despite official statements made by psychoanalysts, symptoms certainly affect our diagnostic positions to a greater or lesser extent. Although we regularly assert that the same symptoms are associated with different psychopathological personality organizations, it is clear that we can quickly draw similarities between certain morbid behaviors and specific types of diagnosis. Studies in clinical psychopathology are used as a support when we consider, for instance, that compulsive and addictive conducts are often based on borderline or narcissistic behaviors, and that drifts in the modalities of the relation to reality or massive identity impairments are generally present in psychotic functioning. We then have to take the contradictory position – that is, not only in the projective productions – to look for elements that reinforce a given clinical intuition or conviction, but also, beyond that, to look for contradictory, paradoxical, odd, or strange elements that do not occur as expected.

Narcissistic and obsessional behaviors share the same strong investment in limits, which in the Rorschach translates into an increase in formal determinants. In some patients, the overinvestment in contours and boundaries gives evidence of the defense of boundaries between inside and outside, to avoid any risk of confusion. The fact that such reliance on forms is very often effective (high F+%) should not come as a surprise. Indeed, in these patients, the distinction between the ego and the object must be maintained at all costs, as it notably allows the refusal of dependence, the fear of mingling, and especially the negation of the internal sources of instinctual movements. The F, and the objectivation that it attempts to preserve, is a key factor, and as far as it is associated with specific contents such as the skin responses that I mentioned previously (see the section The Rorschach: From Self-Representation to Narcissism, above), it protects the person from being affected by the excitement that would come from the outside – from the object and from others! To some extent, it is a double defense against instinctual movements: not only the refusal of the source of internal drives, but also the equally unbending refusal of objects that might solicit it.

In severe obsessional neuroses, we may find a similar mode of defense in the attachment to the "objective" external reality, the same fear of invasion by drives, and it is known that, in such situations, the fear of being caught up in the excitement is massive. The idea of engaging it in small amounts is unbearable, and it rapidly gives way to anxiety over an overwhelming surge. The increase in F% is therefore just as recognizable, and it takes on the meaning of a fight against the instinctual emergence, with a significant mobilization of isolation. Therefore, it is sometimes difficult to differentiate between the isolation that serves a neurotic compromise and the isolation that is closer to splitting the ego, of course, but which is also clearly linked with isolation.

It is well-known that the distinctive characteristic of neurosis is revealed in the expression of internal conflicts between agencies inside the mental scenery. In contrast, borderline functioning is less able to create such scenery, and these patients primarily manage conflicts externally, through interpersonal realities or even through the body and behavior. Narcissistic functioning, however, can reveal some forms of internal cathexis that can merge with the prevalence of the ego libido, and their high intellectual competencies are capable of symbolizing performances, to the extent that the differential diagnosis is not always that simple, especially with the Rorschach. Add to this the existence of ritual behaviors, a certain meticulosity, and a strong sense of superiority, and the differentiation is even more difficult.

It is then that the TAT – through the relational deployment that it calls for – may be of assistance in a complicated assessment. Indeed, the processes of elaboration of the narcissistic type of discourse, as constructed and elaborated based on the seminal work of Brelet-Foulard (Brelet, 1986), are highly reliable indicators for identifying narcissistic functioning, and not merely the narcissistic traits that are more or less substantially present in all psychopathological personality organizations (with the exception of schizophrenia). With the use of the TAT scoring grid (see Appendix 3), we can quite clearly understand the level of investment, the mobilization, and the efficiency of the obsessional mechanisms within a neurotic personality organization, through toing and froing, oscillations between desire and defense, through the part that is left to the object cathexis and through sexuality in its potential for binding the aggressive instinctual movements.

It is particularly interesting to consider this dimension when analyzing protocols, as the brutal instinctual emergence with a destructive connotation may appear both in obsessional neuroses and in narcissistic functioning: sometimes as an untangled aggressiveness that is carried by death drives and subject to destructive forces. Sometimes, highly solicited by the Rorschach and generating an unexpected emergence of primary processes, death drives are also reflected in the TAT context where sadomasochistic eroticization, pleasure in object relationships, and emergence of fantasy scenarios are all arguments that point to the even temporary binding capacities that are likely to be revealed with careful listening and reading.

Metapsychology and Projective Clinical Practice

Carrying on with these correlations this time on the metapsychology side, we find ourselves mainly addressing the narcissistic defenses that are part of the analytical concept of skin-ego, the fecundity of which has proved exceptional. The skin-ego, as Didier Anzieu (1985) developed it, provides, yet again, surprisingly relevant illustrations.

The Rorschach, the Body, and Dreams

It seems necessary to briefly mention two dynamic references involved in the Rorschach in particular, but also in psychoanalysis and treatment: dreams and the body. The *imaging reverie* as defined by Daniel Lagache (1957) requires the observance of a double constraint: the substantial or evanescent solicitation of representations and affects, the call for the dreamer in their original subjectivity – narcissistic constraint if any – and, at the same time, the required respect for the perceptive "realities," objects that are caught in the paradox of excitation and its limitations. If indeed the projective situation must allow for respect of the two principles of the course of thought, it is then involved in a double consideration: considering the person themselves, as a projective being, a dream producer that is here mobilized in their ability to say what they think, imagine, feel, experience, and desire, as well as considering an object, unknown at first, then to be recognized in the singularity of its being.

The Rorschach – as Nina Rausch de Traubenberg clearly demonstrated by particularly stressing perceptive and projective interferences, mainly in self-representation (Rausch de Traubenberg & Boizou, 1978) – can provide valuable support for the comprehension of associativity and of the implication of the body and images in the production of the discourse.

The Rorschach inkblot – black, gray, or colored – appears in contrast with a white base, outlining the contours and limits of the image, between inside and outside. It has been strongly argued that the Rorschach involves the body, this being particularly justified by the effect of how the inkblots are designed symmetrically around a vertical axis like the human body, thus providing – and this is an observation – a privileged spot to project its representations. The prospects that are opened by the skin-ego widen the scope of this argument to consider the impact of the contours of the inkblot – through the opposition between the figure and the background and the inside and the outside – that is thus used as a spatial medium for originally corporeal images – a Freudian mirror of the ego: "The ego is first and foremost a body-ego; it is ultimately derived from body sensations, chiefly from those springing from the surface of the body" (Freud, 1923/2001, p. 26). Thus the Rorschach proves to be an identity test, an assessment of limits through the suggestion of a more or less represented container–bag, through the stress on the barriers of contact, the recognition of which is particular in each case and accounts for the quality of the capacities of containing and exchanging in a person: firm contours, clearly outlined or unstable, simmering, discontinuous, interpenetrations between the figure and the background; clear, precise or the entanglement of more or less comprehensible forms.... In short, this material requires a labor of figuration in the psychoanalytic sense of the word, insofar as the person tested is confronted with the same requirement for symbolization as the dreamer: Thoughts and feelings that are awakened by the Rorschach cards must be selected and transformed in order to enable them to be represented by visual images. This work is possible if the skin-ego is established: As with dreams, the person must have a filtering, screening system and protective shield, ensuring an effective differentiation between the inside and the outside. Furthermore, the impressionability of the projective layer must be sufficient in order to conserve the traces of the object and to be organized as stable images.

In some situations that rather involve the clinical observation of limits in the broad sense of the term, beyond the visual, there is a polysensoriality of images, the shock of which is poorly understood: Carried by the words that preserve the enigma, they are no longer about vision, but rather about awakening unprecedented sensations, the opacity of which is indefinable. In such particular situations, the visual and representational communication appears as broken: Words aim at concealing what cannot be depicted, to stand in the way of the listener, because they can no longer see. The fading and the disappearance of containers – when there is no recognition of delimited and identifiable entities, when the body of the thought itself is fading – makes associative activities and the creation of images almost impossible.

In the Rorschach there are inevitable correspondences between the dynamics of reverie and the ability to depict representations of the body: Could the basis for the association or the construction of images in the Rorschach be precisely the possible investment in a space, as a locus of projection of the body surface, that is the surface of contact between the inside and the outside, between the subject and the object? The (perceptive) identification of the body and its metaphorical derivatives would be the original approach that may give sense to this highly enigmatic material. The encounter between the real and the imaginary (Rausch de Traubenberg, 1994; Rausch de Traubenberg & Boizou, 1978) is possible and necessary if the use of the transitional area can be updated at the very moment of the testing (Chabert, 1997). Indeed, the person's ability to position themselves in between reflects a space, a locus of projection of the psyche, the topic of which is the essence of the feeling of continuous existence, a temporal binding that is essential for recognizing duration, supported by the establishment of the skin-ego. The transitional work in the Rorschach is primarily represented by M-responses as a representation of the living, as they express what moves, animates, and moves forms, and as body containers, they convey the scenarios that may give sense to representations and affects. These characteristics can more than raise awareness of the listener: The connection between transitionality and associativity is clearly demonstrated through projective tests, especially through the Rorschach. The regression that is generated by the material opens in a surprising way, insofar as it can be understood as analogous to regression in the analytical process. As a result, regression can no longer be considered a pathological sign; it reveals the mysteries of a mental functioning that lets itself go in a flexible and harmonious way or of another functioning that severely decompensates this regressive movement.

The question remains in the Rorschach whether the image that is given a meaning, the image that is expressed in words may open a seemingly infinite associative field, a surprising visual and sensory liberty that is supported by a vast scope of illusion. Sometimes, however, the image remains closed on itself, trapped in a discourse that could have provided a belief in the image's having a meaning, a belief that is triggered by the anxiety of emptiness and annihilation.

It is around these different configurations that the question of the skin-ego, its precariousness and/or significance, is built. Beyond the transitionality that constitutes an intermediary space and thus a space for exchange, the skin-ego supports the deployment of scenarios, the sense of which – sexual and seductive – feeds the symbolic quality of the associated contents. Put differently, the object-libidinal openness may take a leap: It will always reflect, on the one hand, the more or less solid, precarious, or nonexistent establishment of boundaries between the inside and the outside and between the subject and the object, while, on the other hand, it also reflects an investment in the relations between this inside and outside and between the subject and the object within a system of communication in which the *meaning* of the message has a crucial function. The precariousness of the skin-ego can lead to the disappearance of the object in the mental space because no sense can be given to its absence, since it cannot find any container that might be able to provide a space for the construction of fantasy, enabling the pain of loss to be associated with a representation that could help its elaboration.

The Rorschach and TAT: Representations of Relationships and Object Loss

Thus arises the question of the representation of relationships, driven by a double trend – an associative trend that shifts from one person to another, and a scientific trend that changes from subjective to intersubjective. We will briefly examine some of the current reflections on the analysis of the issue of object loss using projective data, and we will identify the key issues. Indeed, the question of representation is central to the construction of the ego, as much as representation and ego are consubstantial when it comes to absence and loss.

> Would the most unbearable loss be the loss from view? Would it announce the complete withdrawal of love from the other, and our concern about any fundamental infirmity: the inability to love the invisible? Above all we must see. Not only see but see above all in order to calm the anguish caused by absence, to reassure ourselves that the loved object is within our field of vision, reflecting our identity back to us. (Pontalis, 1988, p. 275)

This proposal deserves a deep reflection on the role of the image in the projective situation (and also in mental functioning): Indeed, the stimulus in both the Rorschach and the TAT is first and foremost visual, as a tangible reality that is sensitive to the lens of the person. Yet will they provide an object presence as recognizable, identifiable, and at the same time as sufficiently invested to "reflect" the subject in their identity?

What about the role of the image in the psychoanalytic cure? When there is no external stimulus to be used as support and target for perception and projection? How does each patient – according to their mental organization – experience this loss of view? I remember a patient who told me, after the preliminary interviews, while the decision had just been made to enter psychoanalytic therapy: "But then, will I not see you again?"

These are certainly the key terms on which the question of loss in the depressive problematic is based, a loss that could lead – with the disappearance of the other – to the loss of self or, conversely, to the loss of the visible other while preserving its existence as an internal object within the psyche, thus ensuring the sense of continuity of being in the person. This dialectic inevitably binds together the other and the ego, image and representation that are involved in an associative discourse from a perceptive material.

> We must recollect that all representations originate from perceptions and are repetitions of them. Thus originally the mere existence of a presentation was a guarantee of the reality of what was presented.... It only comes into being from the fact that thinking possesses the capacity to bring before the mind

> once more something that has once been perceived … without the external object having still to be there. (Freud, 1925/2001, p. 237)

Mental rearrangement for thinking the absence, and hence to think, can be identified through the associations and responses in the Rorschach and the narratives and stories in the TAT. When the most common reference points – both spatial and temporal – are lost, the person is confronted with "things," the extreme strangeness of which results in a surge of catastrophic anxiety. The psychotic parade – as clearly demonstrated by P.C. Racamier (1978) – is the denial of the sense of these things in an insanitation process. Negativism denies any "sense" in the projective material: No figuration that identifies or even brings meaning is truly achievable with the Rorschach, and no construction of narratives in time and space, as elements from the mental scene, is recognizable in the TAT.

In other modalities of depressive rearrangements, there is an overinvestment in objects and in the external reality: Manifest elements are all essential perceptual references that support the boundaries between inside and outside, as well as the essential support for the concealment of the inner void. The iterative use of concrete or tangible elements is an attempt to fill this void, this gap, when solicited by the cards – when white is predominant in the Rorschach, and when using all the relational figurations as a support in the TAT. Yet, in psychotherapy or in the psychoanalytic cure, there is the same use of concrete and material elements, the excessive attachment to places as much more reliable references than those which, in terms of representations, ensure a sense of continuity of being and of permanence of objects, once the mechanisms of internalization have accomplished their task.

Conversely, narcissistic functioning displays an overinvestment in self-representation and in its productions. As previously mentioned, absence or the object gap are generally filled with the specular and excessive construction of idealized figures. The mirror serves as a key support for the representations of narcissistically qualifying relationships – whether positive or negative – that may explicitly be reflected in the qualification of the transference. The purpose of all of the significant indicators of these modalities is to negate the desire for the other who following the narcissistic logic would denounce the inability of the person to be self-sufficient. The only suitable partner is the person's double, so as to bypass the recognition of differences, of lack and absence.

Furthermore, when the castration anxiety is dominant, the narcissistic threat is also present. Yet, its effects are transitory, temporary, or functional. So the acceptance of gender differences, even when painful, deals differently with the ability to think of the other in their absence and to keep them within the psyche as the object of desire.

The density of projective data is clearly and consistently revealed when these data are developed and analyzed from psychoanalytic perspectives: The material, as a container for thinking contents, solicits at the same time an associative work that mobilizes complex mental operations that outline the relationships between the person and their very objects that may unfold in the analytical process.

This transitional activity is part of an intermediate space that is both a paradoxical space, between *inside* and outside, and a mediator space; *intermediate* here is to be understood as the bearer of messages between the patient and the clinician – that is, beyond their involvement in a diagnostic evaluation, these "translations" are essential for a metapsychological elaboration of the mental functioning, the necessity of which cannot be ignored. Once again, we must stress the importance of these productions as an extremely fruitful and precious contribution to the clinician's training and to the practice of listening.

Acknowledgments

This chapter was originally published in French and is reprinted here in English with permission: Chabert, C. (2014). Les méthodes projectives en psychopathologie clinique: développements, confirmations, contradictions. *Psychologie clinique et projective, 20*(1), 59–78. © Erès Editions.

References

Anzieu, D. (1985). *Le moi-peau* [The ego-skin]. Paris, France: Dunod.

Brelet, F. (1986). *Le TAT: Fantasme et situation projective* [The TAT: Fantasy and the projective situation]. Paris, France: Dunod.

Chabert, C. (1997). *Le Rorschach en clinique adulte: Interprétation psychanalytique* [Rorschach Test in adults: A psychoanalytical interpretation] (2nd ed.). Paris, France: Dunod.

Freud, S. (1923/2001). The Ego and the Id. In J. Strachey (Ed. & Trans.), *The standard edition of the complete psychological works of Sigmund Freud* (*Vol. 19*, pp. 3–66). London, UK: Vintage Classics. (Original work published in 1923)

Freud, S. (1925/2001). Negation. In J. Strachey (Ed. & Trans.), *The standard edition of the complete psychological works of Sigmund Freud* (*Vol. 19*, pp. 233–239). London, UK: Vintage Classics. (Original work published in 1925)

Freud, S. (1930/2001). Civilization and its discontents. In J. Strachey (Ed. & Trans.), *The standard edition of the complete psychological works of Sigmund Freud* (*Vol. 21*, pp. 57–145). London, UK: Vintage Classics. (Original work published in 1930)

Lagache, D. (1957). La rêverie imageante, conduite adaptative au test du Rorschach [Imaging Reverie, Adaptative conduct at Rorschach Test]. *Bulletin du Groupement français du Rorschach, 9,* 3–11. http://doi.org/10.3406/clini.1957.1554

Pontalis, J.-B. (1988). *Perdre de vue* [Losing sight]. Paris, France: Gallimard.

Racamier, P. C. (1978). Les paradoxes des schizophrènes [Paradoxes of schizophrenic patients]. *Revue française de psychanalyse, 42*(5–6), 877–971.

Rausch de Traubenberg, N. (1994). Le Rorschach, lieu d'interactions entre le percept et le fantasme [Rorschach: Space of interaction between percept and fantasy]. *Bulletin de la Société du Rorschach et des méthodes projectives de langue française, 38,* 123–136.

Rausch de Traubenberg, N., & Boizou, M. F. (1978). Interférences entre activité perceptive et activité fantasmatique dans les Rorschach d'enfants [Interferences between perceptive activity and phantasmic activity in children's Rorschach]. *Psychologie française, 23*(2), 127–140.

Additional Suggested Reading

Boizou, M.-F., Chabert, C., & Rausch de Traubenberg, N. (1978). Représentation de soi: Identité et identification au Rorschach chez l'enfant et l'adulte [Self-representation: Identity and identification in Rorschach among children and adults]. *Bulletin de psychologie, 32*(339), 271–277.

Brelet-Foulard, F., & Chabert, C. (2003). *Nouveau manuel du TAT: Approche psychanalytique* [New TAT manual: Psychoanalytic approach]. Paris, France: Dunod.

Chabert, C. (1987a). *La psychopathologie à l'épreuve du Rorschach* [Psychopathology in the Rorschach Test]. Paris, France: Dunod, 1998.

Chabert, C. (1987b). Rorschach et TAT: Antinomie ou complémentarité [Rorschach and TAT: antinomy or complementarity]. *Psychologie française, 32*(3), 141–144.

Chabert, C. (1998). *Psychanalyse et méthodes projectives* [Psychoanalysis and projective methods]. Paris, France: Dunod.

Chabert, C., & Azoulay, C. (Eds.). (2011). *12 Études en clinique projective: Approche psychanalytique* [Twelve case studies in projective psychology: A psychoanalytical approach]. Paris, France: Dunod.

Rausch de Traubenberg, N. (1970). *La pratique du Rorschach* [The practice of the Rorschach Test]. Paris, France: PUF.

Shentoub, V., & Debray, R. (1970–1971). Fondements théoriques du processus-TAT [Theoretical fundamentals of the TAT process]. *Bulletin de psychologie, 24*, 292(12–15), 897–903.

Shentoub, V., & Debray, R. (1978–1979). Que faire d'une excessive richesse fantasmatique? Interprétation d'un protocole inhabituel de TAT [How to deal with excessive phantasmic richness? Interpretation of an unusual TAT protocol]. *Bulletin de psychologie, 32*(339/3–7), 309–322.

2

Dynamics of the TAT Process

Psychoanalytical and Psychopathological Perspectives

Benoît Verdon, Catherine Chabert, Catherine Azoulay, Michèle Emmanuelli, Françoise Neau, Sarah Vibert, & Estelle Louët

Whereas the Rorschach is a universally known projective test acknowledged for facilitating the collection of significant clinical data, the Thematic Apperception Test (TAT) is not as widely used and deserves to become better known. The French School, which has been working for decades on identifying the modalities of the psychoanalytic interpretation of these two methods, underscores their complementarity. Nevertheless, whether the results are congruent or inconsistent, they allow for an analysis that is as accurate and comprehensive as possible of psychic functioning in its plurality or even the heterogeneity of its components.

Theoretical and Clinical Foundations

According to Murray (1943), identifying with the hero of the story expresses one's needs and relationships with the environment through the projection, in the narrative, of the person's behavior in real life. In France, the studies carried out by Shentoub in 1950 – whose collaboration with Debray began in 1970 – offered a different perspective, by referring to the psychoanalytic model of psychological functioning from a clinical and theoretical viewpoint. The method focused on the notions of manifest and latent content (of discourse and stimulus materials), and led to the development of a grid of discourse construction procedures, as well as on the analysis of 18 cards selected due to the significance of the associations that the pictures initiate. This grid records the discourse that the participant addresses to the psychologist within a TAT setting (administration of test, and fantasies the participant is projecting on the card) structured by the psychologist's instructions and specificity of the transference phenomena. Indeed, "as in the psychoanalytic situation, the instructions that give a subject the greatest freedom also impose a constraint on him. He is condemned to be free, condemned to reveal himself" (Anzieu, Chabert, Louët, 2017, p. 23).

Like a dream that conceals latent content under manifest content, "conscious-induced fantasy" (in the form of TAT narratives) is different from the unconscious phantasmic; the former makes it possible to rediscover the latter, provided that every effort is made to formally analyze the narratives, based on discourse construction procedures (how the story is told; Schafer, 1958, 1967) and their manifest content (what is told). The main assumption is that the TAT narrative reflects – based on how the discourse is organized – the psychic operations used in the associative process: Underlying the processes of narrative construction are defense mechanisms that enable the problems evoked or solicited by the material to be processed.

Moreover, analyzing this in terms of manifest content and latent evocations makes it possible to observe the play – or the challenges or even the impossibility of playing – between external reality and internal reality, and therefore the participant's degree of freedom with respect to the conflicts that drive them (Verdon, 2011). It also makes it possible to capture the manner in which participants can address these fundamental psychological conflicts that latent evocations confront them with, reactivating fantasies and affects, and mobilizing – in response to the instructions – defense mechanisms. It is not the content but rather the modalities of the construction of a theme that are analyzed to assess the position that a given issue holds in the person's psychic life: Staging a libidinal or aggressive conflict reflects nonintegrated conflict only if the narrative itself becomes distorted, or even disorganized, by the impact of fantasy and defenses. What ultimately matters is how the issue is developed in the discourse transmitted to the clinical psychologist.

Analyzing individual psychic functioning within a dynamic perspective makes it possible to assess identifiable psychic processes, their singular relationships, and their potential for change. This implies analyzing the mental operations implemented during the application of the test, assuming they reflect the participant's psychic operational modality. This is where theoretical references that constitute the interpretation framework come in: The choice of a psychoanalytic model is part of a clearly defined position involving the theoretical foundations of the analysis of psychic functioning within the field of applied psychoanalysis. This leads us to readapt the concepts we have selected in order to use them within the specific projective psychology field. The application of projective tests makes it possible to collect comprehensive information that is difficult to access in complex psychopathological situations, and, as such, it joins other methods of investigation that seek to establish a relevant treatment plan.

The French School gives great importance to the clinical analysis of the projective situation from a psychodynamic perspective. This is perceived as an encounter between the patient and the clinical psychologist, likely to be expressed in two different and complementary scenes: one relating to both participants' intersubjectivity, in terms of preconscious/conscious functioning in this encounter, and the other drawing its force and associative content from unconscious sources of issues activated by the presentation of the picture cards. Consequently, through the mediation of the stimulus materials, each testing session reactivates the patient's unconscious relational modalities using singular transference manifestations determined by transient intrapsychic and situational influences, as well as by structural elements inherent in that person's psychic functioning. The clinical psychologist's cathexis of their function, the characteristics of their personality, and the "singular" mobilization of each testing session determine countertransference participation. Analyzing manifest content and latent evocations of the cards constitutes an "objective" fulcrum that makes it possible to avoid overly subjective assessments when applying the discourse analysis grid and interpretations to develop the diagnosis.

Today, the method of analysis and interpretation of TAT protocols introduced by Shentoub (1973, 1987), Shentoub and Shentoub (1960), and Shentoub and Debray (1970–1971) continues to grow in the French School, and notably through the studies of Brelet-Foulard and Chabert (2003) – Freudian metapsychology lays the foundation for this method. Reference to the psychoanalytic model of psychic functioning is supported by the fact that both the projective stimulus material and the respondents' discourse can be analyzed in terms of manifest content (perceived content) and latent evocations (arising from the preconscious or the unconscious). In addition, psychoanalytic psychopathology provides a clinically descriptive study of symptomatology – very similar to the description of symptoms in contemporary classifications such as the *Diagnostic and Statistical Manual of Mental Disorders,* 5th edition (DSM-5) and the *International Classification of Diseases,* 11th edition (ICD-11). In addition, the psychoanalytic approach investigates underlying psychic organizations. Indeed, each psychic organization triggers specific defense mechanisms and adjustments; their observation can help clinicians gain a deeper understanding of the patient's difficulties. These difficulties can be ascribed to specific forms of psychic organization (neurosis, psychosis, borderline functioning) that produce different modes of psychic functioning, although the symptomatology may sometimes seem similar or even identical. In this sense, psychoanalytic psychopathology can be seen as complementing phenomenological or behavioral approaches. The classification of psychic disorders according to the psychoanalytic model provides an original and dynamic perspective, which leaves room for contradictory phenomena; the criteria for analysis are rigorously developed, tested, and sustained by both theoretical (metapsychological) elaboration and clinical experience. We will, therefore, review some important Freudian constructs here that are central to our approach.

The Psychic Apparatus

The *psychic apparatus* is a model whose functioning is governed by three perspectives: First, the *topographical perspective* structures data analysis: The conscious/preconscious/unconscious system (first topic) is regularly summoned in the instructions, which, based on a visual stimulus (external), consists of associating images sustained by unconscious representations (internal); the ego/id/superego agencies (second topic) play a central role in facilitating understanding of the intrapsychic conflict, and in particular, in terms of desires and defenses.

Second, the *dynamic perspective* establishes the hypothesis of a mobile psychic functioning, driven by contradictory movements underlying conflict, which provides an essential development in the analysis of protocols, as it underlies the organization of associations during storytelling.

Third, the *economic perspective* is consistently taken into account to assess the intensity of excitation: sometimes unbridled, exuberant, impossible to contain; sometimes incorporated into the associative process through efficient defense mechanisms.

Dialectics of Inside/Outside: Perception/Projection, External Reality/ Internal Reality

Perception

All individuals are subject to stimuli that come from outside, from external reality, as well as from those that come from within, from one's internal reality, in terms of representations and affects. Individuals establish and develop themselves around this dialectic between the inside and the outside, through networks of exchange with their environment, as well as with the self and with one's inner world.

In the psychoanalytic context, *perception* refers to the perception–consciousness system: From a topographical point of view, this system is situated at the periphery of the psychic apparatus, to receive information from both the internal and external worlds. From an economic perspective, this information is expressed in terms of feelings of pleasure and displeasure. Two principles govern this mode of functioning: Consciousness is assimilated into perception in its ability to receive sensitive qualities; on the other hand, the unconscious system is governed by the modalities of quantitative functioning.

The relationship between perception and consciousness often led Freud (e.g., in *Project for a Scientific Psychology;* Freud, 1895/2001) to reunite them within a single system. From an operational point of view, the perception–consciousness system opposes the unconscious and preconscious mnemonic trace systems. From an economic perspective, the perception–consciousness system is characterized by the provision of freely mobile energy that is likely to attach itself to an element by investing in it. The perception–consciousness system clearly plays a fundamental role in how reality is considered, and consequently, in the regulation of two operational principles mentioned by Freud, known as the *pleasure principle* and the *reality principle*.

Projection

Projection features prominently in psychic studies and can be defined as the "operation whereby qualities, feelings, wishes or even 'objects,' which the subject refuses to recognize or rejects in himself, are expelled from the self and located in another person or thing" (Laplanche & Pontalis, 1988, p. 349). Projection introduces a process that is not only internal, but that inevitably plays out between two organisms. From a metapsychological viewpoint, projection is essentially rooted in the theory of instincts. The organism is subjected to two forms of excitation: those from which it can protect itself by flight, and those from which there is no escape – at least in early life – before the development of the protective shield. This distinction makes it possible to initially differentiate between the interior and the exterior. Projection offers a defensive solution with regard to internal excitation, by placing unpleasant stimuli in the exterior, and avoiding them along with all external dangers.

Projection also plays a decisive role in generating judgment, opposition, and differentiation between subjects and objects. Introjection/projection mechanisms initially place differentiation between the internal and the external, and associate it with a judgment value (good and/or bad), on the basis of which the judgment of existence is established. While no distinction initially exists between the subjective and the objective, this is eventually established when the mind acquires the ability to render absent objects present through the construction of representations. These representations – relying on the memory of objects perceived as providing real satisfaction – develop through reproduction and deformation because they are part of psychic reality.

TAT Perception/Projection

Perceptive and projective interferences, as formulated by Rausch de Traubenberg when speaking of the Rorschach (Rausch de Traubenberg, 1970), also apply to the TAT. The difference is linked to the quality of the TAT cards and the instructions that mobilize particular psychic behavior: TAT provides the participant with figurative material, while the Rorschach mobilizes figurative activities from the outset. As "real" objects, the TAT picture cards solicit discourse that reflects perceptive apprehension, while promoting the construction of a narrative through the associations that the pictures initiate. Thus, appealing to perception that is consistently present in the instructions enables an anchoring on "reality" that is essential in accessing the surrounding world. The description of the TAT cards that is as close as possible to an objective one was achieved by Shentoub and Debray (1970–1971) and serves as a reference to define the manifest content of each card presented (see the section Analysis and Interpretation Methods, below). Moreover, as an activator of unconscious memories, the TAT makes it possible to interpret perceptions depending on the participant's main concerns, the organization of their relationships with the self as well as with both internal and external objects, representations, and the resulting affects.

Shentoub and Debray's central hypothesis is that the different TAT picture cards they selected, considering them to be the most significant, refer to the structural model of the oedipal situation; because of the characteristics of the characters and the situations, the double reference to the differences in gender and in generation is present in a manifest or latent manner. This hypothesis has largely been validated since its implementation (Brelet, 1986; Chabert, 1998, Emmanuelli & Azoulay, 2008; Neau, 2002; Shentoub & Debray, 1970–1971; Verdon, 2011) and demonstrates oedipal configurations – structuring or otherwise – that establish a set of highly valuable reference points with regard to psychopathological diagnostics. Whether they relate to instinctual ambivalence, to the struggle between desire and forbidding, to the intensity of castration anxiety, or to the greater or lesser severity of the superego and its effects, the different components of the nuclear complex are likely to be revealed through the narratives of each person.

In the 1980s, Brelet (1986, 1987) proposed an alternative hypothesis, which was not exclusive of that of Shentoub and Debray. This hypothesis highlights the strength of narcissism as well as the discourse construction mechanisms used when in a TAT setting, leading to the study of the behaviors that valorize ego cathexis, sometimes leading to a form of excessive self-sufficiency. Lastly, Chabert (Brelet-Foulard & Chabert, 2003; Chabert, 1998) analyzed the TAT material with reference to issues associated with object loss: Whether in terms of anxiety regarding loss of love, or revealed in the impossible elaboration of the renouncement of oedipal objects, these references to loss are likely to be regularly captured by the different TAT cards.

Four major and complementary cathexes can constitute the dynamics of the picture cards and the associated narratives. Involved in the vagaries of libidinal and aggressive, narcissistic and object cathexes, they interact at the heart of psychosexuality between narcissism and depression, between oedipal conflict and identificatory patterns.

Analysis and Interpretation Methods

The TAT Analysis Method According to Shentoub

The method proposed by Shentoub is based on the analysis of both stories and stimulus material in terms of manifest content and latent evocations (see Appendix 2) as well as on the development of a TAT analysis grid regrouping all of the discourse procedures (see Appendix 3) that are likely to be used by the participant when they engage in a narrative induced by the material. Both are the result of research carried out among populations divided between a "random" group and different groups with proven psychopathological disorders. In 1960, Shentoub and Shentoub conducted a widespread study to determine the ordinary responses to the different TAT cards (Shentoub & Shentoub, 1960). They suggested the hypothesis that certain themes are prominent, given the degree of structure of the TAT images. The test was administered to 100 persons with no psychopathological disorders, recruited in the context of career counseling, and to 60 persons with various psychopathological disorders (depression, anxiety, obsessive ideas, schizophrenia, etc.). In this comparative study, they found that certain themes were repeatedly brought up by most participants, both with and without disorders. Nowadays, patients are still grouped under hysterical neurosis, obsessive–phobic disorders, and psychosis, and, with the evolution in psychopathological studies, have also been grouped under borderline and narcissistic disorders.

Analyzing a protocol involves observing the patient's intrapsychic issues confronted with latent evocations, and identifying the discourse procedures that reflect them. These are summarized in an analysis grid. Associating these data leads to a summary of psychic functioning by revealing potential psychopathological elements. Referring to the stimulus material's latent evocations makes it possible to situate the patient by assessing the conflictual categories that they can address. This assessment is crucial for the diagnostic hypothesis, if one considers that a dominant issue will correspond to each psychopathological personality organization. Neurosis is characterized by the tensioning of the oedipal conflict, anxiety, or the castration complex, as well as secondary identification disorders (Freud, 1916–1917/2001). Whereas borderline functions are primarily organized around object loss (Bergeret & Reid, 1986), depressive anxiety and narcissistic fragility call forth specific defensive arrangements (Green, 1990; Kernberg, 1975; Kohut, 1971). Psychoses are defined by archaic anxiety, which primarily concerns the patient's identity and the loss of relationships with others and with the self (Klein, 1935/1968; Winnicott, 1958). Moreover, depending on their particular associations and specific configurations, discourse procedures reveal a normal personality organization or a specific pathological organization (see the section Analyzing Discourse Procedures for examples). The analysis of data obtained from intrapsychic issues and discourse procedures used by the patient is required. These data are analyzed throughout the protocol while taking into account the unfolding associative dynamics, the game of defense mechanisms enlisted when confronting or addressing issues, the quality of the patient's relationship with reality, and the quality of thought processes; these result in a diagnostic hypothesis closely linked to psychoanalytical psychopathology.

Take neuroses, for example. These are characterized by three interrelated dimensions: the reference to childhood history – sexuality where conflict originates, in the versions in which patients construct themselves; intrapsychic conflict and the notion of compromise (between desire and defense, between the pleasure principle and reality principle); and symbolic expression.

The *conscious–preconscious/unconscious conflict* can be identified in the TAT through the dialectic of manifest content and latent evocations. One can interpret the characteristics of the perceptual approach to the material, based on the procedures reported by the psychologist using the discourse analysis grid, based on Appendix 3 (some A1 procedures, CF procedures, E procedures). Relying on A2 procedures, the relationship with reality is prevalent, and what emerges in the primary procedures (procedure E) rarely reflects the persistent transformation of perceptions. Compromise between perceptual reality (manifest content of the cards) and the expression of fantasies (inner and psychic reality) is thus possible for neurotic patients. Lastly, the operational quality of the preconscious, characteristic of the neurotic category, is revealed in discourse through the symbolic significance of narratives and the fact that the plays of desire and defense involve a psychic elaboration activity that makes it possible to contain and process the excitation provoked by using the picture cards. Unlike neurotic patients, borderline or psychotic patients who have trouble maintaining a distinction between internal and external reality are usually unable to establish such a compromise.

The *conflict between agencies* results in the use of specific rigid (A2) and labile (B2) mechanisms that apply to sequences developed in contradiction or opposition. In addition, they join forces with predominantly rigid or labile mechanisms associated with obsessionality (A3) or hysteria (B3), underpinned by the defense mechanisms characteristic of these personality organizations. The intrapsychic account of conflict, confirming neurotic functioning, can be seen in the ability to stage representations and affects – that is, to dramatize them. Through its instructions inviting individuals to make up a story, as well as through its figurative material, the TAT promotes the development of stories. Highlighting the affects associated with representations and addressed to the other, which is characteristic of hysteria, is reflected, for instance, in the procedures that place emphasis on relationships (B1-1), dramatization (B2), and in relation to the erotization of relationships (B3-2). In obsessional neurosis, dramatization relies on the active behavior of construction that shows the hypercathexis of thought (intellectualization, A2-2). The oedipal conflict, in its most comprehensive configuration, is displayed by the numerous picture cards that solicit it, revealing the different components on the identification and relationship representations level that are highly conflictual.

The analysis of a TAT protocol involves two stages. The first consists of an analysis of discourse form – that is, how the story is told, based on the discourse analysis scoring grid, with a view to identifying these procedures and evaluating their importance and function. The second stage is devoted to the analysis of content: What are the issues addressed by the patient? Are they consistent, or not, with the card's specific latent content?

Analyzing Discourse Procedures

The expression of defense mechanisms can be identified through language and its discursive organizations: With the TAT, they are likely to be analyzed and drawn out from discourse procedures (TAT Scoring Grid, see Appendix 3). Defense mechanisms are varied and used with varying intensity to deal with the psychic conflicts triggered by the cards' latent evocations. The identification and analysis of these forms of discourse enable us to observe their degree of efficiency, flexibility or rigidity, and in some cases, their pathological dimension.

The different discourse procedures are identified in a discourse analysis grid, enabling analysis. To determine a specific discourse procedure, the clinician selects a segment of speech. The segment can consist of a few words, an entire sentence, or several sentences. A single segment can be simultaneously ascribed to several different procedures (e.g., anonymous characters and establishment of a relationship, sexualized discourse and verbal deviance). The clinical examples given here provide a clearer understanding of our approach.

Far from being a comprehensive list of the operational modalities present in all psychical organization, this grid is a tool that can be regularly modified, in particular with regard to the evolution of clinical analysis and to the issues it raises (Azoulay, 2002; Azoulay & Emmanuelli, 2000). It serves as a reference for assessing and rating the construction specificities of each narrative. Divided into four broad categories, it is complete only when the entire protocol has been analyzed.

These categories were originally devised by Shentoub and Shentoub (1960) on the basis of psychopathological categories (see the section The TAT Analysis Method According to Shentoub, above): A procedures (rigidity) were determined on the basis of analyses of patients with obsessional neurosis, B procedures (lability) were mainly derived from patients with hysterical neurosis, and E procedures (emergence of primary processes) were present mainly in the protocols of psychotic patients. The C and D procedures concern mostly conflict avoidance and recourse to behavioral responses, observed in most protocols regardless of psychopathological category. Over the years, the D section was included in the C series, since it also reflected conflict avoidance.

Series A (Rigidity) and B (Lability)

The first two series (A and B) bring together the discourse procedures initially considered to refer to neurotic defense mechanisms. However, the evolution of clinical psychopathology understanding has led to a more accurate differentiation. Moreover, the distinction among three specific groups within these two broad process categories makes it possible to distinguish the modalities of expression in line with the neurosis of those engaged in other operational modalities.

A1 (reference to external reality) and B1 (cathexis of the relationship) procedures refer to the modalities of discourse – rigid and labile, respectively – likely to be encountered in any form of psychical organization.

A2 (cathexis of internal reality) and B2 (dramatization) procedures refer to the modalities of expression of an intrapsychic conflict assuming that there is an existing differentiated internal space that acts as the scene for the deployment and dramatization of conflicts. However, these procedures alone cannot be considered to signify neurotic functioning.

A3 (obsessive-type) and B3 (hysterical-type) procedures reflect the mechanisms typically present in obsessive neurotic functioning or hysterical neurotic functioning. In both cases, the psychic scene confronts desires with defenses. When associated with other A and B procedures (mainly, but not exclusively), the actual presence of these specific procedures makes it possible to put forward a diagnostic hypothesis of neurotic functioning.

Series C (Conflict Evasion)

This series of discourse procedures, which includes five differentiation groups, corresponds to the expression of a difficulty that is more or less massive and pathological, in reflecting and addressing the conflicts on the psychic scene.

The C/F procedures (overcathexis of external reality) identified by Debray (1997) focus on the elements of external reality; factual, everyday life; and received ideas that replace a faulty internal world. Used in the majority of procedures they correspond to operational modalities characterized by the absence of intrapsychic conflict, as was described by Deutsch (1942) in relation to *as if* personalities and by Marty (1976) in the *operative thought* notion.

C/I procedures (inhibition) generally fall under phobic adjustments in which avoidance and flight dominate. Present at low levels they are a transitional arrangement that enables the pursuit of the narrative and reentry into the conflict. Analyzing how they interact with the other series enables us to identify the neurotic, borderline, or psychotic nature of the inhibition.

C/N procedures (narcissistic cathexis), developed by Brelet (1986), can reflect narcissistic libidinal withdrawal that takes the place of instinctual conflict. Used on a limited basis (they can be found in all of the protocols), they sometimes act as a stepping stone for the evocation of an intrapsychic conflict.

C/L procedures (instability of borders), identified by Brelet-Foulard et al. (in Azoulay & Emmanuelli, 2000), can reflect the relational modalities characteristic of borderline functioning: personality organization marked by dependence on the external object, and porosity and vacillation of borders between self and the other, as well as psychic operational heterogeneity that is likely to underpin splitting. Nevertheless, the limited presence of these procedures can be found in various operational modalities.

C/M procedures (antidepressive) refer to manic-type mechanisms as expressed in Klein's antidepressive struggles. Emphasis is placed on the more or less intense and lasting difficulty to regulate loss and separation by focusing on pirouette, irony, etc. (Brelet, 1986).

Series E: Emergence of Primary Processes

Series E combines discourse procedures that refer to thought modalities saturated with primary process. At low levels the presence of the discourse procedures of series E places an emphasis on a certain amount of flexibility of the agencies that allow the emergence and flow of more massive fantasies and/or affects without disrupting the person. Present at higher levels they can reveal a real fragility of the ego; if they appear in a dominant and iterative manner, they can take a clearly pathological connotation within the psychosis registry.

In this series, we can distinguish four procedures each grouped into its own category:

- E1 procedures: *Perceptual distortion* underscores the shortcomings of perceptive behavior and the relationship to the external reality.
- E2 procedures: *Massive projection* refers to profound disruption linked to an invasion by fantasy.
- E3 procedures: *Disorganization of identificatory and object landmarks* places emphasis on the major difficulties linked to object relations and/or identity.
- E4 procedures: *Impairment of speech* relates to the disorders linked to the disorganization of thought processes and discourse.

Manifest Content and Latent Manifestations of the TAT Material

The current development of manifest contents and latent evocations by selected TAT cards is presented in Appendix 2. We focus on the dual orientation of the underlying issues: those referring to the oedipal organization and those referring to object loss. The psychologist must then pay attention to two kinds of data. First, did the respondent take into account the card's main perceptive elements (age difference, gender, objects, etc.)? Secondly, is the story consistent with the latent evocations of each card? For example, in Card 1, does the story refer to the presence of a little boy and a violin – that is, the central elements of the manifest content? Does the story address the main issues suggested in the card – that is, the boy's feeling of powerlessness when confronted with an object difficult to master; his internal conflict between the desire to use the object and his frustration at not being able to do so (conflict between desire and prohibition); the necessity of having to renounce immediate gratification and the possibility of delaying this gratification thanks to a project in the future (accepting the necessity of a difficult learning process)?

Data Synthesis

This phase involves completing the TAT discourse analysis grid to determine the discourse procedures characteristic of the entire protocol for each story. It also involves accounting for defense mechanisms and putting forward hypotheses of psychic functioning.

Grouping Discourse Procedures

Grouping discourse procedures refers to selecting them on the discourse analysis grid while taking into account the frequency of their appearance and/or their economic weight, in other words, their proportion in comparison with other procedures. This approach is both quantitative and qualitative. However, we do not have as yet any statistical data concerning scores or procedure combinations. The detailed analysis of protocols aims first and foremost to determine the occurrence, relative frequency, and links between different procedures. More than the actual occurrences of one or another procedure (some are very frequently used, such as A3-1 – verbal precautions – while others are used more seldom, such as E2-2 – evocation of the bad object), what is important are the quantitative and qualitative relationships between them. Quantitative in the sense that the prevalence of one type of discourse over another provides us with valuable information on the patient's psychic functioning. Qualitative because it is through the analysis of their combination in the construction of a story, their use in the development of conflict or conversely for more disorganized or destructive purposes, that we can grasp the respondent's resources and vulnerabilities. The same emphasis is not placed on processes involving behaviors that, undoubtedly, are involved in the application of the test (such as the description of the stimulus material) and processes resulting from more active or structured defense mechanisms such as the emphasis on intrapsychic conflict or dramatization. No discourse and no series possess unequivocal validity, because everything depends on how they are distributed and their association with the procedures in the other series.

On completion of this phase, an analysis of the defensive organization is required. It is also necessary to identify the defense mechanisms and the underlying psychic behavior, and to interpret these in psychopathological terms: neurotic, borderline, narcissistic, psychotic, etc. (Brelet-Foulard & Chabert, 2003; Chabert, 1998).

Psychic Issues Tied to Latent Evocations

Respondents can process the latent content suggested in the cards in several ways: They can focus on the oedipal dimension, or react to object loss, or combine both aspects. In the last case, separation from oedipal objects reactivates earlier forms of anxiety, tied to the difficulty of working through primary object loss. The analysis of discourse procedures and latent evocations can thus enable clinicians to determine the respondents' basic psychic problematics (see Appendix 2).

Hypotheses Concerning Psychic Organization

The last phase consists in formulating a hypothesis regarding the patient's psychic organization: neurotic (obsessional, phobic, or hysterical), psychotic (schizophrenia, melancholia, paranoia), or borderline or narcissistic functioning. This classification is based on the psychoanalytic approach to psychic dynamics. In other words, it is an approach focusing on modes of psychic functioning (nature of anxiety, quality and specificity of defense mechanisms, ego structure) rather than on a semiological description. This hypothesis is based on the quality of associative processes, of defense mechanisms and their flexibility, the distribution of narcissistic and object cathexes, and the ability to develop conflict. However, the principle of the complexity of psychical organizations has not escaped the attention of contemporary authors, who suggest that the coexistence of partial structures within a single psychopathological organization is possible. Assessing this personality organization not only facilitates the refining of the diagnostic, but also makes it possible to consider the prognosis and the terms of therapeutic care, with its overtures and metamorphoses (Chabert, 2008–2010; Chabert & Verdon, 2008).

Clinical Illustrations

The clinical material presented here was necessarily selected for the specific purpose of illustrating our approach. Based on a homogeneous clinical sample of women aged 25–35 years showing depressive symptoms, our aim is to demonstrate how the identification and analysis of dominant discourse procedures and psychic issues can contribute to the distinction between the different forms of psychic functioning in neurotic, psychotic, and borderline patients. The three female patients selected for this article were diagnosed by a psychiatrist as suffering from a major depressive episode, according to the Mini International Neuropsychiatric Interview. However, it soon became clear that despite the shared diagnosis, these patients showed very different forms of psychic functioning. For this reason, they were given the Rorschach Test and the TAT. Consequently, our analysis focuses on Cards 2 and 3BM (see Appendix 2). Although confirming the diagnosis could, undoubtedly, only be achieved through the analysis of the entire protocol.

Neurosis

Barbara, aged 28, on sick leave for the last 3 months following a major depressive episode immediately makes highly conflicting representations between the mother figure and the girl figure for Card 2, under the guise of verbal precautions that mitigate the aggressiveness of her speech (A3-1, B2-3):

> The young girl, she wants to leave her village, carry on with her studies and find happiness elsewhere, the mother looks as if she was resigned to her fate, dressed in black, perhaps hoping for something, she looks weighed down, she has never known anything else. (Barbara, 28-year-old patient)

(Here the rival is disqualified, CN-2 with negative valence; the motive behind the disenchantment remains unclear, reflecting that there is both avoidance and repression at work, CI-2.) Simultaneously, shifting the father figure to the brother figure – "this must be the brother ... not the father" (verbal precaution and negation, A3-1, A2-3) – Barbara supports the attractive dimension with all the more force ("young, very athletic, happy, he likes nature," narcissistic details with seductive value, B3-2), which is nevertheless forbidden for both the young woman and the mother figure. She therefore assembles representations that, reflecting the intensity of the oedipal desire (frustration and rivalry), maintain conflict between desire and forbidding; man is the object of desire but woman cannot conquer him; while the mother remains devalued and frustrated, the young girl is endowed with intellectual curiosity and a desire for pleasure from object cathexis far from this dissatisfying scene.

Processing the 3BM card confirms the intrapsychic nature of the conflict. Indeed, the young girl's aspirations and the mother figure's fate in Card 2 lead to punishment on the part the superego: "This is a child or an adolescent who has been reprimanded; he wanted something denied by his parents." Under the pretext of an uncertain identification with regard to the character's age (B3-3), Barbara thus places emphasis on the use of labile procedures indicating object cathexis (introduction of characters who are not present, B1-2; contrasted representations and affects, B1-1, B2-3): One character conveys desire, the other, prohibition. Hesitating between several interpretations (A3-1), she thus initially attempts to mitigate this conflicting object impact through narcissistic withdrawal (CN-1, CN-2 with negative valence): "Or maybe he has been confronted to [*sic*] academic disappointment." However, under the pretext of anaclitic representation (CM-1+), it is the cathexis of the relationship (B1-1) that enables Barbara to restore the satisfaction of the oedipal desire: "In the future he will go back, his mother will comfort him."

Processing singular latent evocations from Card 2 and 3BM in this way highlights rigid and labile procedures of discourse as well as – to a lesser degree – discourse that is narcissistic, inhibited, and even an antidepressive struggle. It reflects the diversity of processes likely to be mobilized in neurosis. The quality of the psychic issues addressed demonstrates the intrapsychic value that structures desire as opposed to defense, as well as the fundamental oedipal conflict and its depressive impact.

Borderline Functioning

Aged 31, Christina has come for a consultation owing to persistent depression over the last 4 years. For Card 2, she conceptualizes a libidinal relationship between the man and the young girl in the forefront (B1-1/B3-2) whose deployment remains confined by rigid procedures (description with attachment to detail A1-1; temporal precisions, A1-2): "So this scene takes place before the War in 1914. The young girl is the teacher. So she is in love with the person who's sowing, the young man sowing behind her." However, excluding the female/maternal character through isolation (A3-4) shows the impossible deployment of interpersonal conflict on a triangular model, in favor of the use of narcissistic mechanisms seeking to maintain differentiation between the characters whose identities tend to be mixed up: "And there's a pregnant woman who looks quite serene" (emphasis on the subjective experience, CN-1), "and the young girl seems to have difficulty expressing herself" (CN-2 with negative valence). "She dares not tell him" (CI-2, the motive of the conflict is unspecified; identity confusion is likely → E3-1).

The use of narcissistic procedures is followed by a focus on sensory cathexis ("It's a beautiful evening," "a beautiful light"; CN-2 with positive valence and CN-4) and confirms the lack of ambivalence and Christina's difficulty in mobilizing an intrapsychic conflictuality where desire and prohibition can confront each other. At the end of the narrative, separation and the potential permanent disappearance of the male character are two themes that illustrate the threat of disruption that weighs on the singular object relationship depicted by Christina; this she attempts to stop through idealization: "Just before he leaves for the war. So she might never see him again. He's handsome" (B2-1, A3-1, B1-1, CN-2+).

Following up on Card 2, Card 3BM sets off the issue of object loss in which the impact of narcissistic injury reflects a melancholic dimension. Indeed, it is difficult for Christina to clearly identify an affect and associate it with the representation of loss: "This person is suffering. He or she is not sleeping but is curled up. I think it's probably a girl." The word she uses ("suffering") suggests – in French – both physical and psychological pain. Emphasis is on the subjective experience (CN-1), without object cathexis, as well as on the apprehension associated with identifying the character on the card, first anonymous (CI-2), then identified as female. There is neither intrapsychic conflict nor cathexis of a reassuring or comforting object but rather a fixation on a still composition (CN-3): "It's more an image of anxiety, of closure." Despite the use of verbal precautions seeking to mitigate the significance (A3-1), the highly projective fatal representation that ends the narrative shows the narcissistic impact from confrontation to the problem of loss, and the hopeless elaboration of a depressive position: "There may even be a gun there. Maybe she's killed herself."

In view of the succession of these two cards and the inhibition of rivalry conflict for Card 2, it is worth questioning whether expressing a self-destructive fantasy for card 3BM is not a mask against an attack on the object in which the ego appears poorly differentiated. Indeed, processing Cards 2 and 3BM draws attention to a prevalence of discourse procedures, reflecting the difficulty of managing conflicts in an intrapsychic scene. Analyzing psychic issues highlights that the problem of loss is fundamental. This is linked to the instability of the internal object that confers to the oedipal conflict a nonstructuring character dominated by the prevalence of narcissistic cathexis within a system of dual relationships.

Psychosis

Patricia, aged 35, says she has been depressed since her divorce 5 years ago. She presents a symptomatology that is both multiple and charged, associating auditory hallucinations with persistent suicidal ideas that have led to several serious suicide attempts.

The story for Card 2 begins in a descriptive mode by focusing on the character in the forefront: "This is a woman with books" (A1-1). However, the following part of the story immediately reveals the failure of rigid defenses: "She's either leaving high school, or going to high school, or there's a woman next to her who I don't know." Indeed, while she initially hesitates between the different interpretations "leaving" or "going" (A3-1), the following part of the story shows that this hesitation does not oppose desire and defense, but rather focuses on the need to spatially situate the characters by insisting on their position (A1-1) and their difference, without associating them (with a disruption of syntax, E4-1). Attention then shifts to the woman in the background, maintaining the expression of sexual fantasy that is frequently mentioned ("She's expecting a baby," B3-2). This leads to further language discrepancy (E4-1) that is very significant in French, because it leads to a change from singular to generalized meaning; here "the" stomach is no longer the woman's stomach but a stomach: "because there is, all the same, a stomach." Patricia can use a coordinating conjunction (*but*) that could support disparate and confrontational representations. But in fact, her story is characterized by anonymity (CI-2) and factual information, reflecting the impossibility for her to represent the investment of libido in a movement toward an object:

> She's resting and there in the center there's a man working with a horse. But the girl with her book, she's either waiting for a bus or a coach.... The man in the center, he's working and the lady whose standing is tired, she's resting. (Patricia, 35-year-old patient)

It is nonetheless worth noting that after all of these differentiation attempts, Patricia is still able to propose a relationship that makes it possible to mobilize the representation of a libidinal relationship while avoiding conflict: "She looks at her husband" (B1-1, B3-2).

Sensitivity to the depressive evocations of Card 3BM is instant, calling for the use of narcissistic defenses that freeze all form of libidinal investment, denying its internal source: It is the picture, rather than the character in the picture, that is sad: "It's a very sad picture" (CN-3). What follows shows the extent to which character identification is problematic and unstable: "It's a lady, it's a person" (CI-2, anonymity of character), "I don't know if it's a man or a woman. In any case, she must have lost someone she cares a lot about" (introduction of a character who is not present B1-2, and establishing relationships, B1-1, all the while maintaining anonymity CI-2). The potential evocation of the fantasy of object loss expresses a libidinal relationship, which, as soon as it is expressed, immediately leads to the emergence of a persecutory projection ("She has been mistreated," E2-2), extreme narcissistic injury ("She's poor," CN2-), and reveals the intensity of depressive anxiety and the absence of the potential projection of a supportive object: "Or she's very sad because no one understands her. She's in a lot of pain" (strong affect B2-2, associated to the representation of a bad object E2-2). The clinical psychologist then notices that Patricia has tears in her eyes.

The intense suffering, which may have a melancholic dimension, seems literally experienced and shows her loss of distance when faced with the projective situation.

While there is no doubt that Patricia is suffering from schizophrenia from a clinical perspective as well as from the results of the projective tests, processing the two TAT cards reveals the intensity of her suffering that is linked to her attempts to maintain a relationship with both lifesaving and destructive objects. Indeed, while the struggle for life reflected by the maintenance of contact with her affects also feeds her self-destructive behavior, her processing of object loss faces obstacles due to an inconsistent identity and highly fragile narcissistic defenses.

Conclusion

The French School, founded by Rausch de Traubenberg for the Rorschach Test and by Shentoub for the TAT, is founded on the legacy of the American School of the 1950s and 1960s as represented by Rappaport, Holt, and Schafer, and of course, first of all, on the legacy of Rorschach, Murray, and their colleagues. These eminent predecessors all received psychoanalytic training. They underscored the importance of paying attention not only to the content of the TAT story but also to how the story is told. They developed Murray's approach, which was to perform a rigorous formal analysis of the story (accuracy of perception, coherence of the narrative, tendency to describe, imagination, quality of syntax, etc.). They were particularly intent on observing how the fluidity and construction of the narrative were either enhanced or disorganized, not by the events of the person's daily life, but by the unconscious conflicts mobilized by the material. In addition, they addressed the question of the status of the story's content – neither an uncontrolled product of the imagination, like daytime dreaming or even a nighttime dream, nor a purely cognitive product devoid of emotional and unconscious content.

As we have tried to show here, Shentoub's approach, both in its original form and in its contemporary variations and applications, deepens this perspective through the use of psychoanalytic theory as a support for interpretations: The analysis of psychic processes thanks to the discourse analysis grid and the identification of latent evocations makes it possible to pinpoint the issues positively or negatively affecting the patient's psychic life (Brelet, 1986).

Based on narratives constructed by subjects using TAT material, the scoring of discourse procedures and the identification of psychic issues, clinical psychologists can highlight the diversity of psychic problems and defense mechanisms in a rigorous and objective manner. The reliability of the assessments is primarily empirical: It is based on the experience of clinical psychologists specialized in projective techniques, and on the consistency of results of blind scorings of the same protocols. One of our studies was devoted to a quantitative analysis (univariate analysis) of the validity of interrater scoring and analysis (Louët,

Consoli, & Cohen, 2010), based on expert guidelines: Two psychodynamic-oriented psychologists scored blindly the same psychological protocols; inter-rater reliability was high and significant.

Thus, this tool provides psychologists with a precise description of each patient's specific functioning depending on psychopathological organization (neurosis, psychosis, borderline functioning) as well as on the resources and psychic fragility of each patient. In combination with the analysis and interpretation of a Rorschach Test, this method makes it possible to produce a synthesis of the psychic functioning of the patient, while taking into account both the psychopathological elements and the patient's resources and potential for working through and change. Thus, this approach to projective testing can be seen as inherently clinical, in the fullest sense of the term.

Acknowledgments

This chapter appeared in a similar form in the *Rorschachiana*: Verdon, B., Chabert, C., Azoulay, C., Emmanuelli, M., Neau, F., Vibert, S., & Louët, E. (2014). The dynamics of TAT process: Psychoanalytical and psychopathological perspectives. *Rorschachiana, 35,* 103–133. https://doi.org/10.1027/1192-5604/a000056 © Hogrefe Publishing.

We would like to thank F.D. Camps for granting us access to Patricia's protocol, collected over the course of his doctoral thesis defended under the supervision of Prof. C. Chabert, titled "The Psychic Processing of Loss Within Schizophrenics. A Psychoanalytic and Projective Approach," University Paris Descartes, 2013.

References

Anzieu, D., Chabert, C., & Louët, E. (2017). *Les méthodes projectives* [The projective methods]. Paris, France: PUF.

Azoulay, C. (2002). La feuille de dépouillement du TAT: Des origines à nos jours [The TAT scoring grid of the TAT: From its beginnings until the present]. *Psychologie clinique et projective, 8,* 21–59. http://doi.org/10.3917/pcp.008.0021

Azoulay, C., & Emmanuelli, M. (2000). La feuille de dépouillement du TAT: Nouvelle formule, nouveaux procédés [The TAT scoring grid: A new formula, new procedures]. *Psychologie clinique et projective, 6,* 305–327.

Bergeret, J., & Reid, W. (1986). *Narcissisme et états-limites* [Narcissism and borderline conditions]. Paris, France: Dunod.

Brelet, F. (1986). *Le TAT. Fantasme et situation projective* [The TAT: Fantasy and the projective situation]. Paris, France: Dunod.

Brelet, F. (1987). On cherche un metteur en scène [A film director is looked for]. *Psychologie française, 50*(32), 137–140.

Brelet-Foulard, F., & Chabert, C. (2003). *Nouveau manuel du TAT. Approche psychanalytique* [New TAT manual: Psychoanalytic approach]. Paris, France: Dunod.

Chabert, C. (1998). *Psychanalyse et méthodes projectives* [Psychoanalysis and projective methods]. Paris, France: Dunod.

Chabert, C. (Ed.). (2008–2010). *Traité de psychopathologie de l'adulte («les névroses», «narcissisme et dépression», «psychopathologie des limites», «les psychoses»)* [Treatise of adult psychopathology ("neuroses," "narcissism and depression," "psychopathology of limits," "psychoses")]. Paris, France: Dunod.

Chabert, C., & Verdon, B. (2008). *Psychologie clinique et psychopathologie* [Clinical psychology and psychopathology]. Paris, France: PUF.

Debray, R. (1997). TAT et économie psychosomatique: un bilan actuel [A current assessment of the TAT and the psychosomatic economy]. *Psychologie clinique et projective, 3,* 19–37.

Deutsch, H. (1942). Some forms of emotional disturbance and their relationships to schizophrenia. *The Psychoanalytic Quarterly, 11,* 301–321. http://doi.org/10.1080/21674086.1942.11925501

Emmanuelli, M., & Azoulay, C. (2008). *Pratique des épreuves projectives à l'adolescence. Approche psychanalytique* [Using projective techniques with adolescents. Psychoanalytical approach]. Paris, France: Dunod.

Freud, S. (1895/2001). Project for a scientific psychology. In J. Strachey (Ed. & Trans.), *The standard edition of the complete psychological works of Sigmund Freud* (Vol. 1, pp. 281–397). London, UK: Vintage Classics. (Original work published in 1895)

Freud, S. (1916–1917/2001). Introductory lectures on psycho-analysis (Part III). In J. Strachey (Ed. & Trans.), *The standard edition of the complete psychological works of Sigmund Freud* (Vol. 16, pp. 243–476). London, UK: Vintage Classics. (Original work published in 1916)

Green, A. (1990). *La folie privée* [On private madness]. Paris, France: Gallimard.

Kernberg, O. (1975). *Borderline conditions and pathological narcissism.* New York, NY: Jason Aronson.

Klein, M. (1968). A contribution to the psychogenesis of manic-depressive states. In *Essais de Psychanalyse* [Contributions to psychoanalysis] (pp. 311–340). Paris, France: Payot. (Original work published in 1935)

Kohut, H. (1971). *The analysis of the self: A systematic approach to the psychoanalytical treatment of narcissistic personality disorders.* New York, NY: International Universities Press.

Laplanche, J., & Pontalis, J. B. (1988). *The language of psychoanalysis* [original in French]. London, UK: Karnac Books.

Louët, E., Consoli, A., & Cohen, D. (2010). Psychodynamic-oriented psychological assessment predicts evolution to schizophrenia a 8-year follow-up in adolescents hospitalized for a manic/mixed episode: Interest of an overall subjective rating. *Journal of Physiology, 104,* 257–262. http://doi.org/10.1016/j.jphysparis.2010.08.004

Marty, P. (1976). *Les mouvements individuels de vie et de mort. Essai d'économie psychosomatique* [Individual movements of living and death: Contribution to psychosomatic economy]. Paris, France: Payot.

Murray, H. A. (1943). *Thematic Apperception Test.* Paris, France: Centre de Psychologie Appliquée.

Neau, F. (2002). L'exigence narrative au TAT dans des protocoles d'auteurs d'agressions sexuelles [The narrative particularity of the TAT in the protocols of authors of sexual aggressions]. *Psychologie clinique et projective, 8,* 157–181. http://doi.org/10.3917/pcp.008.0157

Rausch de Traubenberg, N. (1970). *La pratique du Rorschach* [The practice of the Rorschach Test]. Paris, France: PUF.

Schafer, R. (1958). How was this story told? *Journal of Projective Techniques, 22*(2), 181–210. http://doi.org/10.1080/08853126.1958.10380840

Schafer, R. (1967). *Projective testing and psychoanalysis*. New York, NY: International University Press.
Shentoub, V. (1973). A propos du normal et du pathologique dans le TAT [Study on the normal and pathological in the TAT]. *Psychologie française, 18*(4), 251–259.
Shentoub, V. (1987). Thematic Apperception Test (TAT). Théorie et method [The TAT: Theory and method]. *Psychologie française, 32*(3), 117–126.
Shentoub, V., & Debray, R. (1970–1971). Fondements théoriques du processus-TAT [Theoretical fundamentals of the TAT process]. *Bulletin de psychologie, 24, 292*(12–15), 897–903.
Shentoub, V., & Shentoub, S.A. (1960). Recherche expérimentale et clinique du thème «banal» dans le TAT [Clinical and experimental research on the "popular response" theme in the TAT]. *Psychiatrie de l'enfant, 3*, 405–524.
Verdon, B. (2011). The case of thematic tests adapted to older adults: On the importance of differentiating latent and manifest contents in projective tests. *Rorschachiana, 32,* 46–71. http://doi.org/10.1027/1192-5604/a000015
Winnicott, D.W. (1958). *Collected papers: Through paediatrics to psychoanalysis*. London, UK: Tavistock.

3

From Self-Representation to Narcissism ... and Back Again?

Françoise Neau

This chapter focuses on the relationship between the notion of self-representation, adopted by French projective psychologists in the approach of Nina Rausch de Traubenberg (Rausch de Traubenberg & Sanglade, 1984; Rausch de Traubenberg, 1990), and the psychoanalytic concept of narcissism. By *narcissism,* I refer to the essential component of psychic functioning officially introduced by Freud (1914/2001) in psychoanalysis and widely studied in post-Freudian metapsychology, rather than to the pathologies of narcissism. While the concept of *self-representation* is part of the common heritage of projective psychologists, French and French-speaking psychoanalysts hardly use it today. However, at the time when Rausch de Traubenberg proposed her "self-representation grid," this notion was widely referred to in American psychoanalytical theorizations: The latter undoubtedly influenced the importation and adaptation of this concept, which is still used in projective psychology and teaching today.

I will therefore begin with a brief presentation of the history of the concept of self-representation, as Rausch de Traubenberg developed it in Rorschach analysis from a both theoretical and a methodological perspective, and primarily on the basis of content analysis. Today, if we look at the research conducted or directed by Catherine Chabert, Michèle Emmanuelli, and Catherine Azoulay (not to mention many others), or at their pedagogical tools, we cannot but observe that the methodological and theoretical landscape has changed: Thus, in the schema of interpretation of projective data (see Appendix 1), self-representation, with its two aspects of identity and identification, is presented under the aegis of narcissism. What, then, has remained of the concept of *self-representation* other than its name? In other words, and here I am also concerned with epistemological issues, what do we mean when we speak of *self-representation* in projective tests today?

During the annual conference of the French Language Society of Rorschach and Projective Methods held in Brussels in 1988, Alex Lefebvre described self-representation as a "portable concept": For a concept, this can be both an advantage and a disadvantage. During his presentation with Françoise Hermalsteen on women who had sought cosmetic surgery, the term *self-representation* was used to refer to "unconscious, preconscious and conscious endopsychic representations of the bodily and mental self in the Ego system" (Lefebvre & Hermalsteen, 1990, p. 56). Edith Jacobson (1897–1978) is central to the authors' article. (This important figure of American psychoanalysis, a figure of great moral and ethical standing, was appointed as a training analyst at the Berlin Institute in 1934, and imprisoned by the Nazis the following year for refusing to give information on a patient. For the historical details, see A. de Mijolla (Ed.), *International Dictionary of Psychoanalysis*, 2005). Jacobson had a great interest in the clinical analysis of depression and psychosis, and perceived self-representation as the mental organization that represents an individual as they consciously and unconsciously perceive themselves; this mental organization is part of what Jacobson referred to as the "representational world" – that is, a represented world – capable of representation – created by the child through the use of the symbolic function, based on their perceptual–cognitive world. Thus conceived, *self-representation* becomes a concept at the center of a psychoanalytic system.

Other authors who were present at the same conference defined *self-representation* differently. For instance, for Anne Andronikoff-Sanglade, who understood it as "a psychological version of the psychoanalytic concept of skin-ego, which embodies the psychic apparatus" (Andronikoff-Sanglade, 1990, p. 12), self-representation was "the subject's fundamental fantasy container, an expression of his unity and coherence, reflecting his level of development and narcissistic investments, the primary agent of all relationships" (Andronikoff-Sanglade, 1990, p. 15).

With regard to this "portable concept," another question arises: What do we mean when we speak of the "self"? Logically, Lefebvre and Hermalsteen refer to the conception of the self developed by Jacobson. For Jacobson, the self is "the whole individual, including the body and body parts as well as the psychic organization and its parts" (quoted by Lécuyer, 1978). Thus defined, the term *self* means a person, an individual, or a subject, in the psychological sense of the word.

In the late 1960s and early 1970s, after the "return to Freud" advocated by Jacques Lacan, the notion of self became the topic of heated debate in French psychoanalysis: During the International Psychoanalytical Association (IPA) conference held in Rome in 1969, Jean Laplanche challenged the idea of introducing the self as a separate agency, because, he said, for Freud, the ego and the self were one and the same. In contrast, Pontalis intervened at the Symposium of the French language of Psychological Science Association held in Paris in 1973 to celebrate the "emergence and recognition of the self" (Pontalis, 1977).

"Self-Representation" According to Nina Rausch de Traubenberg: Its Theoretical Sources and Its Expression in the Rorschach

The Concept of "Self-Representation" in the Rorschach

Like words, things, and living beings, concepts have a history and are shaped by it. From the 1970s to the late 1980s, Nina Rausch de Traubenberg gave several versions of the concept of self-representation in the Rorschach and of the grid that goes with it. The publication in 1984 of the article she coauthored with Anne Sanglade titled "Self-Representation and Object Relationship in Rorschach: Grid of Self-Representation" marked an important milestone in her work (Rausch de Traubenberg & Sanglade, 1984). The article reiterated Rausch de Traubenberg's presentation at the Rorschach International Congress of Washington in 1981 and presented one of the versions of the grid in its appendix. Despite its modest title, her last article, "The Development of the Self-Representation Grid in the Rorschach Test" (Rausch de Traubenberg, 1990) – derived from a paper bearing the same title that was presented at the 1988 Rorschach Congress held in Brussels (Rausch de Traubenberg, Bloch-Lainé, & Boizou, 1988), along with the ultimate version of the "self-representation grid," and which was the result of research conducted over a period of 15 years – was fundamental, in that it retraced the history of the concept and its genesis.

Although the epistemological concern does not take center stage, the process of elaboration of the concept as reconstructed by Rausch de Traubenberg provides a wealth of information on how she worked and on the underlying procedures guiding her research, as she describes it once the work is completed; today, this is highly informative for clinical psychologists, researchers, or teachers – and especially if one is all three. Indeed, from the outset, Rausch de Traubenberg identified

> not only the impact of ideas and schools of thought but especially the impact of the encounter between colleagues and teams using different approaches. These encounters and confrontations sparked and even drove exchanges, because I had to explain what was still implicit in my own approach to new interlocutors from other fields of psychology. (Rausch de Traubenberg, 1990, p. 17)

Before we rapidly present these successive developments, we must emphasize from the outset that the *self-representation* concept is an *operational* concept in that it emerges from three sources: clinical work based on projective testing with children, child psychotherapy, and research work on child psychology and psychopathology – indeed, the child seeks to situate, delimit, and "differentiate" themselves (Rausch de Traubenberg, 1990) through a more direct and spontaneous approach to the projective material, less defensive and more sensitive to the symbolism of the picture cards (Rausch de Traubenberg & Sanglade, 1984). This operational concept, then, is not a preexistent psychological or psychoanalytical concept that can be used to interpret a person's responses in the Rorschach. However, it was explicitly derived from a notion proposed by another projective psychologist in the late 1950s – that is, the "self-representation drive, the drive responsible for the choice of content" (Rausch de Traubenberg, 1990). Myriam Orr, who in 1958 wrote a book on the Rorschach and the maternal *imago,* with a preface by Didier Anzieu, spoke of "a universal self-portrait need, or perhaps even a drive" (Orr, 1958).

While the "self-representation drive" now seems somewhat outdated, self-representation might appear as one of the results or outcomes of narcissistic investment. As we shall see later, Rausch de Traubenberg took up the idea of the "need for self-representation in the broadest sense of the term" (Rausch de Traubenberg, 1990, p. 20) – going even beyond mere narcissistic investment.

We must start at the beginning, though. Before the term *self-representation* became prevalent, two analysis grids were developed in the mid-1970s within the framework of the work of the Research Group on the Emotional Development of the Child, led by Daniel Widlöcher and Roger Perron, located in Paris. Together with the clinical psychologists from the child psychiatry service of the Salpêtrière Hospital in Paris, the group conducted the study Differentiation of Parental Images and Identification Movements in the Structuring of the Child's Personality (Perron, Rausch de Traubenberg, & Chabert, 1973); for this study Rausch de Traubenberg proposed a "grid to analyze the evolutionary context through perceptual modes and a grid for the analysis of kinesthetic and non-kinesthetic human representations, their substitutes, their whole or partial nature, whether they are active or not, gendered or not, real or unreal" (Rausch de Traubenberg, 1990, p. 17).

The *self-representation grid* thus emerged following various trials and strove to "systematize the interferences between *perceptual and fantasying activity*" (Rausch de Traubenberg, 1990; emphasis present in the original) and their specificity in children, as described in the book *Le Rorschach en clinique infantile, l'imaginaire et le réel chez l'enfant* (The Imaginary and the Real in Rorschach Testing With Children; Rausch de Traubenberg & Boizou, 1977): by definition, the Rorschach provokes these interferences that can be identified both in the process underlying the response and in the responses themselves, and they are "particularly evident in child protocols" (Rausch de Traubenberg, 1990). Indeed, according to Rausch de Traubenberg (1990), children need to see themselves as "'strong' or 'weak', 'dependent' or 'confident'; they either mold themselves into the offered space, or they alter or damage it." These interactions, which were examined in a study focusing on 160 children's protocols and in the work on human and kinesthetic representations mentioned in the previous paragraph (Rausch de Traubenberg & Boizou, 1977), "led us quite naturally to speak of a need for self-representation," she wrote (Rausch de Traubenberg, 1990). The self-representation grid accounts for this in a "quantitative approach to the qualitative."

Another article published at that time, "Représentation de soi: identité et identification au Rorschach chez l'enfant et l'adulte" (Self-Representation: Identity and Identification in Rorschach Among Children and Adults) (Boizou, Chabert, & Rausch de Traubenberg, 1978) describes this research. With regard to this phase of the study, Rausch de Traubenberg underscored that "everything is centered on the idea that the Rorschach tests for the presence of an 'integrated body image,' according to Catherine Chabert's apt formulation" (Rausch de Traubenberg, 1990). The image of the projected body is not an agency; situated at different levels, from the archaic to the evolved, "loaded with various meanings,"

> this image draws to itself the investments of both self and other, and thus the need for self-representation in the broadest sense of the term. Clearly, self-representation depends on the conditions of libidinal development and how parental images are experienced. (Rausch de Traubenberg, 1990, p. 20)

At this stage, self-representation in the Rorschach associates "fantasized body images" and "established relationships that result from this image and/or structure it" (Rausch de Traubenberg, 1990, p. 20): this self-representation makes it possible to "situate the level of object relations to which it refers" and "determine the stage reached by the subject in his quest to find himself through the phases leading to identification" (Rausch de Traubenberg, 1990).

Before presenting the details of the grid, we must mention the important role played by Rausch de Traubenberg's encounter with American projective psychologists and psychoanalysts, such as Sydney Blatt in particular, but also Martin Mayman, as well as with the work of Jeffrey Urist. Blatt, who was also working on the analysis of object representation "discussed thought disorders, in the context of cognitivism and psychoanalytical theory, in terms of delimitation, self or non-self, real or unreal" (Rausch de Traubenberg, 1990) and assessed "the aspects of internalization of object relations," ranging from most to least differentiated, through perceptual modes and kinesthesia (Rausch de Traubenberg, 1990). She came back from the US with many interesting theoretical ideas. In 1976, Blatt analyzed the "human" responses given by random participants and patients according to their formal quality, their differentiation (parahuman, partial, partial parahuman), and their degree of elaboration (seven categories of attributes enriching the response) and of integration ("meaning the internal source of the motivation for action and the integration of an interaction" depending on its nature and its emotional tone) (Blatt & Lerner, 1984). Similarly, Mayman was undertaking his research at the same time on "the quality of interpersonal relationships based on object representations provided in TAT, Rorschach and early memories" (Mayman, 1967). Drawing on Mayman's methodological developments and the theoretical contributions by Kernberg and Kohut (Lerner, 1998) – whom Rausch de Traubenberg did not mention – Urist analyzed the ability of the Rorschach to "recognize individual differences in the internal self and in object representations" (Rausch de Traubenberg, 1990). Urist, who developed an object relations evaluation scale called the Mutuality of Autonomy Scale (MAS;

Urist, 1977), concluded, according to Rausch de Traubenberg's account (Rausch de Traubenberg, 1990), that the Rorschach was highly sensitive to regressive stimuli and that several projective tests should be proposed to patients.

Rausch de Traubenberg (1990) thus underscored the convergence between her earlier research, conducted with her colleagues, and the American studies in projective psychology mentioned in the previous paragraphs. According to her, these studies all showed that "the essential features of the concept of the internal object" were reflected in three main items: (1) "image categories" (human beings, animals and "objects" and their integrity), (2) the type of relationships between the images, and (3) the objective accuracy. These items thus served as a basis for the development of the self-representation grid, the validity of which Rausch de Traubenberg verified through her clinical work.

Additional Sources for the Concept of Self-Representation in the Rorschach

Without denying the *empirical* dimension of this operational concept, which is closely associated with clinical work and contemporary research in child psychopathology, the notion of *self-representation* appears to have been inspired, though less explicitly so, by two other sources the recognition of which can improve our understanding. The first is the phenomenological conception of the subject, which Rausch de Traubenberg never directly refers to, but which occasionally arises in her formulations. The second are the American post-War theorizations pertaining to ego psychology and object relations. Although I will begin by outlining the former, I will focus on the latter.

The Phenomenological Inspiration

Although the phenomenological inspiration was more apparent in the papers and publications from 1980 to 1985, it was still present in later theorizations. The reference to phenomenology here is limited to the philosophical trend, which had a strong influence on German psychiatry in the early 20th century; I do not aim to address how phenomenology has explicitly inspired the work of projective psychologists since the 1920s. I have as yet found no trace of how Françoise Minkowska (1882–1950), who introduced the *Psychodiagnostik* of Hermann Rorschach in France even before its publication, might have influenced the work of Nina Rausch de Traubenberg.

As still present in later theorizations, indeed, *self-representation* also designates "the subject's fundamental positions as *experienced in his body and his relational world*" (Rausch de Traubenberg & Sanglade, 1984, p. 43; emphasis present in the original). It is both the agent and the outcome of the subject's "positioning," of their "situation" (an echo of Sartre's philosophy is present here) in the face of both objects and the world. According to Rausch de Traubenberg, self-representation, *like Rorschach responses,* has different *components*. The analysis of these components is based on "the identification and recognition of one's lived body as one knows it" and "the projection of one's lived body as it is experienced" (Rausch de Traubenberg & Sanglade, 1984). The dialectic between the lived body as we know it and the lived body as it is experienced, which coincides here with the dialectic between what is perceived and what is projected, between external and internal reality, has met with little success among Rausch de Traubenberg's heirs. Her thinking, however, seems to have been largely inspired by the phenomenological approach, given the emphasis on the notion of "lived body," a sensitive body, determined through apperception, conscience, and the dialectic between the known body and the experienced body.

Further developments would be necessary to clarify what I see as a strong resonance with the theory developed by Merleau-Ponty (1945) for whom the "lived body" takes on an increasingly central role.

> Thus experience of one's own [lived] body runs counter to the reflective procedure which detaches subject and object from each other and which gives us only the thought about the body, or the body as an idea, and not the experience of the body or the body in reality. (Merleau-Ponty, 1945/1962, p. 198)

Rather than "self-representation," shouldn't one, then, speak of a sense of Self even though, in all phenomenological logic, such an indivisible self is unlimited, coextensive with the world and lacking "personal identity"? (For an introduction to Merleau-Ponty's dialogue with psychoanalysis, please refer to Pontalis, 1968. The comparison between the philosophy of perception developed by the author of the *Phénoménologie de la perception* [Phenomenology of Perception] and *Le Visible et l'invisible* [The Visible and the Invisible, Merleau-Ponty, 1964] and Freudian proposals on perception expressed in the "Project for a Scientific Psychology" [Freud, 1895/2001] deserves to be further developed.)

While such a "self" can participate in the *oceanic feeling* in the term coined by Romain Rolland and popularized by Freud (1930/2001), there clearly is an internal contradiction between the use of phenomenological vocabulary and the foundations of phenomenology (as expressed by Merleau-Ponty) in Rausch de Traubenberg's work; in parallel, the distance from Freudian metapsychology has proved significant. From her resolutely psychogenetic perspective, Rausch de Traubenberg postulates that the "sense of personal identity" relies "on a unitary experience which is the point from which all future processes of differentiation, individuation and identification begin" (Rausch de Traubenberg & Sanglade, 1984, p. 43). Consequently, she makes this unitary experience a point of origin which is neither *non-differentiated,* as in Merleau-Ponty's phenomenology, nor *constructed* through the processes of differentiation, individuation, and identification, marked by psychic conflict, as is the case with psychoanalysis.

Self-Representation in the Rorschach, Ego-Psychology, and Object Relations Theories

Blatt, Mayman, and Urvist, the American sources who inspired Rausch de Traubenberg, were influenced, on the one hand, by Hartmann's ego psychology and Kohut's self psychology, through the legacy of Rapaport (a proponent of the theory of ego autonomy), and on the other hand, by the theories of Kernberg, who was the "representative of the neo-Kleinian trend" (Oppenheimer, 1996) and who was engaged in reconciling ego psychology (particularly in its second generation) with Kleinian theories, especially with the positions held by Margaret Mahler and Edith Jacobson (Tessier, 2005).

My question, then, is this: Can this concept be used in projective testing today without referring at the same time to this heterogeneous and complex theoretical background? I will present only a brief outline of these different trends and how they relate to each other.

Ego Psychology

Self-representation, with a capital *S*, was a term that was first used, to the best of my knowledge, by Heinz Hartmann (1894–1970) and was then borrowed by Edith Jacobson. (Born in Vienna like Edith Jacobson, Kohut, Kernberg, and others, like them, Hartmann had to go into exile to escape from the Nazis – first in France and Switzerland, then in the US in 1941. As a brilliant psychiatrist, he had been invited in the late 1920s to lecture at the Johns Hopkins Institute; but he came back to Vienna. To keep him there, Freud had proposed to analyze him free of charge, an offer the aspiring patient accepted. In 1938, a year before he was forced to leave Germany and 3 years after Anna Freud published *The Ego and the Mechanisms of Defense* [Freud, 1936/1993], Hartmann wrote *Ego Psychology and the Problem of Adaptation* [Hartmann, 1939/1958]. Hartmann himself had had to adapt to the US, and he became, as is well known, one of the main promoters of ego psychology in opposition to which, a group of French post-War psychoanalysts, notably including Lacan, advocated a return to Freud.)

Hartmann sought to simplify Freud's concept of the ego, as he found it too complex and somewhat contradictory. While Freud saw the ego as a heterogeneous concept, or rather a concept which underscored the ego's "native" heterogeneity – and even more so since the introduction of narcissism in 1914 – Hartmann preferred to think in terms of a polarity. Freud's ego by definition has more than one meaning and is even deliberately contradictory: It is a double agent or even a triple agent, as it must serve three masters at once – the id, the superego, and external reality (Freud, 1923/2001). The ego is thus at the service of reality testing *and* of the defense against the drives; it is both self-preserving *and* libidinal, the agent of repression *and* an object of love for the individual; the basis of personality *and* a reservoir of libido (at least as formulated until 1923); a surface linked to the perception/consciousness system *and* a mental projection of the body's surface (Freud, 1923/2001); the product of progressive differentiation from the id (Freud, 1923/2001) *and* a concentrate of identifications with infantile objects, loved then lost or abandoned.

Challenging Freudian metapsychology, Hartmann, and after him the supporters of ego psychology, differentiated between the ego and the Self: For them, the ego was only a psychic substructure, entirely devoted to its adaptive functions, which were essential, given that for Hartmann, adaptation regulated the relationships between the environment and the body, while narcissistic investment was directed toward the Self. The Self is the part of the ego that "is opposed to the object": The Self thus becomes "the person him/herself" as opposed to the other. Hartmann's, and later Edith Jacobson's, view of the Self is very close to the notion of individual in classical psychology.

At the same time, Freud's definition of narcissism was called into question: Indeed according to Hartmann, narcissism referred to the libidinal investment not of the ego, but of the Self. As Hartmann said:

> In using the term *narcissism*, two different sets of opposites often seem to be fused into one: the one refers to the self (one's own person), in contradistinction to the object, the second to the ego (as a psychic system) in contradistinction to other *substructures of personality. However, the opposite of object cathexis is not ego cathexis but cathexis of one's own person, that is self-cathexis; in speaking of self-cathexis, we do not imply whether this cathexis is located in the id, the ego or the super-ego*... It therefore will be clarifying if we *define narcissism as the libidinal cathexis not* of the *ego but* of the *self*. (Hartmann, 1950, p. 84–85)

To highlight some of the major trends that have continuously guided our psychoanalytic interpretation of projective tests, it is interesting to compare Hartmann's system and his ego psychology, with the system developed by Kohut, the advocate of self psychology (Kohut, 1971). Kohut does not seem to have had any particular influence on Rausch de Traubenberg, but Catherine Chabert refers to his work in her research on narcissistic pathologies (Chabert, 1987, 1998). Kohut's Self was at first similar to Hartmann's Self: All the self-representations contained in the ego. However, in the 1980s, based on the clinical study of narcissistic pathologies, Kohut developed the concept of self object, referring to narcissistic object relations as opposed to object love, which led him to a "generalized Self psychology." Based on this concept, Kohut founded a new metapsychology that went well beyond the pathologies of narcissism, and a new practice of treatment that was based on the narcissistic dimension of transference and the notion of empathy, on the side of the psychoanalyst. I must refer here to Agnès Oppenheimer's (1996) very illuminating critical interpretation of Kohut's psychoanalytical thought and North American psychoanalytical thought in general. Her posthumously published article (Oppenheimer, 2010) is also worth mentioning. This article presented a historical perspective and an extremely interesting critique of the "the return of identity in psychoanalysis," which is still of great relevance today.

Object Relations Theories

The theories of object relations, as originated in the US by Melanie Klein, directly nurtured the concept of self-representation developed by Rausch de Traubenberg, via the American projective psychology authors she quoted and those who inspired them.

I use the term *theories* in the plural: These theories are united by the fact that they place the internalization, structuring, and clinical reactivation of the earliest dyadic object relations at the center of their model, within a psychogenetic perspective. Even here, however, divergent views have emerged: In the forefront is the issue of the drives and their replacement by object relations, as developed by Fairbairn and Sullivan, for instance, or by Kohut's concept of the self object. In contrast, Jacobson and Kernberg maintained the drives alongside object relations.

Rausch de Traubenberg's approach is in my view closest to the Kernberg model. Indeed, Daniel Widlöcher, who was codirector (with Roger Perron) of the research group at the Salpêtrière Hospital in Paris, in which Rausch de Traubenberg and psychologists from the Child Psychiatry Service participated, wrote the Preface of the French translation of Kernberg's book *Borderline Conditions and Pathological Narcissism* (Kernberg, 1975).

Ego Psychology and Object Relations Theories: Their Unification by Otto Kernberg

Drawing on Hartmann's work, Kernberg (1982) developed his own model by combining two theories that had become popular in America: ego psychology and the theory of object relations. From his point of view, a self-representation, an object representation, and an affect state linking them are essential units of psychic structure; the self is thus an intrapsychic structure, playing a fundamental role in the ego and resulting from the organization of self-representations and their corresponding emotional patterns. It is neither a supplementary agency nor the focus of narcissistic investment as was the case with Hartmann and with Kohut in his early works. Rather, it is a system of self-representations, which is part of the ego. But once again, the ego is a secondary and adaptive ego: Ego activity is what enables the construction of an integrated self and the organization and consistency of self-representations.

What does the term *self-representation* mean for Kernberg? It means outcomes of ego activity rather than its driving force, for "self representations are affective-cognitive structures reflecting the person's perception of himself in real interactions with significant others and in fantasied interactions with internal representations of significant others, that is, with object representations" (Kernberg, 1975, pp. 315–316).

As with Hartmann, narcissism here is the libidinal investment of the self; but it is the result of ego activity and differentiation, which under normal circumstances enables the construction of a coherent and integrated self. A disorder in this organization, according to Kernberg, leads to narcissistic pathology.

Self-Representation in the Rorschach

The Grid

The *self-representation grid* – the product of 15 years of joint work by Rausch de Traubenberg and colleagues – categorizes, on the basis of content analysis, the responses obtained in a protocol in four columns. In the grid's final version (Rausch de Traubenberg, 1990), the first column lists the objects represented, distinguishing among the objects belonging to the human, animal, and inanimate worlds. The first two sections list whole or partial responses, *para-human* or *para-animal* (i.e., monsters, robots, dragons, etc.) and anatomical details. The second column focuses on "how one connects with the object" – that is, the type of interaction (reciprocal or not, active or passive, "positive" or "aggressive," "mirror," "posture" without movements or impossible interaction – statue, mummy, dead human or animal). The third column deals with sexual identification, and the fourth with "differentiation or nondifferentiation between self and others."

The Significance of the Grid

For Rausch de Traubenberg, this grid represented a "unifying principle" of the entire projective space – that is, not only of the person themselves in their relationship to the world, but for the projective psychologist as well; indeed, self-representation "makes it possible to bring together the different moments of qualitative and quantitative analysis by relating them to the subject himself" (Rausch de Traubenberg & Sanglade, 1984, p. 46). In addition to its clinical value, the grid makes it possible to "quantify the qualitative," because "the large number of combinations of data belonging to the four columns ... may be used to develop statistics" (Rausch de Traubenberg & Sanglade, 1984, p. 46) in a far subtler manner than is possible with psychograms, providing the Rorschach with some degree of scientific reliability. I will not discuss the methodological and epistemological issues underlying this view, even if these issues remain relevant today: Indeed, must qualitative data be associated with quantitative data to meet the requirements of science? If so, to what extent and at what price?

This "attempt at systematization" first seeks to *compare groups* of subjects; Thus, in the same article, it is applied to the problem of "aggressiveness in adolescents with somatic disorders" and "mentally disturbed adolescents" (Rausch de Traubenberg & Sanglade, 1984). According to Rausch de Traubenberg, the analysis of the interference between perceptual and fantasying activities can only be conducted on an individual basis. Incidentally, this raises questions for the numerous studies carried out among one or several populations, using a projective methodology. For Rausch de Traubenberg and Anne Sanglade, the self representation grid also allows for individual analysis insofar as it can also highlight "the subject's attitude in the face of his own psychic activity and his representation of the psychic activity of others; it thus reflects the subject's investment of his Self-representation and object relations" (Rausch de Traubenberg & Sanglade, 1984, p. 53). Does narcissism, or rather the narcissistic economy (it is indeed a question of investment), coincide here with a Self defined by its conscious reflexivity, in a psychological tradition derived from philosophy (and more specifically the direction taken by classical metaphysics toward subjectivity), rather than with a Self defined by its unconscious dimension?

In French philosophy, the term *soi* – equivalent to *self,* in English philosophy – is an innovation of the translator of Locke's *An Essay Concerning Human Understanding* (1700): Locke sought to differentiate himself from the ego *(moi)* introduced by Descartes and Pascal. The translator also used the term *soi-même*, which, almost 4 centuries later, Paul Ricoeur turned into *ipséité* (ipseity), *the self proper* (ipse), which, with sameness *(idem),* is one of the two characteristics of identity. It can be defined by what Ricoeur refers to as the "relationship with another" along with the words spoken to this other, the *Nebenmensch* (although Ricoeur does not name it as such). According to Barbara Cassin, this "relationship to oneself, on the part of the individual or the group," defined what, beginning from the 16th century, can be called the European invention of consciousness (Cassin, 2004, p. 260).

Self-Representation Today

Self-Representation in the Rorschach

In the projective psychology studies undertaken at the French School, the factors considered today as reflecting self-representation are divided into two successive but inseparable categories of investigation: identity and identification. These categories are more diversified, better related to one another than in the analysis carried out by Rausch de Traubenberg (Chabert, 1983, 1987, 1998; Emmanuelli & Azoulay, 2001). Self-representation (in the singular form) and the representations of relationships (in the plural form) are studied in terms of conflict resolution, and distinguished from thought processes (even though, owing to their intrinsic polysemy, the same factors are also summoned in the assessment of thought processes: Naturally, I refer to the contribution of movement responses and to the variety of contents).

Today, in the identity category, when summarizing the quality of primary identifications and the underlying narcissistic foundations, our lectures and research are based on the schema of interpretation of projective data (see Appendix 1). We thus briefly examine (1) the integrity of human and animal representations, (2) their degree of reality or life based on the quality of the human and animal responses, whether full or partial, whether purely formal or driven by M (human movement) responses, and FM responses (the movement is projected on animals), to which we pay special attention; and finally, (3) third criterion in the identity category, the quality of inner/outer boundaries, through the formal (F%, F+%) and perceptual (apprehension modes) envelope, as well as content. Particular attention is paid to the "unitary" cards and especially to card V which, from a perceptual point of view, is considered as specifically summoning self-representation.

Similarly, as concerns identification, these studies have led to the reassessment of these human and animal, neutral or gendered, stable or unstable bisexual or unisexual responses, from the perspective of the dynamics of identification and the prevalent type of identification (hysterical, narcissistic, melancholic): Here, again, the analysis of M responses is crucial. From the perceptual perspective, the processing of bilaterality and the responses obtained from the "drive" or "sexual symbolism" cards are also valuable indicators. In the schema of interpretation of projective data, all of the elements make it possible to determine the "quality of the investment of self-representation." The narcissistic position is thus made up of the following two components: self-representation (vs. identity then identification) and the quality of its investment.

The Self-Representation Concept Today

Despite methodological changes, and despite the fact that data collection is today more centered on the analysis of the subject's unconscious libidinal economy and the equilibrium between narcissistic and object investments, the notion of self-representation has not been challenged, or so it seems. There are certainly good reasons for this: The projective psychology tradition, loyalty to the legacy of Rausch de Traubenberg, and the "narcissistic line," which covers the topic of self-representation (with its two aspects, identity and identifications) and its offshoot, "the investment of self-representation"; as though self-representation and narcissism were in the end one and the same.

Even though there is no doubt as to the richness of the legacy left to us by Rausch de Traubenberg through her work on the complex notion of self-representation, can we nevertheless conclude that its current use is ... self-evident? Can self-representation, in a metapsychological sense, preexist its investment? Is it not the result of this very investment? Can it be said that *identity*, a concept that is hardly part of psychoanalytic vocabulary, preexists identification? Or in other words, does not the sense of identity itself (which I personally prefer to "identity"), like the ego, grow on the basis of these layered identifications – which are not all secondary – as described by Freud in *The Ego and the Id* (Freud, 1923/2001)?

The question also arises, even more strikingly, when we turn to representations of relationships: to transform the perception of the other (the perception of the other or, rather, of the *Nebenmensch*, to use Freud's term in the *Project for a Scientific Psychology* written and send in 1895 to W. Fliess; Freud, 1895/2001) into a representation, a fortiori of a relationship, it seems that there has to be a complex system of facilitations, which following various patterns, create mnemonic traces that are invested and reinvested and registered in memory, following Freud's model of the *mystic writing-pad* (Freud, 1925/2001) – that is, within several memory systems. It seems to me, from a metapsychological point of view, that the investment of the self, or of the other – and by other I do not mean a single "block" of otherness but, rather, different figures of otherness, "the other as model, as object, as helper and as adversary" (Freud, 1921/2001) – transforms representation, or even perception, which cannot be reduced to a purely cognitive operation.

Another similar, if not identical, question arises: Is narcissistic investment the investment of self-representation, or – in all loyalty to Freud – is it the investment of the ego as an object of love and hate?

The term *representation* should perhaps be defined in this context. If we use it in the sense of "self-image," we risk losing the living self (the *imago* in Latin often designated the effigy of the dead, and in any case it was a material imitation). If the notion is used in the sense of drive representative, the ideational representative of narcissistic libido, then self-representation regains its driving force (which, once processed, deferred, is the function of all ideational representatives). Is this, however, how the notion of "representation" is used today? Indeed, by viewing Narcissus as no more than a frozen image in the mirror, we risk losing sight of the powerful force of narcissisms (of both of life and death).

The further I advance in my perilous attempt to examine this concept of *self-representation,* the more it seems to me that my objections are actually driven by the treatment that this notion inflicts on the ego, I could almost say on the good old Freudian ego which appears almost confined to the second paragraph on thought processes of the Schema of Interpretation of Projective Data (see Appendix 1). In other words, in this system, the ego invests external reality, it invests the activity of thinking within the internal reality but is itself not invested; it is the self which is invested and is an object of love....

This "good old ego" should not be dismissed so easily. In 1923, Freud showed how the ego can end up encouraging the death drives, because of the desexualization that is part of the work of identification and sublimation, for which the ego is primarily responsible (Freud, 1923/2001). If the ego, whether it is restricted to tasks within the perception–consciousness system or assigned to the activity of thinking, is replaced by the self, then it is cast aside or sheltered from such association with the death drives – and we know that in melancholia, these drives can lead the ego, or the self, to their doom. Of course, identifying one or several narcissistic and melancholic identifications in a protocol, based on the analysis of M or H, does not mean that projective psychologists will not recognize this lethal ego, death's associate – but by speaking of "self" instead of ego, "individual" instead of psychic agency, unity instead of intrapsychic conflict and hatred of the ego, we risk blurring intrapsychic conflict and the division of the ego, and the hatred of which it may be the originator, agent – and object.

Regretting that the Freudian ego has disappeared with the arrival of the post-Freudian self may perhaps mean that the demon of Freudian orthodoxy has caught up with me. In this respect, Pontalis provides useful advice:

> The fact that psychoanalysts from such varying backgrounds such as Edith Jacobson, René Spitz, Winnicott or Guntrip included the self in their conceptualizations was an attempt to respond to the problems encountered during the analysis of some of their patients, rather than an attempt to highlight the insufficiency or shortcomings of Freudian metapsychology. (Pontalis, 1977, p. 162)

Duly noted. But then, another epistemological problem arises: Is not the concept of *self-representation* relevant only for some patients? If so, which ones? Those with identity disorders, identification disorders, or both? Beyond identity and/or identification pathologies, how can one account for the narcissistic line without the concept of self-representation?

The Self According to Pontalis (via Winnicott)

Perhaps all depends on which self, with or without a capital S, in French or in English, we in projective psychology are talking about: Is it the Self theorized by Jacobson, Hartmann, and Kernberg – that is, an American self – or is it a more Anglo-French self, the self whose emergence and acknowledgement, based on the concepts developed by Winnicott, were welcomed by Pontalis? I posit that, over time, and under the influence of the studies undertaken by Chabert, the theoretical background has moved in that direction. And logically, the shift has been from self-representation to Winnicott's sense of self.

Indeed, Winnicott's sense of self is a subjective phenomenon, a subjective description of the sense of existence; it is what makes the psychic apparatus something more than a psychic representation: it is a living reality. According to Pontalis (1977), who discusses the concept developed by Winnicott, the self is a representative of being. It is the self that says "I am" and, in so doing, asserts itself as being, demands to be recognized as being, and affirms the fact of living, of inhabiting a body-ego.

We cannot give a detailed presentation of Winnicott's self in this chapter. But what is worth noting with regard to the concept of self-representation is that the self is what cannot be represented, for two reasons:

- Because the self itself is the representative of the living. It is, first and foremost, something that is experienced, felt; it is not a structure, a substructure, or a sum of representations;
- Because it is a movement, a capacity, or an ongoing process.

Capacity here refers to the capacity to use the object, in the sense described by Winnicott (1971). Just as object-relating is associated with the ego, the capacity to use objects is associated with the self. (The transition from object-relating to object-usage implies that the subject destroys the object in fantasy but that the object survives, develops its own autonomy, and contributes to the subject. Thus, each of us is found–created by the other, creating a strong dialectic between narcissistic and object functioning, in Freudian terms. This, however, occurs in a very different libidinal economy where these different investments, far from competing, complement and enrich each other.)

If the self is neither the equivalent of the whole person, nor of all representations of Self, nor the focus of narcissistic investment, but rather, is the representative of the "living," which includes the capacity to meet the other – in the words of Pontalis – then it seems hardly possible to have representation of such a self. Should we not look for its *presence* rather than its representation?

Drawing on the work of American projective psychologists, Rausch de Traubenberg brought back from the US a reflection on self-representation that contributed explicitly and implicitly, sometimes even unknowingly, to the development of her own research work. The latter was based on clinical experience with projective tests and research in psychopathology, and was also influenced, albeit to a lesser degree, by phenomenology. Today, the psychoanalytic interpretation of the Rorschach developed through the research conducted by Chabert and the French School remains faithful to the legacy of Rausch de Traubenberg. However, this school of interpretation draws more on Winnicott's view of the self, as adapted in France by Pontalis, than on the American *Self*, and more on Freud's concept of narcissism than on the notion of self-representation.

As all of Freud's heirs know – and in this regard Rausch de Traubenberg is perhaps the most Freudian – theory does not prevent things from existing, not even self-representation. However, assessing the tools one works with on a day-to-day basis, including one's operational concepts, is always useful, even for projective psychologists: Freud himself, and before him Kant, clearly showed the value of a critical position. If we are not careful with words (e.g., *self-representation*), do we not risk being careless with things (e.g., narcissism)?

Acknowledgments

This chapter was originally published in French and is reprinted here in English with permission: Neau, F. (2014). De la représentation de soi au narcissisme ... et retour? *Psychologie clinique et projective, 20*(1), 109–129. https://doi.org/10.3917/pcp.020.0109 © Erès Editions.

References

Andronikoff-Sanglade, A. (1990). La représentation de soi: Un concept fécond pour la psychologie clinique et projective [Self-representation: A fruitful concept for clinical and projective psychology]. *Bulletin de la Société française du Rorschach et des méthodes projectives, 34,* 9–15.

Blatt, S., & Lerner, H. (1984). The psychological assessment of object representation. *Journal of Personality Assessment, 47*(1), 7–28.

Boizou, M.-F., Chabert, C., & Rausch De Traubengerg, N. (1978). Représentation de soi: identité et identification au Rorschach chez l'enfant et l'adulte [Self-representation: Identity and identification in Rorschach among children and adults]. *Bulletin de psychologie, 32*(339), 271–277.
Cassin, B. (2004). Consciousness. In B. Cassin (Ed.), *Vocabulaire européen des philosophies* (pp. 260–273). Paris, France: Seuil-Le Robert.
Chabert, C. (1983). *Le Rorschach en clinique adulte: Interprétation psychanalytique* [Rorschach test in adults: A psychoanalytical interpretation]. Paris, France: Dunod.
Chabert, C. (1987). *La psychopathologie à l'épreuve du Rorschach* [Psychopathology in the Rorschach Test]. Paris, France: Dunod, 1998.
Chabert, C. (1998). *Psychanalyse et méthodes projectives* [Psychoanalysis and projective methods]. Paris, France: Dunod, 2013.
de Mijolla, A. (Eds.). (2005). *International dictionary of psychoanalysis* (new revised and expanded edition). Paris, France: Hachette.
Emmanuelli, M., & Azoulay, C. (2001). *Les épreuves projectives à l'adolescence. Approche psychanalytique* [Projective tests in adolescence: A psychoanalytical approach]. Paris, France: Dunod.
Freud, S. (1895/2001). Project for a scientific psychology. In J. Strachey (Ed. & Trans.), *The standard edition of the complete psychological works of Sigmund Freud* (Vol. 1, pp. 281–397). London, UK: Vintage Classics. (Original work published in 1895)
Freud, S. (1914/2001). On the narcissism: An introduction. In J. Strachey (Ed. & Trans.), *The standard edition of the complete psychological works of Sigmund Freud* (Vol. 14, pp. 67–107). London, UK: Vintage Classics. (Original work published in 1914)
Freud, S. (1921/2001). Group psychology and the analysis of the ego. In J. Strachey (Ed. & Trans.), *The standard edition of the complete psychological works of Sigmund Freud* (Vol. 18, pp. 65–143). London, UK: Vintage Classics. (Original work published in 1921)
Freud, S. (1923/2001). The Ego and the Id. In J. Strachey (Ed. & Trans.), *The standard edition of the complete psychological works of Sigmund Freud* (Vol. 19, pp. 3–66). London, UK: Vintage Classics. (Original work published in 1923)
Freud, S. (1925/2001). A note upon the "Mystic Writing-Pad." In J. Strachey (Ed. & Trans.), *The standard edition of the complete psychological works of Sigmund Freud* (Vol. 19, pp. 225–232). London, UK: Vintage Classics. (Original work published in 1925)
Freud, S. (1930/2001). Civilization and its discontents. In J. Strachey (Ed. & Trans.), *The standard edition of the complete psychological works of Sigmund Freud* (Vol. 21, pp. 57–145). London, UK: Vintage Classics. (Original work published in 1930)
Freud, A. (1936/1993). *The ego and the mechanisms of defense*. London, UK: Karnac Books. (Original work published in 1936)
Hartmann, H. (1939/1958). *Ego psychology and the problem of adaption*. New York: International Universities Press.
Hartmann, H. (1950). Comments on the psychoanalytic theory of the ego. *The Psychoanalytic Study of the Child, 5*(1), 74–96.
Kernberg, O. (1975). *Borderline conditions and pathological narcissism*. Lanham, MD: Rowman & Littlefield.
Kernberg, O. (1982). Self, ego, affects and drives. *Journal of the American Psychoanalytic Association, 30*, 893–917. http://doi.org/10.1177/000306518203000404
Kohut, H. (1971). *The analysis of the self.* New York, NY: International Universities Press.
Lécuyer, R. (1978). *Le concept de soi* [Self-concept]. Paris, France: PUF.
Lefebvre, A., & Hermalsteen, F. (1990). Représentation de soi des femmes ayant recours à la chirurgie esthétique [Self-representation of women resorting to cosmetic surgery].

Bulletin de la Société française du Rorschach et des méthodes projectives, 34, 55–63. http://doi.org/10.3406/clini.1990.1684

Lerner, P. M. (1998). *Psychoanalytical perspectives on the Rorschach.* Hillsdale, NJ: Analytic Press.

Locke, J. (1700/1975). *An essay concerning human understanding.* (P. H. Nidditch, Ed.). Oxford, UK: Clarendon Press.

Mayman, M. (1967). Object-representation and object-relationships in Rorschach responses. *Journal of Projective Techniques and Personality Assessment, 31*, 17–24.

Merleau-Ponty, M. (1945, English trans. 1962). *Phénoménologie de la perception* [Phenomenology of perception] (C. Smith, Trans.). London, UK: Routledge.

Merleau-Ponty, M. (1964). *Le visible et l'invisible* [The visible and the invisible] (A. Lingis, Trans.). Evanston, IL: Northwestern University Press.

Oppenheimer, A. (1996). *Kohut et la psychologie du self* [Kohut and self psychology]. Paris, France: PUF.

Oppenheimer, A. (2010). Le retour de l'identité dans la psychanalyse: Perspective historique et critique [The return of identity in psychoanalysis: Historical and critical perspective]. *Champ psychosomatique, 2*(58), 9–53. http://doi.org/10.3917/cpsy.058.0009

Orr, M. (1958). *Le test de Rorschach et l'image maternelle* [The Rorschach test and mother imago]. Paris, France. http://doi.org/10.3406/clini.1958.1566

Perron, R., Rausch de Traubenberg, N., & Chabert, C. (1973). Les images parentales. Niveaux d'expression et niveaux d'expression dans diverses épreuves projectives [Parental figures. Levels of construction and levels of expression in different projectives tests]. *Pychologie française, 18*(4), 175–194.

Pontalis, J.-B. (1968). *Après Freud.* Paris, France: Gallimard.

Pontalis, J.-B. (1977). Naissance et reconnaissance du "soi" [Birth and recognition of the "self"]. In *Entre le rêve et la douleur* (pp. 159–191). Paris, France: Gallimard.

Rausch de Traubenberg, N. (1990). Élaboration de la grille de représentation de soi au Rorschach [The development of the self-representation grid in the Rorschach Test]. *Bulletin de la Société française du Rorschach et des méthodes projectives, 34,* 17–24. http://doi.org/10.3406/clini.1990.1680

Rausch de Traubenberg, N., Bloch-Lainé, F., & Boizou, M.-F. (1988). Etude psychologique des adolescents vietnamiens. Apport du Rorschach [Psychological study of Vietnamese adolescents. Contribution of the Rorschach Test]. *Enfance, 41*(1), 95–104.

Rausch de Traubenberg, N., & Boizou, M.-F. (1977). *Le Rorschach en clinique infantile. L'imaginaire et le réel chez l'enfant* [The imaginary and the real in Rorschach testing with children]. Paris, France: Dunod.

Rausch De Traubenberg, N., & Sanglade, A. (1984). Représentation de soi et relation d'objet au Rorschach. Grille de représentation de soi. Analyse comparée des résultats d'adolescents malades psychiques et malades somatiques [Self-representation and objest relationship in Rorschach: Grid of self-representation: Comparative analysis of results of adolescents suffering from somatic diseases and from psychic disorders]. *Revue de psychologie appliquée, 34*(1), 41–57.

Tessier, H. (2005). *La psychanalyse américaine* [The American psychoanalysis]. Paris, France: PUF.

Urist, J. (1977). The Rorschach Test and the assessment of object relations. *Journal of Personality Assessment, 41,* 3–9. http://doi.org/10.1207/s15327752jpa4101_1

Winnicott, D. W. (1971). *Playing and reality.* London, UK: Routledge.

4

The Utility of the Self-Representation Grid in Differential Diagnosis

Claude de Tychey

All French-speaking projective psychologists know they are indebted to the work and teachings of Nina Rausch de Traubenberg. While I was still a young student in my second year of undergraduate studies in psychology, I read her first reference book, *La Pratique du Rorschach* (The Practice of Rorschach Test; Rausch de Traubenberg, 1970). I was immediately convinced of the value of this instrument. I then sought to better understand Rausch de Traubenberg's work through the support and training she proposed with generosity, availability, open-mindedness, and tolerance for differences, qualities which I truly believe have no equivalent in today's academic scientific community. In my mind, they represent the ego ideal that should be specific to our role as professors.

In attempting to pay tribute to Rausch de Traubenberg's work and her impact on the psychoanalytic interpretation of the Rorschach Test (Chabert, 1983, 1987; de Tychey, 1994, 2012; Emmanuelli & Azoulay, 2001; Roman, 2009; Richelle et al., 2009), I found it difficult to choose only one of the many themes that define her scientific publications, all of which are valuable references for projective psychologists. I finally settled on the grid she developed with Anne Sanglade (Rausch de Traubenberg & Sanglade, 1984). I believe that for Rausch de Traubenberg herself, designing this self-representation grid was an important step in her own research. Along with the affective dynamic grid (Rausch de Traubenberg et al., 1990), her self-representation grid has been used extensively at the University Paris Descartes 5 (today Université de Paris), as well as in projective psychology studies in other French universities. The present chapter will focus on the value of using some of the grid's dimensions within a framework of structural differential clinical diagnosis which, to my knowledge, has never been done before. I am aware, however, that this is a somewhat risky undertaking, insofar as Paris 5 has never used Bergeret's structural approach (1974) as a reference model for interpreting the results of Rausch de Traubenberg's grid.

I will focus on some of the main indicators of this tool likely to be useful in the differential diagnosis of the neurotic, narcissistic/borderline, and psychotic personality organizations. However, I must first point out that, despite significant contributions from English-speaking investigators (Aronow & Reznikoff, 1976), work on Rorschach content has been insufficient, both quantitatively (given that norms are available only for its human content, its animal content, and the anxiety index) and qualitatively. I contend that, through this grid, Rausch de Traubenberg developed an approach at least as rich as Exner's coding guidelines (2003).

Rausch de Traubenberg must first be recognized for her creative and fruitful idea of proposing a more complex way of coding human or animal contents, in order to better understand the avatars of identity building and sexual-identity building, notably using the *Henf* and *Hbarré* codes, and placing *HA* next to *H* and *(H),* the gender-sensitive and gender-insensitive codes (*Henf* stands for human child representation; *Hbarré* stands for human perceived through a function). Moreover, she proposed hierarchizing all content registers, ranging from the most unified in terms of self-representation, to the most fragmented in terms of body image (*skeleton* 001, *bone anatomy* 002, *visceral anatomy* 003, *blood* 004).

Rausch de Traubenberg's second fruitful intuition in developing the grid was the creation of a column to explain phantasmic relationships. The content of this column is very useful for detecting object relationships and their various levels of expression, based on relational representations, whether projected or not, in the Rorschach Test's kinesthetic content.

Indicators of a Neurotic Structural Organization

A neurotic organization implies access to a nonfragile narcissistic identity, the development of gender differentiation, and, at the best level of functioning, a well-formed and stable sexual identity with a structuring and operational oedipal component. For this organization, coding all the contents projected onto the Rorschach seems to imply the following:

- A predominance of undamaged and nondisqualified human and animal contents (Codes 01 and 11) as opposed to fragmented, regressive, or disqualified ones.
- The ability to produce gendered human responses accompanied (in the second column of the grid) by one or more of the following: positive reciprocal interactions (Item 1) with a libidinal facet, opposition–competition interactions that are aggressive in nature (Item 2), or – and this is an item I would like to add to the grid – the expression of an action immediately followed by the impossibility or difficulty of achieving it, reflecting what Chabert (1983) called a back-and-forth movement between the expression of a desire and the impossibility of fulfilling it, because it is prohibited, in the present case, by the typical superego found in the oedipal conflict.
- The ability to give animal responses that are mostly intact (Item 11), even if temporary regressive movements are inevitable (*animal skin* 10, *baby animal*

12, *Walt Disney animal* 16), along with the ability to symbolize the phallic power of the animal figure on Card IV and perhaps on other cards (in particular, in the pink details on the sides of Card VIII).

- The ability to manifest sustained sensitivity to the environment through the production (especially for the pastel cards) of responses to *natural elements* (Item 29), *botany* (Item 30), and *landscapes* (Item 33).
- The ability to give symbolic responses referring to the phallic figure, with perception of pointed objects or pointed parts of animals such as horns or antennae (Items 27 and 18), references to the maternal figure as a container (*cave* 29, *hollow objects* 26, *vase* 26), and positive references to the female figure (Code *F* in the third column).

Indicators of a Narcissistic or Borderline Structural Organization

These two levels exhibit differences, but also similarities. Notably, they both lack a narcissistic identity foundation, cannot be organized around a dominant oedipal mode, and cannot firmly symbolize the female figure in a positive way.

In the first column of the grid, these personality organizations are similar in that subjects produce fewer entire gendered human contents (Code 01 associated with *Male* or *Female* in the third column) and more contents reflecting a degradation of human responses (*Henf* 02, *Hbarré* for function 03), which can be either all-powerful (e.g., a king) or disqualified (e.g., a clown). As Monika Boekholt (1992) has shown, oscillation between these two poles is more characteristic of narcissistic functioning, with *H* (imaginary disqualified objects like witches) or even *HA* at the most archaic levels. In parallel, we find an increase in fragmented human and animal contents, in which case the responses often no longer correspond to the expected norms in the psychogram (in terms of the frequency of the whole, as compared with fragmented parts for both of these registers). And at the levels with the greatest suffering, we find a fragile body image attested to by the more frequent production of responses in relation to anatomy and blood.

In the second and fourth columns of the grid, the narcissistic and borderline organization modes differ in the following ways:

- Fantasized Human and M responses by subjects with a narcissistic personality organization are characterized by more mirror images (Code 11 in second column), especially on the two-sided cards that elicit relationships. There are also more 7 and 3 codes in the second column – that is, more Human and Animal figures with static postures reflecting a simple action or a neutral bilateral action. In the fourth column, these patients' responses are coded primarily U (unilateral), J (duplicates), or E (subjective experience).
- Fantasized Human and M responses by subjects with a borderline personality organization may, in withdrawal contexts, temporarily exhibit the movements of the narcissistic functioning mentioned above. More often, they take on a different form characterized by intense dependence on object

relationships (Code 6 in second column). A dependent orientation is also expressed here – as Roy Schafer (1954) clearly demonstrated quite some time ago – in terms of frequent food content (Code 40 in the first column of the Rausch de Traubenberg and Sanglade's grid) and frequent aggressive oral themes in the M responses, which can have a sadomasochistic orientation (in the grid: Code 5 *passive-aggressive interaction,* and Code 10 *action endured*), as well as more regressive content (R in fourth column) associated with responses *Aenf* and *Henf.*

Indicators of Psychotic Structural Organizations

Although melancholic (or manic depressive) personality organizations are less regressive than paranoid organizations, which themselves are less destructured than schizophrenic organizations, they all share a common point: the impossibility in all three to develop an identity, with a body image that is fragmented.

In the first column of the grid, Animal and Human content, it is extremely difficult if not impossible to maintain a positive Human or Animal response that is entire and nondeteriorated. In the grid, this is reflected by the virtual or total disappearance of Codes 01 and 11, with the degradation of these contents being replaced, in center stage, by images reflecting confusion of the human and animal kingdoms (*H/A* or *HA*), references to unreal, dangerous, or dead humans or animals (Codes 04 and 14), sparse Human and Animal responses, and a fragmented body image (Codes 000, 001, 002, 003, 004, 100, 101, 102, 103, 104, and 105 in the grid). In the most archaic categories, these responses are accompanied by the increasingly pronounced devitalization of contents (Code 13 *prehistoric animals*, Code 60 *symbols*, Code 61 *abstraction*).

In the second column, which reflects how objects are approached, there are significant differences between the three psychotic structures:

- In the melancholic structure, we find fusional identification with dead objects that prevents the mourning process (Codes 07, 001, and 17 in the first column of the grid). This is primarily expressed on Cards II and III via references to skeletons and dead human beings and animals.
- In the paranoid structure, the fantasized interactions (very frequent) in the kinesthetic content are dominated by the menacing aggressive dimension, which has a destructive or persecuting valence expressing distrust or conveying a strong need for protection. (Here, I think it is necessary to adjust Item 5 *passive/aggressive interaction,* Item 8 *aggressive action,* and Item 9 *incongruous, bizarre action.*)
- In the schizophrenic structure, the object no longer exists. Decathexis and withdrawal are such that there is a total lack of human interactive content and no kinesthetic space at all. Nor is there even the ability to see a human being, throughout the entire test in most cases.

Conclusion

My description here could only be very brief. In future research, I think it would be worthwhile to work on the frequency of occurrence of the different items of Rausch de Traubenberg's self-representation grid, using groups of subjects presenting each of these structural organization modes. This approach would help validate the grid, whose sensitivity, I believe, makes it a highly valuable tool for the differential diagnoses of these three organizations.

Acknowledgments

This chapter was originally published in French and is reprinted here in English with permission: de Tychey, C. (2014). Utilité de la grille de représentation de soi dans une perspective de diagnostic différentiel. *Psychologie clinique et projective, 20*(1), 131–137. https://doi.org/10.3917/pcp.020.0131 © Erès Editions.

References

Aronow, E., & Reznikoff, M. (1976). *Rorschach content interpretation.* New York, NY: Grune & Stratton.

Bergeret, J. (1974). *La personnalité normale et pathologique* [Normal and pathological personality]. Paris, France: Dunod.

Boekholt, M. (1992). Modalités narcissiques et registres dépressifs au Rorschach [Narcissistic modalities and depressive contexts in the Rorschach Test]. *Bulletin de la Société du Rorschach et des méthodes projectives, 36,* 51–65.

Chabert, C. (1983). *Le Rorschach en clinique adulte: Interprétation psychanalytique* [The Rorschach in adult clinical settings: Psychoanalytic interpretation]. Paris, France: Dunod.

Chabert, C. (1987). *La psychopathologie à l'épreuve du Rorschach* [Psychopathology throughout the Rorschach]. Paris, France: Dunod.

de Tychey, C. (1994). *L'approche des dépressions à travers le test de Rorschach: Point de vue théorique, diagnostique et thérapeutique* [Approach to depression using Rorschach Test: A clinical, diagnostic and therapeutic point of view]. Issy les Moulineaux, France: Editions et Applications Psychologiques.

de Tychey, C. (2012). *Le Rorschach en clinique de la dépression adulte* [Rorschach Test and adult depression in the clinic]. Paris, France: Dunod.

Emmanuelli, M., & Azoulay, C. (2001). *Les épreuves projectives à l'adolescence: Approche psychanalytique* [Projective tests and adolescence: Psychoanalytical approach]. Paris, France: Dunod.

Exner, J. (2003). *The Rorschach: A comprehensive system.* New York, NY: John Wiley.

Rausch de Traubenberg, N. (1970). *La pratique du Rorschach* [The practice of the Rorschach Test]. Paris, France: PUF.

Rausch de Traubenberg, N., Bloch-Laine, F., Boizou, M. F., Duplant, N., Martin, M., & Poggionovo, M. P. (1990). Modalités d'analyse de la dynamique affective au Rorschach: Grille d'analyse de la dynamique affective [Analyzing affective dynamic in the Rorschach test: The affective dynamic grid]. *Revue de psychologie appliquée, 40*(2), 245–258.

Rausch de Traubenberg, N., & Sanglade, A. (1984). Représentation de soi et relation d'objet au Rorschach. Grille de représentation de soi. [Self-representation and object relationship in Rorschach: Grid of self-representation]. *Revue de psychologie appliquée, 34*(1), 41–57.

Richelle, J., Debroux, P., De Noose, L., & Malempré, M. (2009). *Manuel du test de Rorschach : approche formelle et psychodynamique* [Rorschach Test manual: A formal and psychodynamic approach]. Brussels, Belgium: De Boeck.

Roman, P. (2009). *Le Rorschach en clinique de l'enfant et de l'adolescent : approche psychanalytique* [Rorschach test in child and adolescent clinical field: A psychoanalytic approach]. Paris, France: Dunod.

Schafer, R. (1954). *Psychoanalytic interpretation in Rorschach testing*. New York, NY: Grune & Stratton.

5

Nina Rausch de Traubenberg

In a Line of Transmission ... The Question of Norms in the Rorschach Test

Catherine Azoulay

Introduction: Commitment to a Research Project

After a long period of reflection and a great deal of hesitation, I have chosen to frame my account around a piece of research that Michèle Emmanuelli and I (Azoulay, Emmanuelli, Rausch de Traubenberg et al., 2007) conducted with Nina Rausch de Traubenberg on Rorschach norms for adolescents and young adults. This choice is dictated by the idea that this joint work, from the late 1990s to the early 2000s, enabled me to know Nina on a more personal level. Until then, I had considered her to be an impressive "Master" with an encyclopedic knowledge. She was quite amiable and humanly approachable, but most importantly she was a person whose high status necessarily led me to maintain a respectful distance.

Over long work sessions, mostly at her home in her charming apartment in the VII arrondissement of Paris, I came to know what an admirable person she was. Very quickly, thanks to Nina's investment, questions that might have seemed quite austere – such as coding modes of apprehension, determinants, and contents from the Rorschach protocols of adolescents and young adults between 13 and 24 years of age – became lively discussion topics. Discussing the answer "cat" as a response to Card II from the Rorschach Test and whether to code it as an F+ or F– led to a lively debate on the articulation of perception versus fantasy. Research participants would regularly play along with Nina's infectious enthusiasm and passion for anything related to the Rorschach – such as the history of the Rorschach from yesterday to today, the relation between W and D responses, or the direct or indirect relations between cards. Relations between various psychogram factors – rather austere when we look at it – turned, with Nina, into profound and vibrant meetings. Today, I daresay that without the active participation and benevolence of Nina as well as her genuine love for her object – the Rorschach – the publication of normative data for the Rorschach in adolescents and young adults would certainly not have occurred.

It was also back in those years that Nina allowed me to interview her twice: an audio interview in collaboration with Françoise Neau in 2003 and then a filmed interview with Jean-Yves Chagnon in 2007 (see The Société du Rorschach's website https://www.societerorschach.org/ and the interview on Youtube: https://www.youtube.com/watch?v=8s9zeQaIA6o). Indeed, with such an outstanding personality, surfing the wave of the great history of the last century and facing its jolts, the life of Rausch de Traubenberg could certainly have inspired a novel. Collecting her testimony seemed indispensable to us and to future generations of psychologists.

To illustrate my point, I would like to recall what is meant in projective psychology by the terms *normativity* and *Rorschach normative data,* before briefly reporting on the fundamental parts of the research on Rorschach norms and its extensions.

General Status of Norms in Projective Psychology

In the psychoanalytic field, the question of *norm,* or rather *norms,* has always been a sensitive topic to mention and to deal with. This question causes uneasiness, or even avoidance, which I believe is a matter of three main difficulties which prevent it from being tackled in a more straightforward manner.

Indeed, according to the psychoanalytical methodology of the Rorschach interpretation and the projective methods of the French School, there seems to be a contradiction between the Freudian idea that there is no predefined line between normality and pathology, and the Rorschach idea of norm-referring as a basis for psychogram interpretation, thus contributing to stating hypotheses about mental functioning.

Besides this, over the past 3 decades, a clear separation between "biological" psychiatry and psychoanalysis has been engendered, which is, rather than a dialectical conflict, a split between, on the one hand, a normalizing psychiatry – establishing its own principles with a set of signs indicating pathologic versus normal states – and on the other hand, psychoanalysis which still upholds mental flexibility, variety, and freedom, enabling a human person to evolve through the vagaries of life, over a large continuum between normality and pathology.

Finally, since the events in Paris of May 1968 and with the antipsychiatry movement, psychological tests and their methods have been subjected to widespread criticism in France and elsewhere. Among the most important criticisms were the idea that tests reduce individuals to "objectivized" measures and only serve the purpose of categorizing and typecasting individuals, by denying each individual's specificity. Hence, psychological tests are seen as serving the prevailing "bourgeois" ideology of a society, which is held responsible for the insanity of those it decides to lock up, going against any freedom to be oneself – indeed, any freedom to be mentally ill – without any hindrance (except perhaps for artists!). Since then, one or two generations of psychologists have followed, and from what I now understand, it is no longer a fight to ensure that the voice of the presumed *mentally ill* is heard and respected in the same way as that of the so-called *healthy,* but rather a fight against the dominance of numbers over words, or in other words, in such a case, psychiatric nomenclature over speech. Socially and culturally, numbers have invaded the world of thought and reflection because the so-called "hard sciences" have moved away from the human sciences and, even worse, began to despise them.

It is important to note that in antiquity, philosophy, medicine, and astronomy shared common ground to further the progress of humanity. Nowadays, a discourse from a study in the humanities cannot be recognized as scientific – that is, serious – unless it comprises numbers, percentages, curves, and mathematical and statistical formulas. We would almost forget two basic principles: On one hand, in a reflection, whatever reflection it is, a number offers no guarantee that the reasoning is accurate, and on the other, a number that is isolated from a discourse that can justify it is itself meaningless – such as, for example, an IQ number or even any calculation from a Rorschach psychogram. It seems evident that measurement tests that use scales to quantify an individual's intelligence or personality may "compress" the subject into an isolated number. The same would be true with projective test codifications, numbers, calculations, and formulas that are, for instance, used in a Rorschach psychogram, without their being based on an informative discourse explaining their meaning and ensuring their connections with the exploration of mental functioning that they are meant to serve.

Norms and Normativity in the Rorschach and the TAT

According to Rausch de Traubenberg and to me, understanding normative data and their justification in the Rorschach are part of the same quest for meaning of mental functioning, with due regard to the individuality and originality of each person. This should not be confused with a normalizing approach, which is quite the opposite.

To briefly review the work of Hermann Rorschach on norms: In his book *Psychodiagnostik,* published in 1921, Rorschach gave a report on "average" or "normal subjects" (Rorschach, 1921). At the beginning of his book, he described the reference population on which he based his comparative clinical findings. His sample included a total of 405 persons (231 males and 174 females), with 117 "normal–educated" (n = 55) and "noneducated" (n = 62). The rest of his reference population (n = 288) was considered "mentally ill," mainly comprising schizophrenic patients (n = 188). Rorschach did not define what "normal" meant to him, while it is clear that "mentally ill" patients were those who had been hospitalized following a psychiatric diagnosis. It is our understanding that "normal" was for the time of Rorschach the same as the term "general population" is for our time – that is, any person who is not consulting a psychiatrist or mental health care organization at the time of the study.

Some 40 years later, based on his medical thesis which he defended in 1943, the philosopher, physician, and science historian George Canguilhem published a large study comprising reflections on "normal" and "pathologic," in which he elaborated on the notion of *normativity*. Projective psychology, as we shall see, would later build its own reflections on these studies, which are still authoritative in the field. The philosopher–physician Canguilhem noted the existence of the "subordination" of average to norm in medical research. He questioned whether, if a normal way of life is what conforms to norms, should straying from the norm be considered abnormal? He declared that there is no way that statistics can tell us this. He went further with his critique of the conception of normality in medical practice by developing the notion of normativity from the study of living versus dead – that is, the study of health and its uncertainties, rather than statistical studies on biological criteria: "A human trait would not be normal because it is frequent but rather frequent because it is normal, that is, normative in a given kind of life" (Canguilhem, 1966/2005, p. 18). For Canguilhem, *normativity* meant that the human organism could stay alive and healthy in a particular living environment, by integrating physiological conditions that are constantly interacting to create a balance, but that are also likely at any moment to challenge this balance with disease – and by recovering. Therefore, he was not in agreement with medical norms claiming that someone is either ill or healthy, but rather saw the human body as a tightrope walk, continually striving to maintain a dynamic balance and adapt – constantly at risk of falling. Establishing such a normative balance throughout life is the basis for the ongoing creation of new norms by a given organism.

This innovative and constructive definition of norms in the medical sense, close to the Freudian definition in reference to mental functioning, was adopted by projective psychology as it was developed by the French School. Let us recall the text of Vica Shentoub "About Normality and Pathology in the TAT" (Shentoub, 1973), in which she explicitly made reference to Canguilhem and his definition of normativity to develop the notion of creativity in the stories that are told in the TAT. Just like the organism that needs to create its own norms by adapting to change to stay healthy, mental functioning needs to tolerate change to be creative. Hence, for Shentoub,

> the notion of normativity, excluding any axiological or statistical reference, is based on a set of criteria that could converge towards the notion of creativity, which is the antithesis of pathological organizations that are confined by the defences, which are driven by the repetition compulsion. (Shentoub, 1973, p. 257)

She also stressed that "the problem of normative behavior in TAT – and probably of normative behavior in general – is part of the issue of relative balance between conscious and unconscious structures that is continuously challenged during the test" (Shentoub, 1973, p. 258).

For Nina Rausch de Traubenberg, the psychogram is part of a "reductive and static ensemble compared to the richness of the protocol and does not suffice in any way to appreciate the personality of a subject" (Rausch de Traubenberg, 1970/2000, p. 204). She continued: "Indeed, we know that all the factors in a psychogram are not of equal importance in terms of diagnostic purposes, as for similar psychograms, subjects can display different modes of functioning" (Rausch de Traubenberg, 1970/2000, p. 205). She consistently advised caution when using factors in a psychogram, by suggesting that the prominent personality traits in the psychogram should be highlighted in the form of "a brief assessment of how numerical results stray from norms, how they may be contradictory or how they may differ from one another" (Rausch de Traubenberg, 1970/2000, p. 205).

Besides the idea that the psychogram and the comparison of quantitative data are but a stage in the qualitative interpretation of the protocol, caution when using normative data in the psychogram was based on the recognition of a lack of French statistical norms for the general population.

Therefore, it was also to compensate for this lack that Rausch de Traubenberg supported us in realizing this research, of which I am merely going to mention the outlines, particularly the results and the extensions.

An Ambitious Study

In our laboratory and under the direction of Catherine Chabert, Michèle Emmanuelli and I initiated a research protocol that was aimed at updating the Rorschach normative data in the French population. This protocol focused on a population of 700 subjects from seven age groups (ages 13–15, 16–18, 19–24, 25–34, 35–44, 45–54, and 55–65) and three socioprofessional categories (SPC-1: "above or equal to a baccalaureate +2 years," 30%; SPC-2: "from final year of high school leading to the baccalaureate level to the level of a baccalaureate +2 years," 30%; SPC-3: "strictly under final year of the high school," 40%). For the age groups 13–15 and 16–18, we considered the highest educational level of both parents.

The methodology consisted of four stages:

- Stage 1: Data collection: all nonpatients from companies, administrations, schools, secondary schools and high schools or organizations, cultural centers, universities and controls from students completing their PhD theses.
- Stage 2: Coding protocols and input of data on a computer.
- Stage 3: Statistical processing of data; performed by the Psychology and Statistical Analysis of Data Unit, at the University Paris Descartes, and coordinated by Denis Corroyer, assistant professor.
- Stage 4: Interpretation of results of the research, and publication.

Thus far, results from the statistical processing of the Rorschach protocol factors that cover the first three age groups of the population – corresponding to adolescents and young adults (278 protocols of subjects with age range between 13 and 24) – have been interpreted and published (Azoulay et al., 2007).

Analysis of results was carried out, on the one hand, in comparison with the normative data in effect in France since the 1960s, and on the other, according to the considered variables of age, gender, and sociocultural levels of these groups. Compared with the normative data in effect, we observed notable differences in the Apprehension Modes (equal ratio D/W) and in the quality of formal responses (F+%). Change in the D list, and modifications in popular responses are also to be noted. There was no significant difference between age groups, genders, and SPC with regard to these elements.

For these results and particularly for the drop in D% and F%, the question arises as to whether it is a functional difference between adolescents and adults, or an evolution of the population in general.

It is worth noting that the new Whole Response/Detailed Response (W/D) ratio of 1/1 was exactly identical to that in a study of 150 adults (both males and females) with an average age of 34, conducted in Russia and published in 1992 (Belyi, 1992). Yet the population was not the same. Another study, published by our colleagues from Algiers (Si Moussi et al., 2004), had a similar outcome: It also showed no difference among children, adolescents, and adults in this regard. In addition, in a study conducted by Rausch de Traubenberg and collaborators (Rausch de Traubenberg et al., 1993), of a population of 73 adolescents, nonpatient boys and girls between the ages of 16 and 19, we reached the same conclusion (W%: 40; D%: 47).

Can we attempt to understand this consequential increase in W%, which modified the W/D ratio and was noted to be extending to other populations and cultures? Is the world that is awash in images – with effortless and immediate access to information through multimedia networks – behind these changes in perception activities? We could then connect the increase in the proportion of W compared with that of D to a more passive attitude in front of images – in a population that is now overloaded with a variety of visual information and is therefore less focused on data discrimination and data selection. However, a systematic qualitative analysis of the elaboration of W (simple W or elaborated W?) is required to gain a better understanding of the increase in the proportion of W compared with that of D.

In general, the lack of significant differences – even moderate ones – regarding the various pointers by gender, age, and most often SPC is an important point.

However, a few comments are necessary about certain aspects of SPC, which all-in-all are the ones that most call for thought: Indeed, for SPC-1 and SPC-2, the average number of responses was 31, for SPC-3 the average number of responses dropped to 21. The Animal Response% (A%) was 38% for SPC-1 and 51% for SPC-3. The extended A% fully confirmed the 13-point gap between

SPC-1 and SPC-3 (40% and 53%). The Human Response% (H%) results show that for young people between age 13 and 15, SPC-3 is the only population category in which H% = 0 for some subjects. The number of M responses and responses that integrate sensory data (Color, Vista, Black–White) also drops from SPC-1 to SPC-3, although it is statistically a weak effect.

These quantitative or statistical data reflect on clinical observations that highlight the perceptible importance of inhibition in the underprivileged population categories (SPC-3), whether in children, adolescents, or adults. In our research, all psychologists in charge of the collection of protocols have pointed out this inhibition aspect in SPC-3 subjects. Still, the question has to be raised: What inhibition are we talking about? Is it an intellectual inhibition, an inhibition of imaginary expression, a verbal inhibition, or an inhibition of creativity? If so, should we stick to the – at the very least – upsetting idea that inhibition, regardless of its nature, is part of the norm in socioeconomically underprivileged populations?

Extension

Besides updating French normative data in a population of adolescents and young adults between ages 13 and 24, our research enabled us to update two important complementary tools:

- A new list of D (main common details): based on the list that was collected from the population aged 13–24, a calculation of the confidence interval was performed to create a list of D concerning the whole French population.
- A new coding manual for forms in the Rorschach (Azoulay, Emmanuelli, & Corroyer, 2012), which was much awaited by projective clinicians, to replace the somewhat obsolete *Coding Manual for Forms* by Cecile Beizmann, dating back to 1966 (Beizmann, 1966). The new manual differs from the older manual in that it reflects both the statistical frequency of a given form (criterion: 2.16% of total subjects) and the qualitative criterion of Form, based on the judgment of four experts. Hence, an original and nonfrequent form (quantitative F–) may be considered as a qualitative F+, and a statistically frequent form (quantitative F+) may be considered as a qualitative F by experts.

This dual approach to qualitative and quantitative coding enhances reflections on the interaction between perception and fantasy, a matter dear to the heart of Nina Rausch de Traubenberg.

Furthermore, our methodology has been used extremely rigorously by our Turkish colleagues from the University of Istanbul, led by Prof. Tevfika Tunaboylu-Ikiz (Tunaboylu-Ikiz, Zabci, Pirim-Dusgor, Eredm-Atak, & Kalem, 2013), who recently established Rorschach norms for populations of children, adolescents, and adults and have published a Rorschach coding manual for the elderly (Ikiz, Bengi Pirim, Atak, Mete, & Kalem, 2013) and by our Brazilian colleagues (Jardim-Maran, Pasian, & Okino, 2015).

We shall also mention a recent study by our colleagues Claude de Tychey and collaborators (de Tychey, Huckel, Rivat, & Claudon, 2012) on Rorschach norms in a French population of nonpatient adults, comprising 310 subjects between 25 and 65 years of age, for which the quantitative results have been compared with our results, as well as with the results of other studies (Blomart, 1998; Exner, 2003; Sultan et al., 2004; Sultan, Andronikof, Réveillère, & Lemmel, 2006; Réveillère, Sultan, Andronikof, & Lemmel, 2008). Remarkably, we can see that the quantitative results in the population of adolescents and young adults are close to those in the adult population that de Tychey and collaborators studied; with regard to values such as the number of responses of W%, A%, H%, F%, or F+%, the last having apparently dropped in a significant way compared with the older norms in both studies (61% for adults, 65% for adolescents and young adults). On the other hand, in this study, the authors did not find any difference between the different socioprofessional categories we questioned, and they analyzed both quantitative (notably the increased W% and attenuated F+%) and qualitative results from a social evolution perspective, reflecting fragile narcissistic foundations in the general population.

Conclusion

How to understand the question of norms in today's society and in different cultures? This is not a new issue, but it can be debated in different ways without ever exhausting the topic. If the term *norm* is understood in reference to the normativity that Canguilhem defined, and if rather than talking about Rorschach norms we prefer the term *normative data,* we would then be in line with a thinking approach that includes the idea that normality – to use the expression of J. Y. Chagnon – is the balance between permanence and change, the core idea of this definition reflecting tolerance to change. This definition, in line with the Freudian notion of a continuum between normality and pathology is the opposite of the definition of normality as an average.

Nina Rausch de Traubenberg, who perfectly understood this point, always prompted caution regarding averages and statistical calculations in the extensive research she conducted on the clinical approach to normal. She rather talked about tendencies, and with absolute loyalty to clinical psychology, she strove for the defense of human individuality and the recognition of its original unicity. Her teaching helped many teacher–researchers, who in turn transmit her values and continue her work in France but also in many other countries. Hence we recognize the lively nature of thoughts, permeating work with no boundaries, just like the wind, the clouds, and streams.

During the interview conducted by F. Neau and myself, Nina confided in us her joyful surprise at hearing the response of a Vietnamese adolescent to card V: "A butterfly, flying to reach its future." That's how I would like to imagine the Rorschach, in line with the way Rausch de Traubenberg invested herself in it throughout her career, sharing her passion in a line of transmission.

Acknowledgments

This chapter was originally published in French and is reprinted here in English with permission: Azoulay, C. (2014). Nina Rausch de Traubenberg, le long d'une transmission: La question des normes au Rorschach. *Psychologie clinique et projective, 20*(1), 139–153. https://doi.org/10.3917/pcp.020.0139 © Erès Editions.

References

Azoulay, C., Emmanuelli, M., & Corroyer, D. (2012). *Nouveau Manuel de cotation des formes au Rorschach* [New Rorschach workbook for coding list of forms]. Paris, France: Dunod.

Azoulay, C., Emmanuelli, M., Rausch de Traubenberg, N., Corroyer, D., Rozencwajg, P., & Savina, Y. (2007). Les données normatives françaises du Rorschach à l'adolescence et chez le jeune adulte [French normative data in the Rorschach test for the adolescent and young adult]. *Psychologie clinique et projective, 13,* 371–409. http://doi.org/10.3917/pcp.013.0371

Beizmann, C. (1966). *Livret de cotation des formes dans le Rorschach* [Coding manual for forms in the Rorschach test]. Paris, France: Ed. Du Centre de Psychologie Appliquée.

Belyi, B. I. (1992). *Test Roršacha: Praktika i teorija* [Rorschach Test: Practice and theory]. Saint Petersburg, Russia: Izdatelstvo Dorval.

Blomart, J. (1998). *Le Rorschach chez l'enfant et l'adolescent: Etude génétique et liste de cotation des formes* [Rorschach with the child and adolescent: Genetic study and coding list of forms]. Paris, France: Editions du Centre de Psychologie Appliquée.

Canguilhem, G. (2005). *Le normal et le pathologique augmenté de Nouvelles Réflexions concernant le normal et le pathologique* [Normality and pathology: New considerations on normality and pathology] (9th ed.). Paris, France: PUF. (Original published in 1966)

de Tychey, C., Huckel, C., Rivat, M., & Claudon, P. (2012). Nouvelles normes adultes du test de Rorschach et évolution sociétale: Quelques réflexions [New adult normative data in the Rorschach test and social evolution: Some reflections]. *Bulletin de psychologie, 65*(5), 453–466. http://doi.org/10.3917/bupsy.521.0453

Exner, J. (2003). *The Rorschach: A comprehensive system.* New York, NY: John Wiley.

Ikiz, T., Bengi Pirim, D., Atak, I. E., Mete, L., & Kalem, E. (2013). *Kodlama kitabi 3. Yasli normlari.* [Rorschach coding manual for elderly sample]. Beyoğlu, Turkey: Baglam Yayincilik.

Jardim-Maran, M. L., Pasian, S. R., & Okino, E. T. (2015). Normative study of Rorschach (Parisian School) for Brazilian adolescents. *Paidéia, 25*(62), 333–342. http://doi.org/10.1590/1982-43272562201507

Rausch de Traubenberg, N. (2000). *La pratique du Rorschach* [The practice of the Rorschach Test]. Paris, France: PUF. (Original published in 1970)

Rausch de Traubenberg, N., Bloch-Lainé, F., Duplant, N., Martin, M., & Poggionovo, M. P. (1993). Le Rorschach à l'adolescence: La clinique du normal [The Rorschach Test in adolescence: Clinic of normality]. *Bulletin de la Société française du Rorschach et des méthodes projectives de langue française, 37,* 7–39. http://doi.org/10.3406/clini.1993.1640

Réveillère, C., Sultan, S., Andronikof, A., & Lemmel, G. (2008). Étude de la stabilité des scores au Psychodiagnostic de Rorschach sur un échantillon de sujets francophones non consultants [The stability of Rorschach psychodiagnostic scores in a nonpatient French-language sample]. *Bulletin de psychologie, 61*(6/498), 577–590. http://doi.org/10.3917/bupsy.498.0577

Rorschach, H. (1921). *Psychodiagnostic*. Paris, France: PUF.

Shentoub, V. (1973). A propos du normal et du pathologique dans le TAT [About normality and pathology in the TAT]. *Psychologie française, 18*(4), 251–259.

Si Moussi, A., Benkhelifa, M., & colleagues (2004). Production et banalités au Rorschach en Algérie [Production and popular responses in Algerian Rorschach]. *Psychologie clinique et projective, 10*, 339–357. http://doi.org/10.3917/pcp.010.0339

Sultan, S., Andronikof, A., Fouques, D., Lemmel, G., Mormont, C., Réveillère, C., & Saïas, T. (2004). Vers des normes francophones pour le Rorschach en système integré: Premiers résultats sur un échantillon de 146 adultes [Towards French norms for the Rorschach comprehensive system: First results from a sample of 146 adults]. *Psychologie française, 49,* 7–24. http://doi.org/10.1016/j.psfr.2003.11.002

Sultan, S., Andronikof, A., Réveillère, C., & Lemmel, G. (2006). A Rorschach stability study in a nonpatient adult sample. *Journal of Personality Assessment, 87,* 330–348. http://doi.org/10.1207/s15327752jpa8703_13

Tunaboylu-Ikiz, T., Zabci, N., Pirim-Dusgor, B., Eredm-Atak, I., & Kalem, E. (2013). Les normes adultes de la population turque au Rorschach [Normative data in adult Turkish population in the Rorschach Test]. *Psychologie clinique et projective, 19,* 303–319. http://doi.org/10.3917/pcp.019.0303

Part 2

Clinical Applications & Case Studies

6

How to Deal With Excessive Reality?

Regarding Bodily Sources of Subjectification

Monika Boekholt

"How to Deal With Excessive Reality?" was the title of my speech, delivered at a symposium on January 29, 2011, titled Le Rorschach: de la perception au fantasme (Rorschach, From Perception to Fantasy) in honor of, and in the presence of, Nina Rausch de Traubenberg. *How* to deal with an *excessive* paucity of phantasmic life when the psyche is unable to disengage itself from the perceptual constraint of the projective material – that is, both the Rorschach and thematic tests? *How to deal,* a fortiori, with the "excessive reality" of bodily and/or mental suffering? This question, which is still relevant today, can be traced back to the question raised by Vica Shentoub and Rosine Debray in their article "How to Deal With Excessive Phantasmic Richness? Interpretation of an Unusual TAT Protocol" (Shentoub & Debray, 1978–1979), in which they commented on the possible psychopathological implications of the luxuriant phantasmic activity in the protocol of a man named Gaétan.

As I was about to write the text of this chapter, another chapter was closing: Rosine Debray passed away and left us, too quickly, too soon, which was apparently her only faux-pas in her faithful commitment to the model of the École Psychosomatique de Paris (Psychosomatic School of Paris). Soon afterwards, Nina Rausch de Traubenberg, the last representative of her generation of the university teaching that she had initiated, followed her.

Today, it is still with great sadness and gratitude that in tribute to these great pioneers of the psychoanalytic approach to practice and research in clinical and projective psychology, Vica Shentoub, Rosine Debray, and Nina Rausch de Traubenberg – in order of departure from the scene – I propose to revisit their impact through links between percept and fantasy, psyche and soma, that have now become central in my own trajectory as a psychologist and researcher.

Issues: Excess and/or Deficiency of What?

Excessive reality, "too much" somatic reality, is an expression borrowed from Rosine Debray' article: "When Too Much Reality Ossifies Rememoration" (Debray, 1990). In this remarkable article, our colleague accurately comments on the impact of "somatic urgency" on recall and mental elaboration during analysis, by showing how these crisis situations from acute or lasting episodes might modify or alter their conditions.

Subject to the epistemological specificity of each context, we know that somatic urgency reestablishes interaction between percept and fantasy in projective situations, usually leading to the increased abrasion of associative capacities, as though these capacities might be unable to "detach" themselves from the *manifest content*. This is how, with her figurative expression, Shentoub described these TAT protocols as *dull* – shall we say, with a *boring* purpose, fixed to conscious processes alone, hardly mobilizing the associative activity of the clinician – unlike that of "Gaëtan's," which was filled with the emergence of primary processes, with the risk that at times protagonists might lose track of secondarization, which is the minimum requirement of the narrative, at least in adults.

Catherine Azoulay (2002) noted that after the first scoring grid that was developed in 1958 with Salem Shentoub based on psychopathological criteria, Vica Shentoub's text, cowritten with Rosine Debray in 1978–1979, removed the "emergence of primary processes" from the so-called factors of failure, to give them an economic and dynamic perspective on possible interactions between primary and secondary processes. Later on, echoing the modalities of "operative thinking" that P. Marty and M. de M'Uzan (1963) had stressed, Debray introduced the *F factors* – *F* for factual, as an emphasis on the everyday, the factual, on doing, flattened reference to external reality, circumstantial affects, references to external norms – in the scoring grid, of which the value of concealment or emergence of thoughts and affect is to be measured on a case-by-case basis, depending on the overall dynamics of each person at any given time (Debray, 1987).

The same observations and issues could be applied using the Rorschach Test when, as a "potential space," the responses fit in with the *form* of the blots at the expense of fantasy, as the ability to fantasize – provided it guarantees a certain identity cohesion and a function pleasure – fades under the weight of perceptive reality that "somatic urgency" dictates. What could be done with this greater adherence to external reality if it no longer allows the expression of affects and representations, at the expense of a costly somatic symptomatology? Thanks to the contribution of psychosomaticians, we now know that we should examine the *boredom* affect that the clinicians experience during the monotonous testing process, in view of the *depression without sadness* – called *essential* – in patients that they may reflect. Yet, what should be done, a fortiori, in contexts of generalized alterations when clinging to perceptive reality, the ultimate anti-instinctual shield, seems to be itself at risk of disappearing? This is certainly a matter of diagnosis and therapeutic choices to which projective tests, among other contributions, may provide some answers.

Unlike analytic situations, projective situations and especially the Rorschach Test, as discussed further, are unique in that they trigger references to the body in various aspects, "normal" and pathological in both children and adults, known to be part of the construction and deconstruction of identity. Faced with the excessive and often astounding reality that serious bodily disorganization represents and the effects of *un-psychization* (lack of fantasy) whatever their origin, one may wonder to what extent the symbolic or even direct reference to the body, as an implicit reference to *Homo erectus*, is likely to underlie the (re)animation of mental activity that might be mobilized in situations where care is provided through a body approach.

What Can Mental Activity Do When Dealing With the Reality of the Body?

This question dates back to 1967–1968, when I came across clinical psychology at the Institute of Psychology of University Paris 5 (now the Université de Paris), as part of the Certificate of Projective Techniques. As a freshly graduated student of psychopathology, I was studying again after practicing psychology full-time for 1 year at the psychiatric hospital in the Hautes-Alpes department, holding but a Licence (bachelor's degree) from the Aix-Marseille University. My studies were conducted in excellent internships in psychiatry and paediatrics and with recommendations from Simone Cotte. I had also just taken a 2-year detour as a teaching assistant in social psychology at the Sorbonne, regarding access to, and the future of, the BA degree in French language and literature. While studying for the psychopathology degree, students were taught by Thérèse Lempérière, Jean Delay, Pierre Pichot, and Jacques Perse how to identify, separate, and classify nosological entities, which was an absolute necessity. Projective psychology helped me discover a new world of multiple intertwined substructures as close as possible to individual reality, including those coming from the articulation between mental and bodily activities. It was actually a glimpse of the subtlety of this approach that was based on a psychoanalytic model in which notions of conflict and defensive modalities nuance the diagnostic and prognostic issues. I have since adopted this model on both personal and professional levels, and I have an unwavering commitment to it.

In the year 1967–68, with the unusual enthusiasm she shared with her students, Nina Rausch de Traubenberg presented protocols to her students, including those from her doctoral dissertation, involving individuals with congenital cardiopathy (Rausch de Traubenberg, 1965a). Among these were the preoperative and postoperative Rorschach protocols of a certain Marie-Thérèse, aged 22, that are still among the prototypes of hysterophobia today: "A flower petal

… I don't like this red stain, I hate red with a passion … an iris torn for pleasure." The report underscored "the importance of the emotional charge and the expression of fantasies, giving second place to the issue of bodily integrity that is experienced as an aggression that is similar to sexual assault" (Rausch de Traubenberg, 1965b). The expression of the assault seemed more remote in the postoperative protocol of this young woman. Contrary to the fears of the medical profession, the existence of a mental symptomatology not only did not aggravate somatic disorganization, but it could also contribute to its reorganization.

In the following years, appointed as a teaching assistant with Michèle Martin, at the request of Rausch de Traubenberg, we presented the Marie-Thérèse case on numerous occasions, always with the same enthusiasm, yet without being able to analyze the conducive mental mechanisms to somatic reconstruction. Using the Rorschach Test to differentiate "real" hysterical neurosis from its less structuring imitations in patients we encountered in the department of Prof. Widlöcher, later became the subject of my thesis (Boekholt, 1985) supervised by Rausch de Traubenberg, sealing my commitment to university research. Through this voluminous work, which I find unreadable today, I was trying, based on statistics – with the help of Matty Chiva – to differentiate between "good" and "poorly mentalized" functioning, inexpertly following the assumptions of the École Psychosomatique de Paris. I focused on issues of the future of neurosis and structural changes with age. This was followed by further studies on the psyche of adults and children, from a dynamic and economic perspective, in most cases in light of a more diversified and better developed projective perspective.

Regarding children assessed within the context of cardiac surgery, Rausch de Traubenberg commented on the protocol of Jérémie (aged 7 years and 10 months) among the so-called normative examples, in the book that she wrote with Marie-France Boizou (Rausch de Traubenberg & Boizou, 1977). Their conclusion valued the ability in that child "to express justified anxiety and overcome it," and further stated that "unlike many severely affected children, Jérémie does not seem to be at risk of taking refuge in mental retardation and emotional impoverishment" (Rausch de Traubenberg & Boizou, 1977, p. 139). The praise for mental activity and anxiety in the face of the reality of the suffering body which is explicit in this report sheds light on psychosomatic clinical research, the theorization of which emerged much later on my own path.

When the time came for me to face the severity of the illness in hospitalized children and adolescents in neurosurgery (Recasens et al., 1997), I reproduced, as closely as possible, the test–retest methodology that Rausch de Traubenberg had used in her thesis to assess the implications and effects of the invasive intervention they were forced to undergo. Except in urgent cases, a comprehensive psychological assessment was carried out before the intervention and then repeated after intervals of 6 months, 1 year, and 2 years later. Welcomed by most children and their families, the assessment was perceived as a playful and/or soothing moment: "when I play with you," "when I speak with you," "I feel less pain," said young patients who experienced intolerable pain before surgery.

After the intervention, many of them expressed the joy of "playing" with me again and enjoying a privileged moment. Ultimately, however, only young people with previous solid components of "infant" or "child" neurosis could subsequently rediscover the enjoyments, with a mental and somatic benefit. Others, particularly those who had persistently denied all painful affects in the face of their new bodily reality inherent in the intervention, were not able to rediscover such enjoyments. The effectiveness of the mental activity that was proposed to some young people and their families proved to be dependent on the acknowledgement of anxiety and the (re)elaboration of the depressive position.

Two sets of conclusions emerged from this research. On the one hand, on the theoretical level, the accuracy of the psychosomatic perspective was evident, not as an a priori underlying premise, but based on the clinical evidence of the experience that was observed in an *après coup* (after the event) and which determined the rules: "Mental activity protects the body from somatic disorganization. When disorganization occurs anyway, mental activities help reorganization," as Rosine Debray (2001) pointed out when I defended my thesis to obtain accreditation to supervise research (Boekholt, 1998), and which she has repeated during the different thesis committees I have attended with her as a rapporteur. The accuracy of the psychosomatic perspective was also evident in the research she conducted, with Catherine Chabert and Michèle Emmanuelli, in gynecology patients (Debray, Boekholt, Chabert, & Emmanuelli, 1993) and in all of my own research with adults, children, and babies.

Concurrently, at the methodological level, the studies that were carried out before and after surgical procedures involving critical implications were consistent with the irreplaceability of the longitudinal approach in clinical studies, to address the subtle issue of prognosis, particularly in children and adolescents. These studies were in line with the thesis by Rausch de Traubenberg and Vica Shentoub (Shentoub, 1967) (led by Didier Anzieu). This promising approach was then adopted by many PhD students, under the direction of Catherine Chabert and others, who, at variance with hasty schematism, focused on the continuities and discontinuities of mental functioning. Because I have closely followed these studies, I will cite the studies of Jean-Yves Chagnon (2002), carried out over the last 20 years on nonpatients, as well as the studies conducted by Geneviève Bréchon and Aline Cohen de Lara, and more recently, Estelle Louët, which reflect the growing interest among the younger generation in the clinical and projective approach. There are many more.

With regard to the assessment of child abuse in child psychiatry (Boekholt, 2000), rather than establishing unnecessary observations which social and legal institutions have made outstandingly well, one of my key objectives was to examine how the psyche might be constructed or reconstructed *in spite of the reality* of the harm inflicted on the body. Consistent with an earlier study by Josette des Ligneris, Duplant, Rucine, and Schwarz (1990), the results have sometimes been disconcerting: Responding to the Rorschach in which traces of suffering may be expected, some children between age 6 or 8 proved to have an early capacity for thorough analysis, without affects, representations of relationships, or any reference to the body. They were thus able to defensively cling to the perceptual reality of form and nothing else but form. However, with the CAT cards and the Patte-Noire projective test featuring bodily convergences that are likely to evoke representations of early relationships, the shaky instinctual references overwhelm their perceptual scope, to the point that it reverses all inside/outside, attacker/attacked, and active/passive references, commensurate with the rupture of "mental envelopes" that was impossible to elaborate without specific and appropriate help. This goes to show the dependence of such modalities of functioning on external objects that are kept, at all costs, in the perceptual field, at the risk of a collapse of identity.

The Reality of the Body: A Springboard for Mental Activity

Some projective situations induce a direct or symbolic reference to the body. Such is the peculiarity of the Rorschach Test, known for its reference, at any age, to body schema, body image (with narcissism and inside/outside boundaries), and self-representation which was a theme dear to Rausch de Traubenberg, or even to the involvement of the body in the relationship representation that the bilateral cards arouse. In the TAT, the body is represented in all of the figurative cards, and Cards 4 and 10 call for an explicit interaction. This is also represented through animal differentiation – big/small, displayed/concealed – in the CAT where Card 10 is the only card that is closely linked to the body whereas 11 out of the 18 Patte-Noire cards have this specificity. The Scenotest material relies on the whole body and motor functions.

Given the high levels of concern regarding the lack of responsiveness to these specific situations that has been observed in adults and children with severe psychiatric, neurological, and/or somatic disorders, I was led to observe that reference to the body, which can be explicit or suggested, verbalized or sometimes simply mimed, involves a minimum amount of differentiating activity – between inside/outside, ego/non-ego – that is likely to be part of the birth or rebirth of mental activity.

What economic sense can be given to the focus on the body that is so common in the Rorschach, the increase or perseveration of which may raise particular concern? With des Ligneris (Boekholt & des Ligneris, 2003), I found it striking to observe in children suffering in different ways – mental and/or somatic disorders – the extent to which the amplified reality of their illness (holed body) and/or the excessiveness of grandiose fantasies that were destined for its denial, could use the perceptive medium as a preferred mode of expression. The alternation between grievance and denials also reflected the quest for restorative or compassionate attention from the clinical psychologist: a touching "look at me" in some children that could lead to psychotherapeutic care. Yet, how often have we been boastfully distanced by the health care teams, acting solely as a good narcissistic foil for the astounding belief in invincibility ("not even hurting") at an age when dependency is essential.

Regarding adults whose projective productions were collected in various clinical contexts, I have argued that the anatomy responses in the Rorschach Test that reflect different degrees of libidinal withdrawal could be a narcissistic regulation (Boekholt, 1983), alongside or in place of, more traditional defence modalities – to help maintain identity cohesion. This sameness function that is also observed in children and adults is particularly striking in contexts that involve psychotic breakdown where verbalized reference to the body or parts of the body, often as a vague or inadequate perceptual perseveration, replaces the clinging to familiar, perhaps experienced dimensions, regardless of changes in external stimuli. "It's something in the body," a young adolescent, in total loss of his references, told us between yawns, before sinking into a puzzling silence.

Faced with Card III of the Rorschach Test, another psychotic patient, an adult, stood up from his chair and placed his hands on both sides of his pelvis. Acted-out responses require clinical psychologists to use highly supportive testing modes and "test the limits," by putting actions into words, if necessary ("you mean that…") in order to maintain associative bonds in mental abilities.

In another psychotic patient, the display of the color red in Card II triggered an impressive wrath: "blood!" that I associated, après coup (after the event), with the creation of Jan Fabre's "I am blood," except that in this particular case, the fragmentation experience of the inside/outside boundaries was not part of any provocative theatrical effects.

Yet, it is the clinical practice with young children that has enabled me to realize the importance of the dimensions of the body, motricity, and sensoriality, in the emergence of identity processes: "from the body to affects, then to the mind," according to the statement by Freud, and to the concept of sensory envelopes by Didier Anzieu. Proposed to all-comers children as soon as they are able to put words to an image, the Rorschach Test proved surprisingly relevant in accounting for the "perceptual evolution echoing the instinctual substrate" (Boekholt, 1996). Indeed, I found that, in children who spoke at the age of 2, sensorimotor language outweighed the use of verbs: The entire body as well as motricity replaced verbal responses to reflect the possible fundamental differentiation between inside and outside. At around 3 and 4 years of age, emphasis is given to fantasy echoing the oedipal emergence, and it is only during the so-called latency period that a more differentiated perceptual activity allows the Rorschach to *become* the Rorschach. It is also during the assumed period of latency that the use of M responses emerges, echoing the ability to forge *representations,* which are particularly significant in children with motor disabilities during their early years of life. This was incompatible with the hyperactive manifestations that were observed in children consulting for this purpose.

Similarly, with regard to the thematic material in the CAT and Patte-Noire, it is striking that young children with a wide verbal palette rely primarily on the motor and bodily sphere, or even on the clinical psychologist, to account for interrelations

– notably aggressive – by miming them using gestures and sound effects. These modalities are part of the mental elaboration that is subsequently put into words in the form of representations of actions that are initially juxtaposed, and then from 4 to 5 years of age are bound together within interactions that make up a "narrative." This explains the meaning of the phrase "from body to mind, from dependence to autonomy, from perception to mentalization" that I adopted, echoing the studies conducted by Debray to develop the grid of analysis of thematic tests (Boekholt, 1993), common to both verbal tests (CAT, TAT, and PN) and test games such as the Scenotest. Pascal Roman drew inspiration from this analysis and skillfully developed La Malette Projective Première Enfance for children aged 6 months to 4 years.

Nothing, however, has been definitively achieved: Encountering severe somatic and/or mental episodes that both break the soul *(die Seele),* notably during life crises and accidents, may, at any age, induce deep ruptures in the identity foundations, the source and future of which must be questioned. What permanence, what changes, and what reorganization might we expect when the sense of the continuity of existence is shaking, especially in adolescence and senescence, or when the individual additionally suffers from dementia? In the face of mental disasters, Chabert and Guedeney (2002) raises the issue of the discontinuous and unpredictable evolution of psychotic adolescents.

Working under the supervision of Chabert and Bernard Golse, Hélène Suarez-Labat (2015) used projective tests to highlight the processes of change in autistic children after a long psychoanalytic treatment. Already in 1991, in line with Donald Meltzer and Frances Tustin, Nicole Jeammet (1991) defended the concept of postautism to account for the change processes hardly expected in adolescents.

Clinical practice with older patients experiencing a loss of autonomy has led Marion Péruchon (1990) and Benoît Verdon (2002, 2012, 2013) to favor a dynamic approach to the unexpected resources that have been identified, for each of them, through projective situations.... Many high-quality studies – I hope the colleagues I have failed to cite will forgive me – are consistent in showing the extent to which the mental work that is undertaken is able, in some cases, to beat the odds of all or part of unfavorable prognostics, or at least soften the edges.

Plea for Bodily Mediations of Subjectification

In extensive institutional care situations, which are difficult and multifocal, mental work prospects become impossible, which requires other modalities, particularly from the body. Indeed, in all or parts of the body, however painful, named or acted out, in projective situations, when the internal reality seems to have been forgotten, fragments of sensorial reactivity still remain: *hoc est corpus meum, ergo sum* (this is my body, therefore I am). This evidence will determine the effectiveness of cognitive stimulations, among others, that are widespread in institutions that Verdon, Kurtz, Rocard, and Toullier (2006) mention when relating to adults and elderly brain-damaged patients. In posttraumatic contexts, however, traces of mental activity may be extremely tenuous, and may reveal their own associative limits to the clinicians and thus minimize, in these patients, the ability to reinvest their internal and relational space. This is why, as Marie-Christine Pheulpin and collaborators (Pheulpin, Benfredj-Coudounari, & Bruguière, 2011; Pheulpin, 2013; Pheulpin, Baudin, & Bruguière, 2017) have suggested, it is important to identify explicit or infraverbal references to bodily axes and/or sensorimotor skills through the bodily and sensory mediation that a projective situation offers, notably with patients with great physical pain – as witnesses of a minimal survival of the body-ego that is necessary for repossession and reanimation of identity reference points, a highly valuable ally for possible therapeutic projects for health care teams.

This experience can be applied to all ages through a curative or palliative team project *incorporating* bodily mediations, along with the multiple modalities of care of adolescents with serious mental disorders, as discussed during the seminar held in the fall of 2012 at the Institut Mutualiste Montsouris in Paris. Must we then prescribe "hot baths and full body massage twice a day," as Freud and Breuer (1895/2001) recommended before psychoanalysis? Why not? Provided we return to psychization paths that do not always – and even less on the first try – rely on the investment of a relational space, based on a verbal exchange. Subject to individual and cultural specificities, the range of bodily approaches – to contain, stimulate, support, and/or elaborate – is broad enough to contribute to the reinvestment of associative processes in the patient–carer interrelationship. Although some would argue to the contrary, body wraps are accurately and preciously recommended for unbearable and indescribable fragmentation anxiety, that is indistinctly experienced at the crossroads of the body and the psyche, while self-injury gestures fall into the illusion of alleviating it. Numerous institutions are now equipped with the Snoezelen environment that is full of promises for sensory revival/appeasement, provided its theorization, and especially the requisite training, are fully addressed.

Concerning young patients with disabling chronic pain who I treated using relaxation alongside the medical care they received (at the Pain Management Unit, Migraine Center for Children, Centre for Paediatric Analgesia, CNRD; director: Dr. D. Annequin, Children Hospital Armand Trousseau, Paris, France), the often spectacular and long-lasting respite from the pain proved to be dependent on the quality of the anaclisis that was jointly provided by the parents and the health care team. These findings were more significant as the symptom – such as retinal migraine, for instance – was blind (i.e., without meaning for the patient), isolated, and without associated mental disorders. Although the pain did not miraculously disappear, it was no longer perceived as an external persecutor but, rather, as an internalized object. Able to tame pain, to "hold" it, according to the metaphor of Winnicott, to "support" pain and manage it by themselves by putting their feelings into words, these children and adolescents were able to space out their medical treatment, get on with their activities, and develop new relationships.

When my colleagues performed a psychological assessment before, and then 1 year after the treatment, the benefits observed were in relation to the capacity to own the "I," and, with the Rorschach test (consistent with the findings of Marika Bergès-Bounes), through the increase in the number of M responses, witnessing better internalization capacities. By transforming the traumatic or painful expression into smaller quantities of negotiable affects, the motor skills and/or sensory solicitations of the projective situation were part of an anaclitic experience, as a "holding–enveloping" helping in the reemergence of a "thinking me/I" within an intermediary space: "It looks like...," "I think...," "It's as though...," "I have the feeling...," "It makes me think of...," "This color reminds me of..." – predicting possible mental reorganizations.

In contrast, children with somatic pathologies – which are often severe, multiple, and long-established – and who, in addition or despite them, display mental symptoms – particularly a type of school phobia with its well-known and sadly confirmed side benefits – gained more benefit from a more or less traditional psychotherapy approach, provided that correspondingly, resourceless families could also benefit from a mental anaclisis.

In cases of crippling pathologies (genetic among others – Marfan, Little, Proteus ... types) that are prone to multiple complications and malformations, based on inconsistent and vulnerable results, any concept of "after" treatment is uncertain. The treatment was spread over several years during which the individual and family psychotherapeutic approach was often discontinuous, with or without relaxation, sometimes as an accompaniment function, as a respite, and/or as a body image replacement.

Conclusion

In the face of bodily injury, one of the most favorable outcomes is to keep or create fantasies, no matter how exuberant, as witnessed in projective creation and in the play space that is maintained with young children; from poetry to fantasy or even sheer madness, from perception to recollection. All mental activities, especially if they remain within the relationship with the clinical psychologist, are likely to facilitate the reorganization of the illness or at least mitigate its intensity.

The projective situation suggests all of these indications that place the suffering individual at the heart of therapeutic projects in order to encourage their path toward subjectification. Unlike the entire educational and cognitive system that refuses to differentiate between individual uniqueness and what has been closed off to the "wounds of the soul" (Chabert, 2009) at the risk of aggravating decompensation through acts or serious forms of withdrawal, there is a need to reconsider the role of bodily mediations among therapeutic and institutional indications (Pinel & Gaillard, 2013), provided they fall within the resources' reinvestment: "body to mind" resources, *from the sense of self to self-representation,* of which the projective situation is a privileged witness.

Acknowledgments

This chapter was originally published in French and is reprinted here in English with permission: Boekholt, M. (2014). Que faire d'une excessive réalité: À propos des sources corporelles de la subjectivation. *Psychologie clinique et projective, 20*(1), 93–108. https://doi.org/10.3917/pcp.020.0093 © Erès Editions.

References

Azoulay, C. (2002). La feuille de dépouillement du TAT: Des origines à nos jours [The TAT scoring grid: From its beginnings until the present]. *Psychologie clinique et projective, 8,* 21–59. http://doi.org/10.3917/pcp.008.0021

Boekholt, M. (1983). Mécanismes de régulation narcissique au Rorschach [Narcissistic regulation mechanisms in the Rorschach Test]. *Psychologie française, 28*(2), 124–128.

Boekholt, M. (1985). *Hystérie et confins de l'hystérie au Rorschach* [Hysteria and borders of Hysteria] (Unpublished doctoral dissertation). René Descartes University, Paris, France.

Boekholt, M. (1993). *Épreuves thématiques en clinique infantile. Approche psychanalytique* [Thematic tests in children clinical settings: Psychoanalytical Approach]. Paris, France: Dunod.

Boekholt, M. (1996). Fondements pulsionnels de l'expérience visuelle: Regard à travers la genèse du processus Rorschach [Drives as foundations of visual experience: Genesis of Rorschach process]. *Psychiatrie de l'enfant, 39*(2), 537–579.

Boekholt, M. (1998). *Normalités et pathologies: Approche clinique et projective* [Normalities and pathologies: Clinical and projective approach] (Thesis for habilitation to supervise research). Université Paris Descartes, Paris, France.

Boekholt, M. (2000). Traumatisme réel, traumatisme fantasmatique. Le Patte-Noire dans l'approche des représentations de relation [Real traumatism, phantasmic traumatism: Black-Paw to understand representations of relationships]. *Psychologie clinique et projective, 6,* 145–154.

Boekholt, M., & des Ligneris, J. (2003). Le narcissisme chez l'enfant: Modalités normales et pathologiques [Narcissism in the child: Normal and pathological modalities]. *Psychologie clinique et projective, 9,* 95–116. http://doi.org/10.3917/pcp.009.0095

Chabert, C. (2009). Blessures du corps, blessures de l'âme. Psychothérapie d'une jeune fille diabétique présentant de graves troubles des conduites alimentaires [Wounds of the body, wounds of the soul: The psychotherapy of a young diabetic girl presenting severe symptoms of eating disorders]. *Psychologie clinique et projective, 15,* 9–26. http://doi.org/10.3917/pcp.015.0009

Chabert, C., & Guedeney, N. (2002). Permanence et changement dans l'évolution d'un adolescent psychotique [Permanence and change in a psychotic adolescent outcome]. *Adolescence*, 183–203.

Chagnon, J.-Y. (2002). *Le pronostic à la preadolescence* [Prognosis in preadolescence]. Villeneuve-d'Ascq, France: Presses Universitaires du Septentrion.

Debray, R. (1987). Le TAT : Aujourd'hui et demain [The TAT Test: Today and tomorrow]. *Psychologie française, 32*(3), 127–130.

Debray, R. (1990). Quand trop de réalité fige la remémoration [When too much reality ossifies rememoration]. *Revue Française de Psychanalyse, 4*(54), 931–945. http://doi.org/10.3917/rfp.g1990.54n4.0931

Debray, R. (2001). *Épître à ceux qui somatisent* [Epistle to those who somatize]. Paris, France: PUF. http://doi.org/10.3917/puf.bonn.2001.01

Debray, R., Boekholt, M., Chabert, C., & Emmanuelli, M. (1993). Modalités de fonctionnement psychique et expression gynécologique chez trente jeunes femmes [Psychic functioning and gynecological expression of 30 young women]. *Revue française de psychosomatique, 4,* 165–184. http://doi.org/10.3917/rfps.004.0165

des Ligneris, J., Duplant, N., Rucine, M. O., & Schwarz, F. (1990). Fonctionnement psychologique des enfants victimes de sévices [Psychological functioning of Children victims of abuses]. *Rorschachiana, 17,* 320–324.

Freud, S., & Breuer J. (1895/2001). Studies on hysteria. In J. Strachey (Ed. & Trans.), *The standard edition of the complete psychological works of Sigmund Freud* (Vol. 2). London, UK: Vintage Classics. (Original work published in 1895)

Jeammet, N. (1991). Le post-autisme: Une figure de la "normalité"? Métamorphoses et permanence de stratégies autistiques [Postautism: Figure of "normality"? Metamorphosis and permanence of autistic strategy]. *La Psychiatrie de l'enfant, 34*(1), 137–170.

Marty, P., & de M'Uzan, M. (1963). La pensée opératoire [Operative thinking]. *Revue française de psychanalyse, 27,* 345–356.

Péruchon, M. (1990). Rorschach et TAT dans la maladie d'Alzheimer: Prolégomènes à une étude du processus démentiel [Rorschach and TAT in Azheimer's disease: Prolegomena to study dementia process]. *Bulletin de psychologie, 44*(398), 2–10.

Pheulpin, M.-C. (2013). *Adultes en détresse: De l'expérience du corps à la scène psychique.* [Adults in distress: from the experience of the body to the psychic scene] (Unpublished thesis for habilitation to supervise research). University Paris Descartes, Paris, France.

Pheulpin, M.-C., Baudin, M., & Bruguière, P. (2017). *Clinique des états du corps. Approche psychanalytique et projective* [Clinic of body states; Psychoanalytical and projective approach]. Paris, France: Dunod.

Pheulpin, M.-C., Benfredj-Coudounari, K., & Bruguière, P. (2011). Les épreuves projectives, un creuset de réorganisation psychique? Quand la clinique du traumatisme crânien léger questionne le traumatisme psychique [Projective tests: A moment of psychic reorganization? When clinical work with moderate cranial trauma makes us question psychic trauma]. *Psychologie clinique et projective, 17,* 221–249. http://doi.org/10.3917/pcp.017.0221

Pinel, J. P., & Gaillard, G. (2013). L'institution soignante à l'épreuve de l'hypermodernité [The hospital and the challenge of hypermodernity]. *Bulletin de psychologie, 526*(l), 333–340. http://doi.org/10.3917/bupsy.526.0333

Rausch de Traubenberg, N. (1965a). *Implications psychologiques des cardiopathies congénitales. Effets des interventions correctives* [Psychological implication of congenital heart diseases: Impacts of corrective operations] (Unpublished doctoral dissertation). Sorbonne University, Paris, France.

Rausch de Traubenberg, N. (1965b). *Pedagogical dossier* (Unpublished manuscript). Sorbonne University, Paris, France.

Rausch De Traubenberg, N., & Boizou, M.-F. (1977). *Le Rorschach en clinique infantile. L'imaginaire et le réel chez l'enfant* [The imaginary and the real in Rorschach testing with children]. Paris, France: Dunod, 1996.

Recasens, C., Chokron, S., Boekholt, M., Gueniche, K., Zittoun, C., Brauner, R., & Féline, A. (1997). Étude du craniopharyngiome chez l'enfant. Sémiologie et psychopathologie pré- et post-opératoire [Study of craniopharyngioma in childhood: Preoperative and postoperative semiology and psychopathology]. *Annales médico-psychologiques, 155*(9), 545–555.

Shentoub, V. (1967). *Le devenir des manifestations phobo-obsessionnelles de la puberté à l'adolescence* [Outcome of phobo-obsessive symptoms from puberty to adolescence] (Unpublished doctoral dissertation). Université Paris 5, Paris, France.

Shentoub, V., & Debray, R. (1978–1979). Que faire d'une excessive richesse fantasmatique? Interprétation d'un protocole inhabituel de TAT [How to deal with excessive phantasmic richness? Interpretation of an unusual TAT protocol]. *Bulletin de psychologie, 32*(339/3-7), 309–322.

Suarez-Labat, H. (2015). *Les autismes et leurs évolutions: Apports des méthodes projectives* [Autisms and their evolutions: Contribution of projective methods]. Paris, France: Dunod.

Verdon, B. (2002). Le TAT: Une épreuve projective heuristique pour la clinique du sujet âgé [The TAT: A heuristic projective test for clinical work with the elderly subject]. *Psychologie clinique et projective, 8,* 83–208. http://doi.org/10.3917/pcp.008.0183

Verdon, B. (2012). *Clinique et psychopathologie du vieillissement: Apport des méthodes projectives (Rorschach, TAT)* [Psychopathology in clinical field of ageing: Contribution of projective methods (Rorschach, TAT)]. Paris, France: Dunod.

Verdon, B. (2013). *Le vieillissement psychique* [Psychical ageing]. Paris, France: PUF.

Verdon, B., Kurtz, A., Rocard, V., & Toullier, M. T. (2006). Éduquer, stimuler, renforcer, revalider, la cognition prescrite [To educate, stimulate, reinforce, revalidate: The prescribed cognition]. *Perspectives psy, 4*(45), 345–352. http://doi.org/10.1051/ppsy/2006454345

7

From Clinical Work on Learning, to Learning Clinical Work With Rosine Debray

Catherine Weismann-Arcache

From Past to Present: Temporal Trajectories

My 1990s With Rosine Debray

From one career path to another and from one generation of projective psychologists to the next, the subtitle of this introduction follows that of an article by Rosine Debray: "My 70s with Vica," which was published in 2002 in *Psychologie clinique et projective* (Debray, 2002). I met Debray in 1994 during my training in educational psychology for the state-registered diploma. It was a very clinical training she led with the infectious vigor and enthusiasm that were so characteristic of her. She had an anticipative and kind hope for me, suggesting that I continue my education with a thesis after completing a *diplôme d'études supérieures spécialisées* (DESS) in psychology and a *diplôme d'études approfondies* (DEA; in France until 2005, both were postgraduate degrees preparing for a doctorate): "Mere formalities," as she said! Driven by this stimulating investment, I signed up for the DESS in clinical psychology and psychopathology in 1995. And while I was still a student, in spite of being a school psychologist since I had completed my DEPS (the French state-registered diploma in school psychology), Debray proposed me to present a case study in her lecture on the psychological assessment. This case study – a disharmonic child with both high intellectual potential and severe dyspraxia – was published in 2000 in her book *Psychological Assessment of Children in the Latency Stage* (Debray, 2000). The following year, I joined the association Clinique des Apprentissages (Clinical Work on Learning) that she had just established and which is currently chaired by Jean-Yves Chagnon (see http://clinap.fr/).

While leading the training in educational psychology, Debray was also involved in the initial curriculum and had introduced the psychoanalytical theory into diversified teachings, reflecting the schools of thought that led to clinical psychology. Some of her axioms are printed in my memory and most importantly, they guide my practice as a psychologist, teacher, and researcher: "In most cases, a single sign does not have a value in and of itself" (Debray, 2000, p. 40) and "The mental apparatus contains, for life, the cognitive apparatus as a reservoir and support for intelligent behavior." She also vividly insisted on the transference–countertransference aspects inherent in all relational measures, whether it be care or research. I would readily add the transmission situations; Debray taught me methodology through the richness and complexity of the psychological assessment. She supported me in the theoretical–clinical elaboration of my thesis (Weismann-Arcache, 2003a), and through her seminars at the Institut de Psychosomatique (IPSO Pierre Marty), she trained me in clinical practice and psychotherapy with children and parents. Her two professions, psychoanalyst and teacher–researcher, molded her remarkable epistemological, methodological, and clinical coherence.

Thanks to the après coup of writing a document for accreditation to supervise research (Weismann-Arcache, 2013a), I became aware of "the phantasmic interactions" (Lebovici & Stoleru, 1983; Lebovici, 2009) that connected me to Debray and nourished my activities as a clinician, teacher, and researcher. I would like to organize my work along three axes that she strongly initiated with her adages, which she always expressed with great conviction and which influenced several generations of students. These adages by Debray are the invisible thread of my journey from French public school to the school of psychoanalysis, then from schoolchild to child, and lastly, from child to parents.

At the School of Psychoanalysis

In most cases, a single sign does not have a value in and of itself.
Rosine Debray

This simple yet powerful formula is worth remembering day in day out with psychology students, as psychological assessment seems to be currently taking a step backwards: It is more and more reduced to a sum of partial measures. However criticized (Weismann-Arcache, 2011a), psychological assessment is based on the simplistic concept of comorbidity, which is used to juxtapose and sum up disorders, leading to a multiplication of diagnoses that are based on descriptive criteria. Debray insisted on the crucial issue of child development and its intravariability and intervariability, by referring to what psychoanalysis considers a genetic perspective, which was extended to cover psychosomatics in an unprecedented way. Two decades ago, at the first science day that was organized by her association Clinique des Apprentissages (Clinical Work on Learning), she concluded as follows:

> For the latter [psychoanalysts], it is impossible to artificially isolate that which is a sole matter of development of intelligence from what comes with it, namely the general psychosomatic development of the subject and particularly, the emotional development that is perceptible through that of the psychic apparatus. (Debray, 1998, p. 113)

In most of her writings, the model of development, which Anna Freud proposed (1962), is used as a reading grid to comprehend the different "styles" of children: motor, cognitive, and language, but also changes in character and behavior (Debray, 2000). Was it her interest in the body, the *soma*, that led her to question the complex organization of praxes, and the role of mental representation of the body image and drawing in the construction of intelligence? She thus presciently developed the very current notion of *suppléances* (replacement) that children with dyspraxia develop to compensate "for something that is missing" when no rehabilitation can fill this gap (Debray, 2000, p. 50).

My work on disharmonic development with its structuring or pathogenic aspects is certainly addressed toward part of the issue of development and its heterogeneous destinies, which I questioned in my study on "development and mental temporality in intellectual precocity," which was a study for my dissertation, which I wrote under the direction of Debray (Weismann-Arcache, 2003a). Psychoanalytic theory sheds light on the dimensional modeling of the development of intelligence, including its deficit dimension (Weismann-Arcache, 2004b), extending from dyssynchrony to disharmony, from intelligence to mental processes, and from creativity to sublimation. Hence, I proposed some indicators of development, creativity, and intelligence in projective tests, exemplified by the projective clinical work on high potential.

From Schoolchild to Child

Of course, the cognitive apparatus is part of the mental apparatus which contains it for life. It goes back to underlining that the quality of intelligent performances remains in close dependence on the emotional state of the subject who makes them.
Rosine Debray

At a time when advances in cognitive and neuroscience fields are centered on neural connections and their organization which resembles more closely that of a network than that in which one functional unit is the subset of another, this vision may now sound schematic, thus simplistic. Nevertheless, it remains heuristically valuable by bringing to mind, in its own way, that intelligent behavior is based on the unique fantasies of the subject. A detailed psychological assessment is then a precious tool for a closer understanding of the nature of the link between intelligence and narcissistic and object investments. Debray developed a grid for reading psychological testing, the purpose of which was to enable the "dynamic appreciation of the mental functioning of the child in relation to his/

her cognitive potential, phantasmic irruptions, and defensive arrangements (Debray, 2000 p. 10). I wanted to extend such a view on intelligence and cognitive potentials to thinking processes and to sublimation in children, as a treatment of anxiety and its variations, whether it is effective or not (Weismann-Arcache, 2011b, Weismann-Arcache & Tordjman, 2012). From this perspective, I have extensively addressed the contribution of a detailed psychological assessment, and the interview, Wechsler scales, Piagetian tasks, drawings, and projective testing that it comprises. Most of these tools are atheoretical and require a theoretical reading grid to give them meaning (Chabert, 1998): Rey Complex Figure Test and drawings are examples to illustrate the point (Weismann-Arcache, 2010a). To this end, I also conducted research into methodological tools – a study that compared the Rey Complex Figure Test with Piagetian tasks, identifying possible clinical interpretations. My clinical meetings with children, who are now labeled as "children with a high intellectual potential," naturally led to patients diagnosed with dyspraxia (Weismann-Arcache, 2010b), hyperactivity (Weismann-Arcache, 2006), and depression (Weismann-Arcache, 2011b; Weismann-Arcache & Tordjman, 2012), who were approached from a transnosographic perspective. I compared the points of view of neurosciences and psychoanalysis with my work on atypical functioning.

From the Child to Their Parents

> *The therapist must resolutely be on the side of the mother,*
> *especially as she is more hurtful.*
> Rosine Debray

Debray expressed the third adage as a rule that is both absolute and difficult when pursuing a treatment with the father–mother–baby or father–mother–child triad: The issue of narcissism and its fluctuations that are related to the challenges of life was her primary concern, and she demonstrated the relevance of this double-sided concept in her clinical work and in parenthood as well as in its manifestations throughout life. One of its manifestations becomes meaningful when it is put in the context of the notion of proficiency that Debray often stressed in her writings. She saw it as the key point in the mother–baby relationship and as the condition on which the maternal hyperparenting may support "the primary maternal preoccupation" (Winnicott, 1969). She considered this anxious hyperparenting as a sign of health that is even greater and inevitable when the first-born is a boy (Debray, 1992; Debray & Belot, 2008).

Other authors have also stressed the stimulating aspect of the intensive mothering that is provided by mothers of great men. This is an intense almost incestuous mother–child relationship, which is normal during the first years, yet it continues through adulthood as far as mothers of creators are concerned: Those mothers are like a Jocasta in the making, libidinally overinvesting in their child, especially when it is a boy (Anzieu, 1981). Conversely, certain mother–child dyads can intensely share similar experiences of incompetence, leading to a disastrous "reciprocal disappointment":

> Injury which is related to having failed to be seen as competent by the mother – and vice versa – would lead to a narcissistic weakness and a sense of incapability that is promptly taken over and aggravated by mechanisms of characterial objection. (Debray & Belot, 2008, p. 167)

These relational modalities can be reactivated in all relationships that necessarily imply narcissistic challenges and would lead to many learning disabilities, which are considered today as neurodevelopmental disorders. Debray stressed "the links that join together narcissism through self esteem and the possibility or not of committing to intelligent procedures" (Debray, 1996, p. 212). As a 6-year-old child learns to read, success builds their self-esteem, and conversely, repeated failures fill the child or the adolescent with incompetence feelings that call for objection mechanisms. This early relational dysfunction may give rise to a variant with "certain babies superficially investing the exterior world and creating a protective blur as a response to what they experienced as great discontinuity of places and persons" (Debray, 1996, p. 168). Debray brought to our attention that this type of organization may coexist with excellent cognitive development, often combined with somatic disorders like eczema, creating a real "somato-psychic divorce": mental processing of excitation being prematurely blocked. All of her work demonstrates how the psychosomatic economy of the baby and the destinies of their development are dependent on the regulation capacities of their parents, especially on the maternal protective shield. Thus, parenting processes shed light on the child development process. My clinical practice with high potential children provides an illustration, which is sometimes striking, of these statements, and I was able to show how hyperparenting may be a carrier of such overdeveloped intelligence, without prejudice to their complexity, sometimes painful, often sublimatory or autosoothing (Weismann-Arcache, 2003b).

These three adages that Debray applied in clinical work are certainly the pillars on which the architecture of my own theoretical-clinical constructions rest organized around issues such as anachronism and disharmony. Now I would like to present my research on development and its heterogeneousness and on the assessment of thought processes extended, in the third section, to cover the clinical work on the parents–child relationship in the hypermodern society.

I addressed mental development and its nonlinear temporality on the basis of clinical work on high potential (Weismann-Arcache, 2013b). This research pitched in the impact of anachronism and its role in mental development: How much unbalance can mental functioning tolerate to stay out of pathology? This issue was very much influenced by Debray's considerations (1989, 1990) concerning "critical states" that may precede disorganization or "precocious maturation phases" in the baby. It is most likely that such interest in the "rapid pace" of development in babies led Debray to propose the TAT for use from the age of 6 years (Debray, 1987). and I followed her by applying the Longeot Scale of Logical Reasoning (applicable to children from the age of 9 years) to test high potential children from the ages of 5–6. My goal was to put the models of intelligence, and particularly the Piagetian model, to the test of psychoanalysis. Precocious intelligence is used for its "metaphorizing" value (Lebovici & Stoleru, 1983; Lebovici, 2009), and it can be extended to two conceptual fields, which have the benefit of being explored by psychoanalysis – that is, the field of epistemophilia or that of the development of thinking or mental development. The object of research is then based on two coordinates – that is, mental organization as the synchronic axis and temporality that affects mental development according to the history of the subject as the diachronic axis. On the basis of these theoretical–clinical relations and the methodological backing, I explored contemporary issues and even new symptomatic expressions (dyspraxia, higher-functioning autism, hyperactivity, or learning disorders) with tools and methods from clinical psychology and with reference to psychoanalysis.

Most of my work was based on the projective methodology that was elaborated by the French School (i.e., by Rausch de Traubenberg, Chabert, Debray, Emmanuelli, Azoulay, Chagnon, and others). Debray must be given credit for having committed, with conviction, to the psychoanalytical interpretation of investments and defensive movements that can be detected through intellectual efficiency tests or through Piagetian tests. And beyond daring in 1987 to propose undertaking the TAT with children from the age of 6, she initiated research on a well-tempered methodology with "a material that is neither too regressive nor too exciting to assess the quality of the defence compromise that a child is able to reach at that age" (Debray, 1987, p. 158).

Contemporary Organizers in Development Processes, Thinking, and Parenting

High Intellectual Potential: An Illustration of the Development Heterogeneity

Dyssynchrony, Heterogeneity, Disharmony

High intellectual potential has a magnifying effect on normal processes as it is characterized by dyssynchrony that accentuates them, *dyssynchrony* being a term that was introduced by J.-C. Terrassier (1981). According to Gibello (2009), this "affective-intellectual dyssynchrony" varies from ordinary affective immaturity to serious psychopathological organizations.

This developmental approach justifies the term *intellectual precocity,* but it remains insufficient to describe adults with high intellectual potential or even the characteristics of mental organization in such children. To avoid reductionism, I favored a concept-centered approach rather than stigmatizing – even in a positive way – the subjects: Using concepts enables emphasis on the complexity and diversity of models to understand human nature. Consequently, I use the terms *high potential, intellectually precocious child,* or even *gifted,* according to a particular point of view: psychometric definition, quantitative definition of a potential that was detected in a particular field (with an IQ greater than 130), a reference to development and to a lead, or even in reference to an overgift as regards the ideal child. A central issue in my work is how *intellectual precocity* – I deliberately use this term – would affect the libidinal development of the child, and its connection with the organization of the psychic instances: Considerations of the dynamic and diachronic point of view enable the consideration of the pathogenic or structuring value of intellectual precocity and its connection with different mental constellations. The key clinical reference is developmental heterogeneity, which I suggest as an alternative to the common usage of the notion of dyssynchrony. Descriptive clinical study, which states an affective immaturity of the intellectually precocious child, in contradiction with intellectual immaturity, does not address the connection between instinctual dynamics, defensive mental organization, and identificatory investments. Would the concept of dyssynchrony remain relevant from the projective tests perspective?

Projective Methodology and Developmental Reference Points

The high intellectual potential issue is foreign to psychoanalysis, but its conceptual underpinnings – intelligence, creativity, and anachronous development – are the components of mental functioning that belong to all children and can be assessed by projective tests. Projective tests could be part of a developmental perspective, since normative data show the occurrence frequency of some responses or certain discourse processes according to age. Hence, young children – before the age of 6 – favor a global approach to a percept that corresponds to their syncretic thinking, whereas during the latency stage, children explore the material in detail. This is not merely a matter of cognitive style, but also a development of defense mechanisms that are necessary for intellectual work: At the age of 6, learning to read, just like reading Rorschach, CAT, or TAT cards, happens through isolation mechanisms which reflect repression – among other things.

Conversely, children with high potential give priority to global responses instead of details, which demonstrates "a projective activity, striving to end and define; and hence overcome uncertainty" (de Mijolla-Mellor, 1992). This reversed proportion to all-comers children demonstrates a great investment of limits and difficulties in separating elements in the card, keeping the percept as a whole. It is an indicator of the intense anxiety of loss or castration and of its processing through the massive and total investment in a problem, a theme, or a relationship, that will be just as quickly displaced into another investment.

In the course of child development, expression modes in the Rorschach evolve, and there is an inverse relation between "the real motor activity and the ability to evoke action or interaction representations" (Boekholt, 1996). At about the age of 6, motor expression wanes in favor of elaborated and appropriate M responses. With relation to oedipal identifications, we expect relationships between differentiated, gendered, and socialized characters, just like the drawings of children.

In gifted young children, M responses are precocious from the age of 3 years, indicating a strong quest for identifications, driven by heterogeneous and mobile parental imagos. Instinctual responsiveness surfaces through great sensitivity to colors. Such diversified processing modalities of excitation are similar to what Emmanuelli and Azoulay observed through the adolescent process emerging "under both narcissistic and instinctual constraints" (Emmanuelli & Azoulay, 2001, p. 40). Contradicting usual assumptions, projective clinical work points to an accelerated psychoaffective development, which condenses and hence challenges developmental temporality and chronology.

According to the themes that highly gifted children approach, the CAT and TAT call for mental work that is triggered by existential questions based on origins and disappearance. Infantile sexual theories also rise, since they remain very active at the cost of less repression, which may be one of the conditions for sublimation (Weismann-Arcache, 2012).

Such fantasy elements reflect the frequency of difficult or delayed conceptions as a result of perinatal bereavements or infertilities, or even enigmatic or exceptional filiations: Precocious children have often been late-in-life babies, long-awaited and greatly invested babies; and we know how such a "Jocasta" mothering brings both creative and pathogenic potentials (Weismann-Arcache, 2009, 2013b). The TAT narratives often revolve around an "initial draft" of a family novel with a narcissistic register including themes that reflect cosmogony: mythology, Egypt, planets, and prehistory. Conversely, the bareness of certain narratives and speechlessness when dealing with the last TAT card demonstrate noncongruence between high cognitive abilities and the possible work of thought. Such projective testing reveals depressions that are masked by advanced cognition and which are often attributed to external causes such as unsuitable schools for these children (Weismann-Arcache, 2011b).

From a developmental perspective, projective testing can highlight different forms of the loss anxiety that shade the object relationships: What is known can be used as a defense against feeling, the exterior against what is represented; and this can be the thetic position of a high potential child, as reflected by the modalities of their responses to projective testing. Based on variants of this special position, clinicians and researchers can answer the questions regarding a high potential, whether that is an educational arrangement or a therapeutic help. In return, contemporary clinical work enhances the projective methodology by increasingly developing its implications.

From Intelligence to Thought Processes

Projective Methods: An Insight Into Nonprojective Tools?

How does the articulation between projective methodology and psychoanalytical theory assist clinicians or researchers when they clinically come across tools (logical thinking tests, Rey figure, drawings) and objects (high intellectual potential, "dys" disorders, learning disorders) that seem very far from the psychoanalytic epistemology? I support the hypothesis that current clinical practices can benefit from the psychoanalytical reading and its projective results, such as that practiced by the French School, supplementing it with its multiple areas of application and experience. In the manner of Debray, I have chosen tools that integrate quantitative and differential elements into a qualitative approach to identify the specifically contrasting vulnerabilities and strengths in high potential subjects. Lastly, the research that I did for my DEA (DEA in French stands for *diplôme d'études approfondies* – that is, a French master of advanced studies degree as a 1-year degree preparatory for a PhD) (Weismann-Arcache, 2000), which was titled Connection Between Intelligence and Narcissism, linked these two concepts together. The first one, narcissism, is derived from psychoanalysis, and the second, intelligence, refers more to Piagetian or neurocognitive epistemology; although all data and material may be highlighted and elucidated in light of a clinical approach, as I subsequently demonstrated through Piagetian testing (Weismann-Arcache, 2004a).

Cognitive Apparatus and Mental Apparatus

Testing in the psychological assessment of children can be put in perspective with this dual cognitive and dynamic approach: When Wechsler scales allow for comparisons on the basis of a norm, it seems to me that they rather assess contents and knowledge, whereas drawings are indicative of the sublimatory or psychopathological ties of this intellectual investment, whether it is underdeveloped or overdeveloped for that matter. Midway between instrumental and projective tests, the Rey figure drawing is a discriminative test to assess the quality of mentalization, the connections between the internal world and the external reality, and the balance between inhibition, which is sometimes necessary, and proneness to fantasy that fuels the desire to know. For that matter, we could transpose to the Rey figure what Debray and Shentoub highlighted about the TAT: "this dual conflicting play between control and slackness during the testing" (Debray & Shentoub, 1978). Debray applied this statement to tests that involve more secondary processes, as the Scale of Logical Thinking by Longeot, which is derived from Piagetian epistemology: "the existence of a significant fantasy may thus emerge as well as the possibility to come back to a rational mode of reasoning, while being supported by the questions and counter-suggestions of the examiner" (Debray, 2000, p. 24).

Rey Complex Figure: When Geometry Bent Meets Intellectual Finesse

Initially, the Rey Complex Figure Test was a graphic test of perceptual organization and mainly memory: In the first phase, the participant is asked to copy the shape of the figure, then 2 min later, without notice being given, they are required to reproduce it from memory. Both reproductions are timed without any time restriction, and the examiner carefully notes the different realization sequences. It was developed by André Rey in 1941 to assess the importance of the memory deficit resulting from neurological diseases: A significant loss between the copy and memory pointed to a memory deficit; and a defective reproduction in the copy phase was about another disorder.

This test was classified as an instrumental test – a bent for geometry – enabling the assessment of the level of perceptual organization, representation, and spatial organization. Debray attached importance to its clinical relevance and to intellectual finesse: She considered

> this dual testing as a somewhat reflection of the unconscious narcissistic organization of the subject which is projected into this meaningless image, first as a present object of perception and reproduction, then as a missing object to retrieve with a vanishing memory, vanishing even faster and with even more alterations when internal cohesion, that is, the narcissistic organization, is more fragile. (Debray, 1983, p. 191)

Referring to the psychosomatic theory and to the concept of mentalization that was developed by Pierre Marty (1976, 1980), she used the first *topic* as an economic model to understand mental functioning, and she considered that the Rey Complex Figure Test was particularly well suited to this task. She focused on the gap between both reproduction times of the Rey figure and on the comparison present versus missing object. Some participants copy the model without any significant alteration, whereas only a few disparate elements and the envelope (contour) remain in their memory: The gap between what can be reproduced when the object is present and what is brought to mind when it is missing can reveal the capacity to retain the internal object and the capacity to evoke missing objects. The Piagetian and Kleinian theories are solicited, as it is from the permanence and continuity of internal objects that the child manages to organize time, space, and causality: The child must have built a stable and solid internal object, which refers to the manner in which they have elaborated ambivalence and the depressive position.

Diagnostic and Prognostic Value of the Rey Figure: Issues Involved in Using the Rey Figure With Children With High Intellectual Potential

It is surprising to observe the extent to which difficulties and reluctance, resulting from the testing, can contrast with the cognitive brilliancy noted in intelligence tests. This gap between verbal tests – calling for reasoning and knowledge – and performance, perceptual reasoning tests, and drawings that generally measure the intellectual investment, which is more defensive than adaptive, leaves little room for "the pleasure of functioning" (Kestemberg & Kestemberg, 1966).

I propose to analyze the Rey figure the same way as is done for projective tests, since it has many analogies with the TAT and with the Rorschach as a test for time and space organization, which is perceptible through binding and unbinding. The pattern of a child is organized in accordance to their development, and types of reproduction are identified on a normative basis, according to age: between the ages of 5 and 11–12, type IV prevails, the child reproduces details by juxtaposition, building a more or less consistent whole according to their age. An analysis of the *drawing processes,* which is equivalent to that of the *discourse processes* in the TAT, will guide the clinical practitioner.

Refusal of the Model and Identificatory Fragility

The Rey Complex Figure Test instructions bring into play mental processes for retention and conservation of an object that must be structured and transformed based on an imposed model, between percept and project. High intellectual potential participants dislike tasks that do not call for reasoning, that require a strict application of a framework which cannot be inferred or deducted, and which is imposed by an adult. Refusal or difficulty complying with a model, along with graphic motor limits, delineate the connections between thought and regulation of intrapsychic conflicts. Projective tests usually confirm the fragility of identificatory processes underlying the refusal of the model. It therefore appears that the type of dysgraphia or dysorthographia disorders, which are relatively common among high potential persons, and for that matter, affect more boys than girls, is part of the impossibility of accepting the constraints that are inherent in the application of collective conventions and in shared codes, which are required for such activities. In this respect, the Rey figure copy is indicative of the adjustment or maladjustment to the model (Weismann-Arcache, 2004a).

The reproduction of the Rey figure brings into play the relation between part and whole, as well as the relation between tempered identification and massive incorporation: It is about moving from contiguity to continuity through a binding work.

Narcissistic Organization

The Draw-A-Person test, draw a family, and the Rey figure can show worrisome splitting in young high potential children: When all parts of the body can be rendered, their missing connections highlight the gap between the known and the corporeal experience. Concurrently, the binding in the Rey figure is ineffective; the drawing outlines are unfinished and cannot cross at any nodal point, thus failing at intersections. During the latency stage, drawings illustrate dyspraxia disorders (Weismann-Arcache, 2010b), with a particular difficulty in the representation of the body in space, and reluctance to draw as a painful confrontation with self-representation and with its imperfections; an insurmountable gap between the infantile ego and the very demanding ego ideal, which in a way demands a photo that reproduces precisely the external reality and refuses to struggle with a drawing that deals with internal reality. An excessively faithful photographic reproduction of the copy hints at the overinvestment in the external reality, at the massive assimilation that is similar to learning by rote to avoid interior work and to avoid metabolizing as required for any appropriation. Expected alterations and omissions indicate repression, transformation, and introjection activities.

Mentally finding and finding again an object that is visually perceived, and accepting the inevitable alteration of the mental reality, involve an internal security that tolerates the replacement of perceptual identity with thought identity, as this was raised by Freud in his article "Negation":

> The reproduction of a perception as a presentation is not always a faithful one; it may be modified by omissions, or changed by the merging of various elements. In that case, reality-testing has to ascertain how far such distortions go. (Freud, 1925/2001, p. 238)

From my perspective, if the judgment of existence reinforces the Self in its functions of adjustment to reality, too much judgment would lead to an intransigent ideal ego.

With regard to the Rey Complex Figure Test, there is a similarity to the favored processes in the Rorschach Test: A dominant global perceptual approach in the Rorschach Test reflects the persistence of copies focusing on the outlines as the organizing and holding element, which is not generally the case during the latency stage. High potential children focus on the so-called Type II global approach, which basically prevails from the age of 11–12 to adulthood, starting with the drawing outlines so that nothing gets lost.

When the loss issue deteriorates the pleasure of thinking, all elements can be present at the reproduction phase, but the absence of a main thread indicates a lack of internal cohesion: Contents without a container are equivalent to accumulated knowledge to fight the loss anxiety. Conversely, a better level of reproduction from memory than copy is a good prognostic revealing adequate mental reorganization capacities: Preferring one's own mental representation to try to modify the external reality is specific to M responses in the Rorschach, and it also reveals creative and sublimatory capacities at the Rey figure testing. This type of mental thought investment is common and precocious among high intellectual potential children – as well as artists, for that matter.

Greenhouse Effect in Infantile Clinical Practice: Narcissistic Issues of Parenthood

Late-in-Life Parents, Precocious Child

Since my approach was not nomothetic, I found what I was not looking for and discovered that most of the gifted children in my sample experienced outstanding or enigmatic conception and birth conditions: I observed an unexpected frequency of medically assisted procreation births or perinatal traumas (Weismann-Arcache, 2013b). A child death or a miscarriage may have preceded the birth of the high potential child, or even, an antenatal checkup may have provoked suspicion – which was refuted afterwards – of anomaly (often cognitive) in the fetal development. This is two thirds of my sample, which currently includes some 100 subjects. These difficult conceptions, which are forbidden or fantasized as transgressive or "contrary to nature," penetrate parental representations and anticipations. We must certainly not correlate high potential and medically assisted procreation, yet we conclude that the gifted child was eagerly awaited and invested in by their parents: Before the real child, their mother having long hoped for pregnancy, could maintain until late the narcissistic and fantasized baby of her dreams. With delight, the mother of a 6-year-old gifted boy told me, "He can sense all my thoughts," while with jubilation, another said, " He knows me by heart" or even "There is nothing I can hide from him!"

Debray highlighted the specificity of the maternal investment in a baby boy (Debray, 1992): carrying, then giving birth to a baby of the opposite sex can be highly rewarding for a young mother, and at the same time, it can be a cause for concern and a feeling of strangeness. These normal ambivalent feelings can sometimes be intense, according to the constitution and the history of the mother, then leading to an anxious and exclusive overinvestment in the child. Other authors have also stressed the stimulating aspect of the intensive mothering that is provided by mothers of great men. This is an intense almost incestuous mother–child relationship, which is normal during the first years, yet it continues through adulthood as far as mothers of creators are concerned. These mothers are like a Jocasta in the making, libidinally overinvesting in their child, especially when it is a boy (Anzieu, 1981). Parenthetically, this overinvestment can also touch girls.

We have to remember that before succumbing to the real seduction, Oedipus was a very long awaited child by his infertile adoptive mother, Queen Merope. He was also the fruit of a forbidden conception, since the oracle told Laius and Jocasta that any son born to them would assault them. Incestuous and mortal passions in this tragedy are based on the infertility of the two women: the infertility of Jocasta through chastity and the natural infertility of Merope who eagerly wanted a child. On hearing the announcement of the curse, Oedipus gave up this privileged relationship, and in an attempt to protect his mother, he reluctantly left "his abode on the bank of the sonorous sea":

> I will never see the very famous Corinth and my abode on the banks of the sonorous sea again, for if I went back to my people I would be but a curse for them. Hence I will go to distant countries, and I will bring benediction to those who are not from my blood. (Buckley, 1931, p. 17)

This passionate mother–son relationship does not always lead to the tragedy of Sophocles that inspired Freud when symbolizing the *Oedipus Complex:* hence he wrote, "If a man has been his mother's favorite child, he retains throughout life the triumphant feeling, the confidence in success, which not seldom brings actual success along with it" (Freud, 1917/2001, p. 156).

He also evoked the seduction that his mother exercised on him when he was a little boy. For this matter, intelligence is a plant that needs to be watered by the maternal love, since "no human being would become intelligent if there had not been previously a mother under the illusion – that is, certainty – that her child is brilliant; for no reason other than to please herself" (Diatkine, 1994, p. 19). Such a "Jocasta mothering" (Anzieu & Besdine, 1974) is specific to the numerous biographies of artistic and literature creators. Thus, Brenot (2007), a psychiatrist and writer, cites Proust, Gary, Barthes, Camus, and even Baudelaire, who have all benefited from the exclusive and intense love of their beloved mothers.

Experiencing such happiness in the first years of life can lead the child to feel very nostalgic and guilty for forming a sort of couple with his mother. From this perspective, although the mother is always the "first seductress" (Freud, 1940/2001), oedipal and instinctual dangers are magnified under the excess of maternal stimulations, resulting in a poor functioning of the protective shield. The mother may also unconsciously respond to the great receptivity of her baby, a constitutional receptivity that is present at the early stages of life. Several older studies (Ajuriaguerra & Marcelli, 1981) or more recent studies (Bessou & Yziquel, 2002) note a majority of eldest children or only children among high potential children.

In Conclusion: Greenhouse Effect in Infantile Clinical Practice

Between 2005 and today, I observed two extreme situations with pathogenic effects or not: so-called gifted children, on the one hand, and new parenthood including medically assisted conception, on the other. At first glance, these two phenomena seem to be independent – and it is not about criticizing medical advances, thus regretting a time long past and idealized – but I linked these two issues together to reflect on the position of children in current families, and on the new conditions of their mental development in relation to modern or hypermodern temporality (Kaës, 2012).

I now consider gifted children, and mainly the representations and fantasies related to them, as a figure of current childhood and as a hyperinvested child position paradigm. I called this contemporary family dynamic *late-in-life parents, precocious child:* It is the child who creates the parents; the child is at the center of the family, whereas the couple is on the periphery (Théry, 2005). The child becomes a narcissistic extension, a double – nothing is too good for them – but there can be a price to pay: The child will have little room to differentiate themselves from parental overinvested expectations. Nowadays, children seek a consultation to express their difficulty in existing, playing, learning, and thinking outside the family (Marinopoulos, 2005).

Such a configuration introduces singular relational modalities into families that I have referred to as the *greenhouse effect in infantile clinical practice*. This is a new conception of child development under forced conditions, similar to the case of the bulbs of plants that are grown in greenhouses to challenge the seasons, with the greenhouse being artificially heated, for instance. From the embryonic stage, and even before, development is under a forced conditions, which is illustrated by the medically assisted conception that has become common and frequent; this phenomenon contributing to define a new representation of children, bestowing an outstanding position on them.

The increasingly systematized resort to medically assisted conception, resulting from unexplained infertilities or simply from delays in conception that are considered too long, is a good social metaphor. Time of growth becomes an unfortunate setback, and time of childhood is shrinking in favor of adolescence, or even a more and more precocious puberty. Hence, development with sector accelerations unfolds in a disharmonic way, in so-called outstanding children: The ideal becomes the norm, and disorders are no longer symptoms, but rather part of a neurological diversity which is claimed to be a genetic specificity that makes the child outstanding.

We hear paradigmatic examples over and over again: high potential, "dyspraxic but fantastic" (Internet website for dyspraxia), "Aspies" (for Asperger autistic), and hyper-super-active. ... These examples question the "greenhouse effect," which reduces the human temporality from its very genesis and that has an impact on the practice of psychologists, teachers, and educators.

Paradoxically, one of the effects conceals the reference to mental development, which seems denied nowadays through the demand for autonomy, predominance of immediacy, and formalized horizontal transmissions. Psychopathology is not left untouched by its classifications freezing into symptoms, disabilities, and genetic or neurological listings, which – provided they might be sometimes real – conceal the *infans* dimension and the scope of their mental development. While my previous research explored mental balance when put under tension and its impact on mental development, the issue that is currently challenging my thought may be phrased as follows: Are the children of today still entitled to development?

To proceed further in my work and to question the impact of contemporary issues on parental functions and on the investment in the child (narcissistic, cultural, mythical ...), I am turning again to Debray to conclude with an adage, which is still in my mind as an inner voice and as the way to go: "Look for the how rather than the why!"

Acknowledgments

This chapter was originally published in French and is reprinted here in English with permission: Weismann-Arcache, C. (2014). De la clinique des apprentissages à l'apprentissage de la clinique avec Rosine Debray. *Psychologie clinique et projective, 20*(1), 199–211. https://doi.org/10.3917/pcp.020.0199 © Erès Editions.

References

Ajuriaguerra, J., & Marcelli, D. (1981). *Psychopathologie de l'enfant* [Child psychopathology]. Paris, France: Masson.

Anzieu, D. (1981). *Le corps de l'œuvre* [The body of work]. Paris, France: Gallimard.

Anzieu, D., & Besdine, M. (1974). *Psychanalyse du génie créateur* [Psychoanalysis of creative genius]. Paris, France: Dunod.

Bessou, A., & Yziquel, M. (2002). Enquête auprès de l'Association d'aide à la reconnaissance des enfants intellectuellement précoces (AAREIP): À propos de 86 cas [Survey of the Support for Intellectually Precocious Children Recognition Association (AAREIP): Regarding 86 cases]. *Approche neuropsychologique des apprentissages chez l'enfant, 67*(14), 125–131.

Boekholt, M. (1996). Fondements pulsionnels de l'expérience visuelle: Regard à travers la genèse du processus Rorschach [Drives as foudations of visual experience: Genesis of Rorschach process]. *Psychiatrie de l'enfant, 39*(2), 537–579.

Brenot, P. (2007). *Le génie et la folie* [Genius and madness]. Paris, France: Odile Jacob.

Buckley, E. F. (1931). *Légendes de la Grèce antique* [Legends of ancient Greece]. Paris, France: Payot & Cie.

Chabert, C. (1998). *Psychanalyse et méthodes projectives* [Psychoanalysis and projective methods]. Paris, France: Dunod.

Debray, R. (1983). *L'équilibre psychosomatique: Organisation mentale des diabétiques* [The psychosomatic balance: Mental organization of the diabetics]. Paris, France: Dunod.

Debray, R. (1987). Qu'apporte le TAT à 6 ans? [Which contribution of TAT for 6-year-old children?]. *Psychologie française, 32*(3), 157–159.

Debray, R. (1989). Des phases maturantes précoces existent-elles chez le bébé? [Do precocious maturation phases exist for a baby?]. *Revue française de psychanalyse, 53*(4), 1149–1153.

Debray, R. (1990). Quand trop de réalité fige la remémoration [When too much reality ossifies rememoration]. *Revue française de psychanalyse, 4*(54), 931–945. http://doi.org/10.3917/rfp.g1990.54n4.0931

Debray, R. (1992). Aléas de l'accès à la position passive ou les vicissitudes de la pulsion d'emprise. [Uncertainties of the access to the passive position or the vicissitudes of the drive of influence]. *Revue française de psychanalyse, 56*(5), 1441–1444.

Debray, R. (1996). *Clinique de l'expression somatique: Psychanalyse des liens psyché-soma.* [Clinical study of somatic expression: Psychoanalysis of the links psyche–soma]. Lausanne, Switzerland: Delachaux et Niestlé.

Debray, R. (1998). *L'intelligence d'un enfant. Techniques et méthodes d'évaluation* [The intelligence of a child: Assessment techniques and methods]. Paris, France: Dunod.

Debray, R. (2000). *L'examen psychologique de l'enfant à la période de latence* [Psychological assessment of children in the latency stage]. Paris, France: Dunod.

Debray, R. (2002). Témoignage: Mes années 70 avec Vica [Testimony: My 70s with Vica]. *Psychologie clinique et projective, 8,* 11–19. http://doi.org/10.3917/pcp.008.0011

Debray, R., & Belot, R.-A. (2008). *La psychosomatique du bébé* [The psychosomatics of the baby]. Paris, France: PUF. http://doi.org/10.3917/puf.debr.2008.01

Debray, R., &Shentoub, V. (1978). Que faire d'une excessive richesse fantasmatique? [How to deal with excessive phantasmic richness?]. *Bulletin de psychologie, XXXII*(339), 309–322.

de Mijolla-Mellor, S. (1992). *Le plaisir de pensée* [The pleasure of thinking]. Paris, France: PUF.

Diatkine, R. (1994). *L'enfant dans l'adulte ou l'éternelle capacité de rêverie* [The child in the adult or the eternal capacity to daydream]. Paris, France: Delachaux et Niestlé.

Emmanuelli, M., & Azoulay, C. (2001). *Les épreuves projectives à l'adolescence* [Projective tests in adolescence]. Paris, France: Dunod.

Freud, A. (1962). *Le normal et le pathologique chez l'enfant* [Normality and pathology in childhood]. Paris, France: Gallimard.

Freud, S. (1917/2001). A childhood recollection from "Dichtung und Wahreit." In J. Strachey (Ed. & Trans.), *The standard edition of the complete psychological works of Sigmund Freud* (Vol. 17, pp. 145–156). London, UK: Vintage Classics. (Original work published in 1917)

Freud, S. (1925/2001). Negation. In J. Strachey (Ed. & Trans.), *The standard edition of the complete psychological works of Sigmund Freud* (Vol. 19, pp. 233–239). London, UK: Vintage Classics. (Original work published in 1925)

Freud, S. (1940/2001). An outline of psychoanalysis. In J. Strachey (Ed. & Trans.), *The standard edition of the complete psychological works of Sigmund Freud* (Vol. 23, pp. 139–207). London, UK: Vintage Classics. (Original work published in 1940)

Gibello, B. (2009). *L'enfant à l'intelligence troublée* [The child whose intelligence is disturbed]. Paris, France: Dunod. http://doi.org/10.3917/dunod.gibel.2009.01

Kaës, R. (2012). *Le malêtre* [Malaise]. Paris, France: Dunod. http://doi.org/10.3917/dunod.kaes.2012.01

Kestemberg, E., & Kestemberg, J. (1966). Contribution à la perspective génétique en psychanalyse [Contribution to the genetic perspective in psychoanalysis]. *Revue française de psychanalyse, 30*(5-6), 580–713.

Lebovici, S. (2009). *L'arbre de vie* [The tree of life]. Toulouse, France: Érès.

Lebovici, S., & Stoleru, S. (1983). *Le nourrisson, la mère et le psychanalyste* [The infant, the mother and the psychoanalyst]. Paris, France: Le Centurion.

Marinopoulos, S. (2005). *Dans l'intime des mères* [In Mothers' Privacy]. Paris, France: Fayard.

Marty, P. (1976). *Les mouvements individuels de vie et de mort: Essai d'économie psychosomatique* [The individual movements of life and death: Essay on psychosomatic economy] (Vol. 1). Paris, France: Payot.

Marty, P. (1980). *L'ordre psychosomatique: Les mouvements individuels de vie et de mort: Essai d'économie psychosomatique* [The psychosomatic order: The individual movements of life and death: Essay on psychosomatic economy] (Vol. 2). Paris, France: Payot.

Terrassier, J. C. (1981). *Les enfants surdoués ou la précocité embarrassante* [Gifted children or embarrassing precocity]. Paris, France: ESF.

Théry, I. (2005). Filiation et parenté: La distinction des sexes dans une société égalitaire [Filiation and kinship]. In M. Delage & P. Pedrot (Eds.), *Identités, filiations, appartenances* [Identities, affiliations and membership] (pp. 25–41). Paris, France: PUG.

Weismann-Arcache, C. (2000). *Des liens entre intelligence et narcissisme* [Connection between intelligence and narcissism] (Unpublished master's thesis). Université Paris Descartes, Paris, France.

Weismann-Arcache, C. (2003a). *«Quand j'étais grand»: Le développement et la temporalité psychique à l'épreuve de la précocité intellectuelle* ["When I was great": Development and psychic temporality to the test of intellectual precocity] (Unpublished doctoral dissertation under the direction of Prof. R. Debray). University Paris Descartes, Paris, France.

Weismann-Arcache, C. (2003b). De l'usage du contretemps chez les enfants surdoués [About the use of setback by gifted children]. *Champ psychosomatique, 30,* 45–56. http://doi.org/10.3917/cpsy.030.0045

Weismann-Arcache, C. (2004a). Quelle clinique pour les apprentissages? [What clinical work for learning?]. In M. Emmanuelli (Ed.), *L'examen psychologique en clinique: Situations, méthodes et études de cas* (pp. 23–30). Paris, France: Dunod.

Weismann-Arcache, C. (2004b). La déficience intellectuelle n'est plus ce qu'elle était [Learning disability is not what it once was]. In M. Emmanuelli (Ed.), *L'examen psychologique en clinique: Situations, méthodes et études de cas* (pp. 241–252). Paris, France: Dunod.

Weismann-Arcache, C. (2006). Les nouvelles équations symptomatiques infantiles ou la recherche du sujet perdu [New symptomatical equations in the child, or in search of the lost subject]. *Perspectives psy, 45*(4), 318–330. http://doi.org/10.1051/ppsy/2006454318

Weismann-Arcache, C. (2009). *Les surdoués, du bébé à l'adolescent: Les destins de l'intelligence* [The gifted, from the baby to the teenager: The destinies of intelligence]. Paris, France: Belin.

Weismann-Arcache, C. (2010a). Le dessin comme support d'étude du développement psychique: L'inscription relationnelle de l'image du corps [Drawing as a tool to study of the psychic development: Relational inclusion of body image]. In G. Nevoux & S. Tordjman (Eds.), *Le dessin des enfants à haut potentiel. De la créativité à la psychopathologie* (pp. 54–73). Rennes, France: PUR.

Weismann-Arcache, C. (2010b). La dyspraxie, un objet neuroscientifique pour la psychoanalyse? [Dyspraxia, a neuroscientific object for psychoanalysis?]. *Neuropsychiatrie de l'enfant et de l'adolescent, 58,* 391–397. http://doi.org/10.1016/j.neurenf.2010.01.001

Weismann-Arcache, C. (2011a). Définition et cadre clinique de l'examen psychologique de l'enfant et de l'adolescent [Definition and clinical setting of the psychological assessment of the child and the adolescent]. In R. Voyazopoulos, L. Vannetzel, & L.A. Eynard (Eds.), *L'examen psychologique de l'enfant et l'utilisation des mesures* (pp. 71–124). Paris, France: Dunod.

Weismann-Arcache, C. (2011b). L'intelligence surdéveloppée, une héritière de la dépression infantile? [Overdeveloped intelligence: The legacy of infantile depression?]. *Psychologie clinique et projective, 17,* 279–296. http://doi.org/10.3917/pcp.017.0279

Weismann-Arcache, C. (2012). Sublimation chez l'enfant et éducation: La sublimation selon les âges de la vie [Sublimation in child and education: Sublimation according to the ages of life]. In S. de Mijolla-Mellor (Ed.), *Traité de la sublimation* (pp. 250–270). Paris, France: PUF.

Weismann-Arcache, C. (2013a). *L'anachronisme et la dysharmonie comme organisateurs contemporains des processus de développement, de pensée et de parentalité* [Anachronism and disharmony as contemporary organizers of development, thinking and parenting processes] (Unpublished thesis for habilitation to supervise research) University of Rouen Normandy, Rouen, France.

Weismann-Arcache, C. (2013b). Parents tardifs, enfant précoce? Assistance médicale à la procréation et haut potentiel intellectuel [Older parents, precocious child? The relationship between medically assisted procreation and high intellectual potential]. *Psychiatrie de l'enfant, 2*(56), 467–484. http://doi.org/10.3917/psye.562.0467

Weismann-Arcache, C., & Tordjman, S. (2012). Relationships between depression and high intellectual potential. *Depression Research and Treatment, 2012*. http://doi.org/10.1155/2012/567376

Winnicott, D. W. (1969). *De la pédiatrie à la psychanalyse* [Through pediatrics to psychoanalysis]. Paris, France: Payot.

8

Prepsychoses in the Work of Nina Rausch de Traubenberg

Contributions and Developments in Projective Psychology

Jean-Yves Chagnon

Nina Rausch de Traubenberg was, after Didier Anzieu and before Catherine Chabert, the clinical psychologist who, through her extensive methodological work and clinical practice, introduced and perpetuated the Rorschach practice in France and in the French-speaking world (Rausch de Traubenberg, 1970), not only as a diagnostic instrument but also as a key clinical tool. She contributed to codifying its present administration, and she left an interpretation method that incorporates phenomenology and psychoanalysis. Her preferred field of work was infant psychopathology within clinical psychology. As part of that work, she produced numerous works throughout the 1970s on prepsychoses, either alone or in collaboration with others. In this chapter, I would like to show that her works had quite an impact, not only on theory, method, and clinical practice, but also on education and research, to the extent that, along with Vica Shentoub's works, they laid down the epistemological lineaments of what would become the School of Paris or French School (Chagnon, 2013).

Texts and Their Methodological, Clinical, and Theoretical Contributions

In 1972 and 1973, Rausch de Traubenberg and collaborators (M.-F. Lambert-Boizou, F. Bloch-Lainé, J. des Ligneris, and R. Ponroy, and with C. Chabert for the penultimate collaboration) released four articles on prepsychoses:

- "Thematic and Contents: Discussion on Prepsychotic Children's Projective Productions," in the *Bulletin de la Société française du Rorschach et des méthodes projectives,* in 1972 (Rausch de Traubenberg & Lambert, 1972),
- "Prepsychotic Organization of Personality in Children, Studied by Means of Projective Techniques," in the *Revue de neuropsychiatrie infantile,* in 1973 (Rausch de Traubenberg et al., 1973a);
- "Prepsychotic and Psychotic Organization of Personality, Studied by Means of Projective Techniques," in *Psychologie française,* in 1973 (Rausch de Traubenberg et al., 1973b). (It should be noted that this article expands upon the previous one by providing a comparative study of prepsychotic and psychotic children's productions. It is co-signed by Catherine Chabert – this article being probably one of her earliest articles.);
- "The Notion of Infantile Psychosis, Studied by Means of Projective Techniques," in *Rorschachiana,* in 1973 (Rausch de Traubenberg, 1973).

These articles fed into specific chapters on prepsychoses in the book titled *The Imaginary and the Real in Rorschach Testing With Children,* which was co-authored with M.-F. Boizou (Rausch De Traubenberg & Boizou, 1977/1996), a book that remains highly relevant today. These same articles also fed into a strong section in her PhD thesis (Rausch de Traubenberg, 1981), which was the equivalent of our modern *habilitation* to supervise research.

These articles reflect the work of the Laboratoire de Psychologie at the Child Psychiatry Department of the Salpêtrière Hospital, which was led by Prof. J. D. Duché and which, at the time, included D. Widlocher. They were joined by the Groupe de Recherches sur le Développement Affectif (Group of Research on Emotional Development), founded and led by Prof. Roger Perron. These studies remarkably linked together clinical practice, methodology, research, and education. From our perspective, they had a major impact for clinical psychologists, psychopathologists, psychoanalysts, and teacher–researchers in (projective) clinical practice for the following reasons:

First, they have significantly helped to show the important contribution of projective tests to a *complete* psychological assessment, at a time when it was not yet conceptualized as a *thorough* psychological assessment, since the term was coined much later by Rosine Debray (2000). We should remember that, at that time, psychological assessment "manuals" did not normally include projective methods. Then, assessment was still only inspired by psychometrics (Zazzo, 1969), even though psychometrics – which was no longer confined to objectivizing quantitative analysis – was opening to a "dynamic" qualitative analysis (Guillaumin, 1965) or was guided by the integration of both intellectual and personality factors (Perron-Borelli & Perron, 1970).

Second, they legitimized, in an equally significant way, the pertinent and heuristic contribution of projective tests to clinical child psychiatric practice, with reference to psychoanalysis. This contribution was not yet fully acknowledged, especially at the Alfred Binet Center in the XIII district of Paris, considered then as the center of psychoanalysis.

Debray, who worked in the XIII district of Paris in the 1960s, has reported on S. Lebovici's and F. Klein's interest in, but also on R. Diatkine's and C. Chiland's reluctance, and even frank aversion, to accept projective tests. Since then, projective tests have been broadly accepted; they have received honors from prominent psychiatrist–psychoanalysts (Jeammet, 1993), and in today's child psychiatry manuals, they have become an important component for diagnostic and prognostic activities within a child psychiatry team (Marcelli & Cohen, 2012).

Third, they were anticipating and paving the way for works on borderline, narcissistic, depressive, and psychosomatic issues that were going to be addressed over the subsequent decades (the 1980s) in adults (C. Chabert, F. Brelet, R. Debray, C. De Tychey, and others), then (in the 1990s) in adolescents (C. Chabert, M. Emmanuelli, and C. Azoulay), and then again in children (M. Boekholt, A. Cohen de Lara, and J.-Y. Chagnon), among others.

Fourth, in a fruitful back and forth movement, they were going to bring new concepts (self-representation) and clinical and research tools (grid of self-representation, self-representation and object relations, affective dynamics, etc.), which, in turn, were going to support much research, including that led by Emmanuelli (1991), which was the starting point for a long series of theses based on grids, in support of clinical practice;

Last, seizing upon a new concept that has been elaborated by child psychoanalysts, works on prepsychoses have certainly left a lasting mark on the French School of psychoanalytic interpretation of projective methods, also known as the School of Paris (Azoulay & Emmanuelli, 2013; Chagnon, 2013), with its efforts to conceptualize the relation between the analysis of mental functioning as a fruitful metapsychological produced theory, and projective methods (Chabert, 1998). Even better, today Chabert does not hesitate to say that the training and practice of projective tests help clinicians and psychoanalysts to listen more carefully to their patients during interviews or sessions, by enhancing their awareness of subtle manifestations, which would otherwise not be heard. In short, it is not only "psychoanalysis supporting projective psychology," but also "projective psychology supporting psychoanalysis" (Chabert, 2013)!

Prepsychoses in Child Psychiatric Clinical Practice

From the perspective of child psychiatric clinical practice, after psychoses were removed from the disabilities category by French child psychiatrists and psychoanalysts (Lebovici, Diatkine, Misès, and Lang), there came a time of better delimitation between normal and pathological based on criteria other than symptomatology, a time of diagnostic refinement, and already, a time of studies on borderline cases between neuroses and psychoses. Symptomatic polymorphism (mainly behavioral and instrumental) and mental process trends in children make diagnostic assessment more complex, combining it with a prognosis in children, which is the only way to enable appropriate assistance.

In 1969, Diatkine published his – magisterial – text on the *prepsychotic child* (Diatkine, 1969). From a purely metapsychological perspective, he presents prepsychotic mental functioning as associated with instability between primary and secondary processes, with regulations that are not fully able to balance inherent anxiety and depression in mental development. During adolescence, psychosis is a major psychopathological risk (in this context, prepsychosis means the period before the onset of psychosis), but there are different possible evolutions (characteropathy, psychopathy, somatizations, etc.), which is why this term has been criticized for its lack of differentiation.

The debates were then very rich and intense (Chagnon & Durand, 2007). Misès proposed the notion of *evolutive dysharmony* to describe a "mosaic" functioning that is often oriented toward deficiency risks. This would be replaced by the notion of *borderline pathologies* (Misès, 1990). More nosography-oriented, J.-L. Lang (1978) prefers the term *para-psychosis* to support the idea that prepsychoses belong to the psychotic structural category, while emphasizing the efficient defensive dimension (*para-psychosis* means protection against frank psychosis). Lastly, Widlöcher (1973) keeps the term *prepsychoses* (near psychoses), but he makes it an autonomous structural organization with a stable evolution, characterized by a phantasmic activity devoid of secondary elaboration and usual neurotic defenses, by anxiety of self-coherence destruction, by a chaotic organization of libidinal development, and by the intensity of aggressive impulses. The last two authors evoke the works of the Salpêtrière team and their interest in projective assessment. Later, Palacio-Espasa and Dufour differentiated prepsychoses from paradepressive organizations or paraneurotic organizations within the broad spectrum of *personality disorders* (Palacio-Espasa & Dufour, 1994). Their theorization focused on the vagaries of the depressive position and their singular managements (maniac, schizoid, narcissistic).

Prepsychosis According to Rausch de Traubenberg

It is in this context that the aforementioned works of Rausch Traubenberg and collaborators took place (see the section Texts and Their Methodological, Clinical, and Theoretical Contributions). They were initially intended to organize the projective material from very complete psychological assessments (intelligence scales, perceptual organization tests, graphic motor level tests, projective tests including Rorschach, and a thematic test and lastly, the Scenotest) in order to highlight the psychological characteristics that are typical of prepsychotic children compared with psychotic children.

On a clinical, adaptive, and relational level, some of these children seem normal, while others appear to be frankly psychotic and delusional. But beyond these immediate aspects, certain features make them stand apart: in particular "the alternation between the conservation of a sense of objective reality and the emergence ... of archaic fantasies focused on the fears of devouring, destruction and annihilation" (Rausch de Traubenberg et al., 1973b, p. 222). Such fantasies imply "very primitive drives, confused identifications with poorly differentiated parental images, dual relations instead of triangular relations and a primary type of anxiety" (Rausch de Traubenberg et al., 1973b, p. 222). Yet, these intense experiences do not prevent a fast recovery; there is never a total loss of control, unlike what happens with psychotic children. But on many occasions, even more markedly in her 1977 book, Rausch de Traubenberg and collaborators point out that "escape to confabulation and imagination" is not only a sign of disorganization and invasive fantasies, but also a matter of primary defenses aiming to "shatter the fantasy" or to introduce omnipotent manic positions (Rausch De Traubenberg & Boizou, 1977/1996). In that sense, they preempt the works of Palacio Espasa and Dufour (1994), which show the centrality of the depressive position in those organizations and how the primary persecuting guilt can result in a dilution and a defensive unwinding of fantasies and death anxieties, through multiple representations, in search of the clinician countenance.

We would like to emphasize how those articles have given credence to the contribution of psychological and projective assessment, particularly in daily child psychiatric clinical practice. The clinical and functional characteristics of prepsychotic patients stems from the fact that they may only display discreet symptoms, particularly instrumental disorders, learning disorders, and "dys" disorders that current trends have excluded from psychopathology on the pretext of their neurodevelopmental origin (Chagnon, Croas, Djenati, Taly, & Weismann-Arcache, 2014).

The specificities of their mental functioning, sometimes equally discreet, may easily go unnoticed by an "ordinary" clinician: Not everyone is a Lebovici, Diatkine, or Chiland! From this perspective, since projective tests are based on a compromise between fantasy/percept, regression/progression, and primary processes/secondary processes, they support a discussion of the connection between intellectual or cognitive functioning and affective functioning, which is essential to consider. Those tools have a great differential finesse, they provide a subtle diagnostic and prognostic assessment and are acknowledged by psychiatrists such as Widlöcher, Lang, and Jeammet.

Further Developments

Research on prepsychoses has raised awareness of the connection between the real and the imaginary, percept and fantasy; and has demonstrated in exemplary fashion how so-called personality factors would influence perception – a recurring debate! Various works of great importance for our community have extended this research:

- A work in collaboration with Perron and Chabert (1973) on an aspect of "the development of a person" – levels of expression and elaboration of parental imagos – which deals fundamentally with identification processes;
- A second work on the assessment of defense mechanisms in clinical practice with children and with adults (Rausch de Traubenberg, Boizou, & Chabert, 1978);
- A well-known study on the characteristics of self-representation, defined as a "unifying principle, centering the study of mental functioning on how

subjects experience their body and their relational life" (Rausch de Traubenberg, 1990, p. 17) "collecting and focusing different moments of qualitative and quantitative analysis on the subjects themselves" (Rausch de Traubenberg & Sanglade, 1984, p. 42);

- And lastly, an equally well-known work on the connection between percept and fantasy (Rausch de Traubenberg, 1983). The *connection* – a key word for Rausch de Traubenberg – is emphasized to point out the need to focus on the child's and adult's overall mental organization, beyond the collection of a static system of signs (factors) likely to result in a diagnosis. The Rorschach Test was developed as a "space of interaction between perceptive and fantasmatic activities, between the external reality of known objects and the internal reality of experience" (Rausch de Traubenberg, 1983, p. 100), as a correlated hypothesis of the integrated body image–specific testing. These successive works have led to a firm psychodynamic foundation for the interpretation of The Rorschach, alongside the phenomenological perspective.

These works have been continued by:

- The elaboration of a grid of self-representation, in collaboration with Sanglade to analyze the contents and "identify the dynamic relationship between the subject and his objects – internal and external, human and material – in order to analyze the subject's identity and identifications through libidinal and aggressive drives" (Rausch de Traubenberg & Sanglade, 1984, p. 44);
- And soon with a second grid, known as the affective dynamics grid (Rausch de Traubenberg et al., 1990), addressing the answer to a precise question: that of the assessment of individual mental functioning through eight dimensions (expression of drives, aggressivity, sexual thematic, body image, narcissism, depression, anxiety, and defense mechanisms).

Note that the study of these notions – at the intersection between clinical practice and research brought together in a mutual enrichment – has formed today's Rorschach scoring grid: thinking process, quality of the construction of identity and identifications, problematic, anxiety and defense mechanisms, object relations, balance between narcissistic and object investment, etc.

From a psychopathological perspective, the interest in differentiating between identity damages, which are less massive in prepsychoses than in psychoses, to study the modalities of narcissistic investment and the defense mechanisms will support future works on borderline cases and on narcissistic and depressive organizations. So will the interest in psychosomatics, from the time that Rausch de Traubenberg (1965) wrote her doctorate thesis on congenital heart defects.

Finally, these works have identified the relationships between the psychologist, the test taker, and the test. They have also identified the manifest and latent characteristics of the materials, which serves the study of the problematic raised and has greater metapsychological coherence.

Conclusions

This whole work is about teamwork, as Rausch de Traubenberg never ceased to repeat (Rausch de Traubenberg, 1990), but without her constant and generous facilitator talents, striving to achieve incomparable creativity, this work would never have taken place. We thankfully acknowledge her contribution and will let her conclude and speak for herself about what has driven her clinical approach:

> My work is founded on a clinical psychology approach, using the psychoanalytical contribution without trying to be a substitute for it. Grasping "the dynamic interactions within a personality" (Lagache) is, from my perspective, equal to identifying behavioral personalization modes, *personalization as a perceptual and conceptual differentiation, personalization as private, subjective and authentic positions in the quality of presence, whether it is asserted or evanescent, glorious or defeated.* This approach that strives toward detecting the individual character of an experience and the singular aspect of behavior only becomes relevant and fruitful when we address data from both construction and perception angles and from the fantasmatic expression. This method might appear presumptuous however, it takes shape when we choose to base it on "a procedure to precisely understand those significations in their subjectivity" (Anzieu): in this case, the Rorschach in its various significations and its specificity is the base. (Rausch de Traubenberg, 1981, pp. 141–142)

Acknowledgments

This chapter was originally published in French and is reprinted here in English with permission: Chagnon, J. (2014). Les prépsychoses dans l'œuvre de Nina Rausch de Traubenberg: apports et développements en psychologie projective. *Psychologie clinique et projective, 20*(1), 155–165. https://doi.org/10.3917/pcp.020.0155 © Erès Editions.

References

Azoulay, C., & Emmanuelli, M. (2013). L'interprétation des épreuves projectives: L'École de Paris: Sources, déploiements, développements [The interpretation of projective techniques: The School of Paris: Sources, deployments, developments]. *Le carnet psy, 169*, 169–170.

Chabert, C. (1998). *Psychanalyse et méthodes projectives* [Psychoanalysis and projective methods]. Paris, France: Dunod.

Chabert, C. (2013). Clinique projective et clinique psychanalytique: Une rencontre féconde [Projective clinic and psychoanalytic clinic: A fruitful encounter]. *Le carnet psy, 169,* 30–33. http://doi.org/10.3917/lcp.169.0030

Chagnon, J.-Y. (2013). L'École de Paris: Bref historique [Paris School: Brief history]. *Le carnet psy, 169,* 27–29. http://doi.org/10.3917/lcp.169.0027

Chagnon, J.-Y., Croas, J., Djenati, G., Taly, V., & Weismann-Arcache, C. (2014). *Approche clinique des troubles développementaux et instrumentaux* [Clinical approach to developmental disorders and learning disabilities]. Paris, France: Dunod.

Chagnon, J.-Y., & Durand, M. L. (2007). La prépsychose: Un concept toujours actuel en psychopathologie de l'enfant? [Prepsychosis: Is this concept still relevant in child psychopathology?]. *Psychologie clinique et projective, 13,* 123–171. http://doi.org/10.3917/pcp.013.0123

Debray, R. (2000). *L'examen psychologique à la période de latence (6–12 ans)* [Psychological assessment of children during the latency period (6–12 years old)]. Paris, France: Dunod.

Diatkine, R. (1969). L'enfant prépsychotique [The prepsychotic child]. *La psychiatrie de l'enfant, 2,* 413–446.

Emmanuelli, M. (1991). *Les processus de pensée à l'adolescence* [Adolescent thought processes] (Unpublished doctoral dissertation under the direction of C. Chabert). University Paris 5, Paris, France.

Guillaumin, J. (1965). *La dynamique de l'examen psychologique* [Psychological assessment dynamics]. Paris, France: Bordas.

Jeammet, P. (1993). Les tests projectifs à l'adolescence: Point de vue d'un clinicien [Projective tests in adolescence: From a clinician's point of view]. *Bulletin de la Société du Rorschach et des méthodes projectives de langue française, 37,* 3–6.

Lang, J.-L. (1978). *Aux frontières de la psychose infantile* [At the frontiers of child psychosis]. Paris, France: PUF. http://doi.org/10.3917/puf.langj.1978.01

Marcelli, D., & Cohen, D. (2012). *Enfance et psychopathologie* [Childhood and psychopathology]. Paris, France: Masson.

Misès, R. (1990). *Les pathologies limites de l'enfance* [Borderline pathologies in children]. Paris, France: PUF.

Palacio-Espasa, F., & Dufour, R. (1994). *Diagnostic structurel chez l'enfant* [Structural diagnosis in children]. Paris, France: Masson.

Perron-Borelli, M., & Perron, R. (1970). *L'examen psychologique de l'enfant* [Psychological assessment of child]. Paris, France: PUF.

Rausch de Traubenberg, N. (1965). *Implications psychologiques des cardiopathies congénitales: Effets des interventions correctives* [Psychological implication of congenital heart diseases. Impacts of corrective operations] (Unpublished doctoral dissertation). Sorbonne University, Paris, France.

Rausch de Traubenberg, N. (1970). *La pratique du Rorschach* [The practice of the Rorschach Test]. Paris, France: PUF.

Rausch de Traubenberg, N. (1973). La notion de prépsychose infantile à travers les techniques projectives [The notion of infantile psychosis, studied by means of projective techniques]. *Rorschachiana, 10,* 21–31.

Rausch de Traubenberg, N. (1981). *Activité perceptive et activité fantasmatique dans les Rorschach d'enfants et d'adolescents* [Perceptive and phantasmic activity in children's and adolescents' Rorschach] (Unpublished doctoral dissertation under the direction of Prof. D. Anzieu). Sorbonne University, Paris, France.

Rausch de Traubenberg, N. (1983). Activité perceptive et activité fantasmatique au test de Rorschach. Le Rorschach: espace d'interaction [Perceptual and fantasy activities of the Rorschach test: Space of interactions]. *Psychologie française, 28*(2), 100–103.

Rausch de Traubenberg, N. (1990). Élaboration de la grille de représentation de soi au Rorschach. [Construction of the grid of self-representation in the Rorschach Test]. *Bulletin de la Société française du Rorschach et des méthodes projectives, 34,* 17–24. http://doi.org/10.3406/clini.1990.1680

Rausch de Traubenberg, N., Bloch-Laine, F., Boizou, M. F, Duplant, N., Martin, M., & Poggionovo, M. P. (1990). Modalités d'analyse de la dynamique affective au Rorschach:

grille d'analyse de la dynamique affective [Analyzing affective dynamics in the Rorschach test: Affective dynamics grid]. *Revue de psychologie appliquée, 40*(2), 245–258.

Rausch de Traubenberg, N., & Boizou, M.-F. (1977/1996). *Le Rorschach en clinique infantile. L'imaginaire et le réel chez l'enfant* [The imaginary and the real in Rorschach testing with children]. Paris, France: Dunod, 1996.

Rausch de Traubenberg, N., Boizou, M. F., & Chabert, C. (1978). Représentation de soi: Identité et identification au Rorschach chez l'enfant et chez l'adulte [Self-representation: Identity and identification in children's and adults' Rorschach]. *Bulletin de Psychologie, 32*(339), 271–277.

Rausch de Traubenberg, N., & Lambert, M. F. (1972). Thématiques et contenus: Discussion sur les productions projectives d'enfants prépsychotiques [Thematic and contents: Discussion on prepsychotic children's projective productions]. *Bulletin de la Société Française du Rorschach et des méthodes projectives de langue française, 27,* 15–22.

Rausch de Traubenberg, N., Lambert-Boizou, M.-F., Bloch-Lainé, F., Chabert, C., des Ligneris, J., & Ponroy, R. (1973a). Organisation prépsychotique de la personnalité chez l'enfant à travers les techniques projectives [Prepsychotic and psychotic organization of personality, studied by means of projective techniques]. *Revue de neuropsychiatrie infantile, 12,* 745–754.

Rausch de Traubenberg, N., Lambert-Boizou, M.-F., Bloch-Lainé, F., Chabert, C., des Ligneris, J., & Ponroy, R. (1973b). Organisation prépsychotique et psychotique de la personnalité chez l'enfant à travers les techniques projectives [Prepsychotic and psychotic organization of personality, studied by means of projective techniques]. *Psychologie française, 4*(18), 213–231.

Rausch de Traubenberg, N., Perron, R., & Chabert, C. (1973). Les images parentales: Niveaux d'élaboration et niveaux d'expression dans diverses épreuves projectives [Parental imagos: Development levels and expression levels in various projective tests]. *Psychologie française, 4*(18), 175–194.

Rausch de Traubenberg, N., & Sanglade, A. (1984). Représentation de soi et relation d'objet au Rorschach: Grille de représentation de soi [Self-representation and object-relationship on the Rorschach Test: Self-representation grid]. *Revue de psychologie appliquée, 34*(1), 41–57.

Widlöcher, D. (1973). Étude psychopathologique des états prépsychotiques, [Psychopathological study on prepsychotic conditions]. *Revue de neuropsychiatrie infantile, 21*(12), 735–744.

Zazzo, R. (1969). *Manuel pour l'examen psychologique de l'enfant* [Handbook of child psychological assessment]. Neuchâtel, Switzerland: Delachaux et Niestlé.

9

Thought Processes in Adolescence

A Projective Perspective

Michèle Emmanuelli

Based on the psychoanalytic theory, the recent focus of research on clinical thought processes in adolescence has led to the emergence of two types of reflections in the field of projective tests: those that cover the contributions of the projective approach to the understanding of the process of adolescence, and those – more innovative – concerning the contribution of projective tests to the study of thought processes, in its shortcomings as in its creative aspects. Throughout their work, each in her own way, Nina Rausch de Traubenberg and Rosine Debray made their contribution to both types of reflection.

Rosine Debray acquired her experience with projective tests in clinical child and adolescent psychology while working as a psychologist at the Alfred Binet Center. During this period, which she describes in an article recounting "her 1970s with Vica Shentoub" (Debray, 2002), she collaborated with the latter in the elaboration – which is often reworked – of the TAT scoring grid, for which, she also participated in several studies that I will mention later with regard to their contribution to the psychology of thought.

While sometimes extending her spectrum of interest to adults, Rausch de Traubenberg carried out her clinical activities and her research in projective psychology in a children and young adolescents department, and most of her studies focus on the use of the Rorschach with children. However, as we will show, some of her studies contributed to the field of adolescents. Moreover, the methodology that she proposed in her lectures and that she used in her practice laid, and reviewed, the essential foundations of thought processes.

I followed the teachings of both Rausch de Traubenberg and Debray, before I started teaching at the University Paris 5 (today Université de Paris), and subsequently joined the team of Debray. In my field of interest, a field in which the process of adolescence and the thought process frequently intersect, the studies I undertook and will present here were first driven by a certain way of viewing clinical psychology, research, and, on a wider basis, those who participated in our research.

Projective Approach to Adolescence

Rightly regarded as "the Cinderella of psychoanalysis" by Anna Freud in the 1960s, adolescence was also the Cinderella of projective methodology. It was many years before adolescence gained recognition and began to be explored as a field of investigation in itself. The first studies launched by the early developers of the first tests (the Rorschach and TAT) were directed toward adults. These were followed by clinical research and writings – with specific tests development – related to children. It was not until 1959, in the US, that a book devoted to the specificity of Rorschach responses in adolescent populations was published (Bates Ames, Métraux, & Walker, 1959); and not until 1988, that a chapter on the Rorschach distinctive features in borderline adolescents was published in a book from the psychoanalytic perspective (Lerner & Lerner, 1988), reflecting the writings of Kernberg (1984).

In France, the work of the French School on adults and children has laid the foundation for research that is centered on the specificity of projective tests during preadolescence and adolescence: The thesis of Vica Shentoub (1967) covers the study of obsessive manifestations during preadolescence, using the TAT. Without undertaking a study on the adolescent process, she identified the characteristics of normative functioning in children from the latency period to preadolescence and compared them with those of children with obsessive-compulsive disorders. Later, concurrently with the development of psychoanalytic studies on adolescence, many articles focused on the characteristics of the Rorschach in adolescence: It was primarily Catherine Chabert who laid the foundations for reflections in this field, both on normal functioning (Chabert, 1983, 1985–1986, 1990a) and on the approach to certain disorders (Chabert, 1990a, 1990b, 1994; Chabert & Emmanuelli, 2001); other studies were based on the specificity of the TAT (Douville, 1987).

Rausch de Traubenberg coordinated two major studies. In 1988, in collaboration with the team of psychologists at the Salpêtrière Hospital, she published an article titled "Psychological Study of Vietnamese Adolescents: Contributions of the Rorschach" (Rausch de Traubenberg, Bloch-Lainé, Boizou, Martin, & Poggionovo, 1988). This article was remarkable for the quality of the methodology on which it relied to explore the traumatic consequences of resettlement of these adolescents and for the significance of the results it presented. The study was based on the comparison of two groups of adolescents: 64 Vietnamese adolescents who arrived in France after 1975 and who were living in three different foster family types (their own families, institutions, French foster families) and 30 French adolescents as the control group. Using the emotional dynamics grid that was developed by this team, the study covered the key lines of instinctual expression, aggressiveness, narcissism, body image, depression, anxiety, and defense mechanisms. Their relevance for the approach to adolescent functioning was revealed, demonstrating that the particularities of the mental functioning of Vietnamese adolescents, under the lens of the Rorschach, were more related to traumatic events than to cultural specificity. These valuable results revealed the extent to which mental functioning, as evidenced by the Rorschach, was based on data that transcended cultural aspects.

Published in 1993 in the *Bulletin de la Société du Rorschach,* the second article presented research on 73 nonpatient adolescents aged 16 to 19 years and provided a valuable study of the issues as they appeared with each card (Rausch de Traubenberg, Bloch-Lainé, Duplant, Martin, & Poggionovo, 1993). Moreover, it allowed a highly detailed differential study of the position of boys and girls. These results are interesting as a touchstone for research on adolescent groups with disorders – as such, a similar study should be undertaken with the TAT.

Indeed, the 1993 issue of the *Bulletin de la Société du Rorschach,* which was edited by Chabert and Rausch de Traubenberg, was entirely dedicated to adolescence, with an approach based on normality and pathology themes (Chabert & Rausch de Traubenberg, 1993). Lastly, the publication of the first French normative data for the Rorschach in adolescents and young adults engaged, with the team of researchers, the passionate participation of Rausch de Traubenberg in this work (Azoulay et al., 2007).

Taking these different studies further, Catherine Azoulay and I published the first book on the use of projective tests in adolescence. It presented the expressions of adolescent mental functioning in their particularities and in their psychopathological drifts, as they appear with the Rorschach and the TAT (Emmanuelli & Azoulay, 2001). Indeed, a fundamental contribution of psychoanalysis lies in the statement that there is no gap, but rather a continuity, between the normal and the pathological within mental functioning. The psychoanalytic approach of projective tests is based on the fundamental concepts of psychoanalytic metapsychology to account for the variety of mental movements that are specific to adolescence and on the key issues that are involved as adolescence progresses: the reemergence of the oedipal complex, narcissistic reorganizations, confrontation with separation, and with the depressive position. From this perspective, the issue of change that is at the heart of adolescent functioning can be understood in a very efficient way, and the shortcomings of adolescent functioning can be revealed.

The issue of change is certainly not unique to adolescents. Primarily focusing on psychosomatics, starting from 1976, Debray conducted a study on the mental organization of diabetics, a study on which her PhD thesis was based (Debray, 1983). She incorporated a case study, using the TAT, the Rey Complex Figure Test, and the Draw-A-Person test of patients whose diabetes had been diagnosed during sensitive life stages that were conductive to disorganization: oedipal conflict age, adolescence, adulthood, midlife, and retirement age.

Regarding patients whose diabetes had been diagnosed during adolescence, the following results emerged: When diabetes appeared to be associated with a sexual etiology, as a result of the pubertal reorganization trauma, it was part of a mental organization that was likely to be of good quality in adulthood, even if the existence of a narcissistic vulnerability might help to understand the disorganizing nature of the economic overload of puberty. All diabetes occurring in adolescence does not fall into this configuration, and for a number of patients, the onset of the disease was mainly driven by the traumatic reactivation of what might appear as their narcissistic vulnerability rather than by an "added-on" sexual factor. In this respect, Debray refers to patients with an unelaborated trauma such as precocious mourning or to those whose narcissistic vulnerability was plugged throughout childhood and even in adolescence by the physical presence of parents, and whose movements of disorganization only appeared in adulthood, during a first long separation or a separation with traumatic valence.

Approach to Thinking

The notion of thinking takes on very different meanings depending on the underlying theory: Essentially understood in terms of its cognitive aspects from the neurocognitive perspective, it becomes increasingly complex in psychoanalytic theory. Indeed, from his earliest works, Freud described the implementation, development, and functioning of the mental apparatus by differentiating opposing systems in terms of *primary and secondary processes,* to further notions of *pleasure principle, reality principle,* and *unconscious and preconscious/conscious*. He progressively built on his studies by developing the relations between these two principles of the course of mental events (Freud, 1911/2001) and the opposition between conscious thought and fantasy, stressing the necessary input of the negative through the introduction of *negation* (Freud, 1925/2001). While the emergence of reasonable and reasoning thinking was carefully described in 1895 (judgment, memory, etc.) – and further addressed in that 1911 article (Freud, 1911/2001) – in addition, the data became significantly more complex in his successive texts as a result of multiple factors: the role of the libido and the object in this functioning, two driving forces, two sources of impetus but also two motives of disorder that were developed in subsequent works by Freud and some of his successors. However, it is not possible to discuss here Freud's articles on the destinies of thought in disorders and sublimation (Freud, 1910/2001, 1913/2001) as well as the contributions of his successors, such as Melanie Klein, Wilfried Bion, André Green, and Didier Anzieu. To achieve the purpose of this present chapter, I would simply point out that in the two fields that Freud identified – thought and sublimation – we find the same factors, whether working positively or contributing to failure, as those that are reactivated and that interfere, either by facilitating or by disrupting the process of adolescence: the libido activity and in particular, the oedipal dynamics, narcissism, and the processing of loss.

Thought Processes in Adolescence: From the Projective Tests Perspective

From this necessarily brief sketch, let us now turn to the contribution of projective tests in this field where adolescence and thought meet. The studies that I initiated and pursued were built on clinical practice with adolescents who had begun to experience difficulties or failure in school after a hitherto untroubled schooling. It was thus necessary to evaluate the process of adolescence and the capacities of mental processing of conflicts that reemerge from the start of puberty (the reemergence of the oedipal complex, narcissistic vulnerability, and the reemergence of object loss), as well as the quality of thought and sublimation capacities. The general hypothesis, tested according to the three axes mentioned (oedipal conflict, narcissistic fragility, and loss of object), is that of the impact of the adolescence process on thought and on sublimation capacities. A supposedly disturbing impact for troubled adolescents: The question is what is precisely the most disruptive element in these issues. Verification of such a hypothesis requires a comparison with a group of adolescents who perform well at school, in order to observe the modalities of the processing of the same issues, as well as to examine the quality of thought and sublimation processes of these adolescents. It is a matter of understanding what helps them maintain their school efficiency and their adaptation despite the impact of the processes of adolescence.

On the Methodological Level

Given the involvement of all three issues in the three areas studied (adolescence, thought, and sublimation), the contribution of the Rorschach and TAT are particularly valuable. Indeed, the clarifications they bring are complementary – the Rorschach focuses on resources and narcissistic failure, and the TAT reveals the mode of access and treatment of the oedipal and object loss issues. The two tests also intersect: Each test is also a useful means of shedding light on what the other primarily reveals.

The use of a highly detailed methodology for research, with specific criteria for each test, allows a subtle and precise investigation of how each of these issues is translated, through its features when dealing with unstructured material that mobilizes sensory and instinctual drives (the Rorschach), or when dealing with figurative images that are still to be transposed into "secondarized" narratives (TAT).

However, the usefulness of such studies goes well beyond research: Certainly, in common practice, clinical analysis does not involve so much detail, yet the identification and publication of these criteria provide clinical psychologists with support and improvement in any case where they wish to deepen their analysis and focus on understanding these issues when necessary.

Methodology With Regard to Thought and Sublimation

Is it possible, and how would one approach *thought* and *sublimation* using projective material? For which aspects? In clinical practice, it is primarily the task of "intelligence" tests – in reality *intellectual efficiency* tests – to reflect what participants can do with their intelligence at the time they are tested with a certain testing type. This is not a question of "measuring" intelligence, but of approaching the manifestation of intellectual capacities that are essentially related to conscious functioning and to aptitudes that are divided into various areas: judgment, knowledge, memory, logical reasoning, and understanding of social situations. The relation to reality is therefore evaluated in situations that are not intended to call for destabilizing productions of the unconscious. Certainly, the Wechsler scales that are the most commonly used for this purpose have the advantage of situating assessed participants in relation to the general population of the same age and country. When approaching the thought process in adolescence, it is important to make use of this assessment that allows us to stress the quality (global or heterogeneous) of efficiency, or highlight difficulties in some of these areas. I will not dwell on the fact that a clinical approach that is nourished by psychoanalysis allows the use of these test responses beyond their quantitative inputs, including by opening them to the qualitative aspects of the functioning of thought (Emmanuelli, 2004). Although precious, this has limitations.

Projective tests prove irreplaceable. Independent of knowledge or reasoning skills, they mobilize the thought processes, understood as the cathexis of thoughts when faced with the need to deal with conflicts and the related affects. Thus, they make it possible to approach their quality and its variations, based on the issues that are reactivated by the material (which varies from card to card).

This approach that is traditionally reserved for the Rorschach involves, on the one hand, factors that investigate the relation to reality, on which the quality of thought processes is based. An example of this is the formal quality of responses and their adequacy with the percept presented, whether they are merely rooted in form or based on more receptive movements (as sensory, vectors of affects in the Rorschach) or more projective (as M responses – that is, attributing a movement to a percept). On the other hand, this approach evaluates that which reflects the capacities for play, for creation, and mental flexibility; that which accounts for the sensitivity to affects and the ability to bind affects and representations (e.g., the personal thought involvement in developing original responses, within organized locations, the variety in responses, the differentiated use of sensoriality, and M responses).

The teaching of the Rorschach as provided by Rausch de Traubenberg – when I took her courses before becoming, a year later, a lecturer on her team and supervising practical work for the thematic part, while she was responsible for the Rorschach (one can imagine my emotions) – was based on the following working hypothesis presented in a handout for her course:

> The interpretative approach that we are presenting is based on the clinical experience and on our working hypothesis. Our hypothesis is that the weight of conflicts, the need for expression and realization have an impact on mental and perceptual elaboration as well as on the issues and affects strictly speaking [...] Two sets of data need to be analyzed: The first set of data is a mode, a manner of using mental equipment according to the stage of maturity: It brings together productivity, its variation and its rhythm, the use of perceptual reality (W, D) and the expression mode (F, M, C). The second set of data relates to the expression of what is experienced, tested, and felt. (unpublished handout from course given by Rausch de Traubenberg)

As illustrated, this is the first point that concerns the approach to thought processes. The essence of this teaching is the idea that is expressed in the quotation from the handout, above – that is, the functioning of thought is closely dependent on the emotional style, both in terms of adaptation to, and investment in, reality to deal with the issues that are triggered by the material.

In her books, articles, and her teachings which she provided in the field of the psychological assessment of children, as well as in the theses she directed – many of which were conducted by school psychologists – Debray vigorously defended the idea of a "cognitive apparatus that is distinct from the mental apparatus in which it is nonetheless immersed" (Debray, 2000, p. 14). On the work of thought, she pointed out the cognitive/affective articulation:

> The required cognitive activity to perform problem-solving tasks is only compatible with little excitement or affects. The mental apparatus must thus clear the mental scene for long enough to allow the establishment of logical reasoning and then run its full course. If the child is agitated by significant conflicting storms, no relevant cognitive activity is possible. (Debray, 2000, p. 14)

Using – for assessment of children – data from Piagetian tests, Wechsler scales, drawings, school assessments, and specialized tests, Debray recommended, in terms of projective tests and in line with the work that she had previously carried out, the use of the TAT. Here we can find the – sometime – pursued option of the Rorschach that was chosen by Rausch de Traubenberg and the reliance on the TAT by Shentoub, with whom Debray conducted her initial researches.

Personally, following the long-standing position of Chabert within the University Degree of Projective Psychology (DUPP) program, supported by Rausch de Traubenberg, I have relied on the use of both the Rorschach and TAT in my clinical practice as well as in my research.

From an existing methodological approach, I have continued to explore thought processes using the Rorschach and incorporating some additional factors that have enabled me to broaden the field of investigation. Moreover, I have focused on also defining criteria in the TAT that could reveal the quality of thought processes.

As regards sublimation, there was no specific methodology to approach it using projective tests. However, I will mention the article that was published in 1978 by Shentoub and Debray as enabling the approach to a particularly creative functioning. This article was titled "How to Deal With Excessive Phantasmic Richness in the TAT? Interpretation of an Unusual TAT Protocol." This is the protocol of a 24-year-old man, a philosophy student, who sought counseling to better assess the relevance of his professional projects as he envisioned them to lie in the creative writing or cinematographic field; it is noteworthy that this appeared to be a well-chosen orientation for him given the projective test results. This protocol was unusually rich. Today, it can even be considered as colored with elements from the CM series of the TAT scoring grid (see Appendix 3), reflecting a struggle with depression, which is not to minimize its richness. Even though these processes were not yet present in the scoring grid at the time, the authors concluded that

> this is a rich organization in which well-mentalized neurotic elements integrate more archaic elements and even enable their sublimation. One would think that if decompensation were to occur, it would be by way of depression with the accentuation of paranoiac defences, yet with good possibilities for subsequent recovery, perhaps in favour of social structures likely to legitimize them. (Shentoub & Debray, 1978–1979, p. 316)

According to the authors, this is a well-mentalized organization. These are the conceptions that were developed from the psychosomatic perspective of Pierre Marty (on which Debray relied), which Shentoub and Debray discussed as "(relative) liberty of functioning that is based … on the presence of sufficient permeability between the sub-structures of the mental apparatus" (Shentoub & Debray, 1978–1979, p. 318).

For the purpose of research, aimed at approaching the functioning of sublimation, my my own studies led me subsequently to develop a new methodology in line with the psychoanalytic definitions of this concept, which according to Freud, reveals the displacement of libidinal energy – and *aggressive energy*, in his final writings – to a nonsexual and socially valued field. In both tests, I identified the factors that are likely to reveal this displacement (which lies behind the sublimation) as well as the processing, or, rather, in projective tests, the capacity of representation of the instinctual conflict (Emmanuelli, 1993).

Results

Again, there should be no question of synthesizing the results of such studies, as they cover several fields. Exploration of the process of adolescence, made possible by the approach to a group of nonpatient adolescents aged 12–18, confirms the impact of the issues at stake in the pubertal process; without getting into overly strict stages, they seem to operate according to the following temporal sequence, which does not exclude overlaps: instinctual reactivation, revival of the oedipal conflict; narcissistic destabilization that requires instincts to fall back on the ego; beginning of separation; and putting the elaboration of the depressive position to the test.

Comparison of the results obtained respectively in tests of efficiency, in the assessment of the quality of thought processes, and in the field of sublimation, shows how the intellectual level (IQ) – in a group that was recruited from the norm to the highest levels – can be independent of the quality of thought processes and sublimation. The part that is devoted to conflicts, to their related affects, and to defenses that – with more or less success – attempt to cope with them, appear to be essential, even more essential than efficiency itself.

With regard to reasons for academic failure, while the significance of various issues appears in varying degrees, what is essential lies in what is at stake in the narcissistic foundations area (Emmanuelli, 1994). The same can be said of creativity. The destabilization that is induced by the beginning of adolescence, with its bodily transformations, instinctual excesses, and loss-related anxiety, appears to be at the heart of two contrasting modes of reaction: on the one hand, mobilization that fosters creative focus, investment of thought processes to represent, and expression of a temporary fragility in some subjects; and on the other hand, destabilization that reveals an earlier fragility of the construction of the ego which, under the threat of losing its anaclitic objects, experiences more or less severe disorganization. Different manifestations that are detrimental to school adjustment then emerge: inhibition or disorganization.

Such a methodological approach enables the identification of the deployment of thought that is impeded by obsessive defenses, or by the dispersion resulting from a hysterical functioning, including, at the level of thought processes, the reflection of borderline and narcissistic disorders that emerge under the traumatic impact of the beginning of adolescence. What about sublimation? At this stage of life, sublimation appeared to be relatively inaccessible to most adolescents, regardless of whether they were consulting a therapist or not. For them, what is essential is the investment of thought, in order to mend or at least to reinforce the threatened narcissism. In some individuals, this mental work appears as a source of intense creativity – echoing what is observed in adolescents who, following their personal interests, write poems, journals, songs, compose music, or draw. ... For some, this mobilization may continue thereafter, which is open to sublimation.

Conclusion

Such research not only provides findings that answer clinical questions but also enables the implementation of a methodology that can subsequently be applied to other populations and used in other research. The approach to nonpatient adolescents thus provides a reference point for research on various pathological disorders. Thus, students from the *grandes écoles* (the highly selective elite higher education institutions in France) or even artists have been included in research using the Rorschach and TAT from the standpoint of thought processes and sublimation (Emmanuelli, 2013). Thus, as fully revealed in the report on the interpretation of projective tests in the work of the Paris School published in 2013 in *Le Carnet Psy* (Anzoulay & Emmanuelli, 2013), the work that was carried out using projective tests drew on the studies that were developed, at the time, by the outstanding clinical psychologists who initiated them, among whom were Nina Rausch de Traubenberg and Rosine Debray – each in her field remaining a key figure.

Acknowledgments

This chapter was originally published in French and is reprinted here in English with permission: Emmanuelli, M. (2014). Les processus de pensée à l'adolescence: L'Éclairage projectif. *Psychologie clinique et projective, 20*(1), 79–92. https://doi.org/10.3917/pcp.020.0079 © Erès Editions.

References

Azoulay, C., & Emmanuelli, M. (2013). L'interprétation des épreuves projectives: L'École de Paris: Sources, déploiements, développements [The interpretation of projective techniques: The Paris School: Sources, deployments, developments]. *Le carnet psy, 169*, 169–170.

Azoulay, C., Emmanuelli, M., Rausch de Traubenberg, N., Corroyer, D., Rozencwajg, P., & Savina, Y. (2007). Les données normatives françaises du Rorschach à l'adolescence et chez le jeune adulte [Normative French data for the Rorschach in adolescence and young adulthood]. *Psychologie clinique et projective, 13*, 371–409. http://doi.org/10.3917/pcp.013.0371

Bates Ames, L., Métraux, R. W., & Walker, R. N. (1959). *Adolescent Rorschach responses*. New York, NY: Paul B. Hoeber.

Chabert, C. (1983). Modalités de fonctionnement psychique des adolescents à travers le Rorschach et le TAT [Psychical functioning of adolescents through Rorschach and TAT]. *Psychologie française, 28*, 187–194.

Chabert, C. (1985–1986). Y a-t-il une spécificité des Rorschach d'adolescents? [Is there a specificity of adolescents' Rorschach?]. *Bulletin de psychologie, 34*(376), 655–658.

Chabert, C. (1990a). Les potentialités de changement chez les adolescents psychotiques: Contribution du Rorschach et du TAT à une étude longitudinale [Potentialities of changing in psychotic adolescents: Contribution of Rorschach and TAT to a longitudinal study]. *Revue de psychologie appliquée, 40*, 113–137.

Chabert, C. (1990b). Entre dedans et dehors: La contrainte au Rorschach [Between Inside and Outside: Constraint in Rorschach]. *Adolescence, 8*, 185–198.

Chabert, C. (1994). Adolescence et fonctionnement limite: Une étude de cas [Adolescence and borderline functioning: A case study]. *Bulletin de la Société Française du Rorschach et des méthodes projectives, 38*, 67–83. http://doi.org/10.3406/clini.1994.1669

Chabert, C., & Emmanuelli, M. (2001). Les épreuves projectives à l'adolescence [Projective methods in adolescence]. *EMC, Psychiatrie, 37-213-B-10*, 6 p.

Chabert, C., & Rausch de Traubenberg, N. (1993). Adolescence [Special issue]. *Bulletin de la Société du Rorschach et des méthodes projectives, 37.*

Debray, R. (1983). *L'équilibre psychosomatique: Organisation mentale des diabétiques* [The psychosomatic balance: Mental organization of the diabetics]. Paris, France: Dunod.

Debray, R. (2000). *L'examen psychologique de l'enfant à la période de latence (6–12 ans)* [Psychological assessment of children during the latency period (6–12 years old)]. Paris, France: Dunod.

Debray, R. (2002). Témoignage: Mes années 70 avec Vica [Testimony: My 70s with Vica]. *Psychologie clinique et projective, 8,* 11–19. http://doi.org/10.3917/pcp.008.0011

Douville, O. (1987). Le TAT à l'adolescence [TAT in adolescence]. *Psychologie française, 32,* 161–168

Emmanuelli, M. (1993). Figures de la sublimation à l'adolescence: Apport des épreuves projectives [Figures of sublimation in adolescence: Contribution of projective methods]. *Bulletin de la Société du Rorschach et des méthodes projectives, 37,* 161–181.

Emmanuelli, M. (1994). Incidences du narcissisme sur les processus de pensée à l'adolescence [Impact of narcissism on thought processes in adolescence]. *Psychiatrie de l'enfant, 37*(1), 249–305.

Emmanuelli, M. (Ed.). (2004). *L'examen psychologique: Situations, méthodes et études de cas* [Psychological assessment: Settings, methods, case studies]. Paris, France: Dunod.

Emmanuelli, M. (2013). L'origine du processus créateur à partir du Rorschach et du TAT d'artistes [Sources of creative process through artists' Rorschach and TAT]. In A. Brun & B. Chouvier (Eds.), *L'archaïque: Création et psychanalyse* (p. 173–186). Paris, France: Armand Colin.

Emmanuelli, M., & Azoulay, C. (2001). *Les épreuves projectives à l'adolescence: Approche psychanalytique* [Projective methods in adolescence: Psychoanalytical approach]. Paris, France: Dunod.

Freud, S. (1895/2001). Project for a scientific psychology. In J. Strachey (Ed. & Trans.), *The standard edition of the complete psychological works of Sigmund Freud* (Vol. 1, pp. 283–413). London, UK: Vintage Classics. (Original work published in 1895)

Freud, S. (1910/2001). Leonardo Da Vinci and a memory of his childhood. In J. Strachey(Ed. & Trans.), *The standard edition of the complete psychological works of Sigmund Freud* (Vol. 11, pp. 57–137). London, UK: Vintage Classics. (Original work published in 1910)

Freud, S. (1911/2001). Formulations on the two principles of mental functioning. In J. Strachey (Ed. & Trans.), *The standard edition of the complete psychological works of Sigmund Freud* (Vol. 12, pp. 213–226). London, UK: Vintage Classics. (Original work published in 1911)

Freud, S. (1913/2001). The disposition to obsessionnal neurosis. In J. Strachey (Ed. & Trans.), *The standard edition of the complete psychological works of Sigmund Freud* (Vol. 12, pp. 311–326). London, UK: Vintage Classics. (Original work published in 1913)

Freud, S. (1925/2001). Negation. In J. Strachey (Ed. & Trans.), *The standard edition of the complete psychological works of Sigmund Freud* (Vol. 19, pp. 233–239). London, UK: Vintage Classics. (Original work published in 1925)

Kernberg, O. F. (1984). *Severe personality disorders: Psychotherapeutic strategies.* New Haven, CT: Yale University Press. (French Trans.: Les troubles graves de la personnalité: Stratégies psychothérapiques. Paris, France: PUF, 1989).

Lerner, H. D., & Lerner, P. M. (1988). *Primitive mental states and the Rorschach.* Madison, CT: International Universities Press.

Rausch de Traubenberg, N., Bloch-Lainé, F., Boizou, M. F, Martin, M., & Poggionovo, M.-P. (1988). Étude psychologique des adolescents vietnamiens: Apports du Rorschach [Psychological study of Vietnamese adolescents: Contributions of the Rorschach]. *Enfance, 41*(1), 95–104.

Rausch de Traubenberg, N., Bloch-Lainé, F., Duplant, N., Martin, M., & Poggionovo, M.-P. (1993). Le Rorschach à l'adolescence: La clinique du normal [Rorschach in adolescence: Clinical field of normality]. *Bulletin de la Société du Rorschach et des méthodes projectives de langue française, 37,* 7–39. http://doi.org/10.3406/clini.1993.1640

Shentoub, V. (1967). *Le devenir des manifestations phobo-obsessionnelles de la puberté à l'adolescence* [Outcome of phobo-obsessive symptoms from puberty to adolescence] (Unpublished doctoral dissertation). University Paris 5, Paris, France.

Shentoub, V., & Debray, R. (1978–1979). Que faire d'une excessive richesse fantasmatique? Interprétation d'un protocole inhabituel de TAT. [How to deal with excessive phantasmic richness? Interpretation of an unusual TAT protocol]. *Bulletin de psychologie, 32*(339/3-7), 309–322.

10

Traumatic Traces and Projective Figures of Catastrophes of Symbolization

Pascal Roman

About 20 years ago, I published an article titled "Somatic Disorders and *Catastrophes of Symbolization*" (emphasis added here), in the journal *Psychologie clinique et projective*, as part of a volume that was dedicated to psychosomatics, (Roman, 1997a). This article is one of the texts that are regularly quoted by young colleagues, particularly as a methodological support in projective approaches related to various issues in which the question of trauma takes center stage – just as was the case for one of the chapters that was published the same year, titled "The Projective Method as a Device to Symbolize"[1] (Roman, 1997b).

On that basis, we may question, working backwards, the foundation of a particular interest in these publications as well as the topicality, pertinence, and meaning of the proposals they contain. If we look back with hindsight, putting these two publications into perspective prefigures the project that included my research over the last 20 years, following the dual line of thinking of Catherine Chabert, on the one hand, and René Roussillon, on the other.

Indeed, in these two texts I defended, respectively:

- At a theory of method level: the assertion of the *symbolizing* function of projective tests; the projective test being considered as "a device to symbolize," in a range from the offer to symbolize, to the obligation to symbolize, from the perspective of tests that invite a review of the traces in the history of the symbolization processes, and which support a "brief psychoanalytic process" (Brelet, 1986).
- At the clinical and methodological level: evidencing the interest in the identification – based on clinical psychosomatics in children – of the traces of

1 This formulation is deliberately ambiguous. It means that both the projective method is a device to be symbolized and that the projective method is a device for enabling symbolization.

> obstacles to the work of symbolization in projective test protocols, from the identification of a number of projective manifestations that I then called *catastrophes of symbolization*.

It is particularly a question here of trying to put into perspective the proposals that are related to the definition and illustration of the catastrophes of symbolization, in view of the topicality of my clinical research that is largely marked by the exploration of the issues of trauma. For what essentially underlies the perspective of catastrophes of symbolization is clearly the revelation, in the projective encounter, of that which traces the trauma – as trauma (i.e., the traumatic experience from the perspective of the subjectivity that is stricken) reflects a failure of the symbolization processes.

It may be recalled that the definition of trauma, in its psychoanalytic sense, comprises two aspects:

1. Mental trauma requires two *ingredients:* The traumatic experience that is characterized by an overflow of excitement that the mental life of the person is unable to process, *and* the feeling of a lack of remedy; in other words, trauma involves a dual experience:
   - A situation that does violence to the person's mental life, such as mistreatment, physical or sexual violence, negligence, inadequacy, absence, or abandonment, which Janin (1996) calls the "hot nucleus of trauma";
   - And the experience of not having been able to rely, in their environment, on a helping adult; according to the wording of Winnicott (1989): "When something should have happened to the child, it is the nothing that he/she experienced" (p. 210), a situation that leads to a feeling – that cannot be expressed through language – of "fear of breakdown" – which Janin (1996) calls the "cold nucleus of trauma."
2. In order for the mental trauma to be established in its deleterious dimension, it is formed in two phases: the initial phase, which that of the traumatic experience strictly speaking, as part of childhood and often kept in a place out of the psyche (by the splitting action), and the second phase (après coup), as part of adolescence or adulthood, a time of sexualization of trauma, a time when trauma takes on its meaning in the genital mental economy.

So this is what I wrote in the journal *Psychologie clinique et projective:*

> In other words, one may wonder how the symbolization deficit involves the body as a scene of the symptom (through a sensory over-investment, an impossible sensory absence) or how the somatic deficit reactivates, to call them into question, the very structures of symbolization. (Roman, 1997a, p. 77)

What I proposed to question then, in the context of psychosomatic affections in children, concerns the singularity of the destiny of the drive in these clinical configurations, a destiny within the complex dialectic between the body and the psyche. It is important to note for that matter, that what is now an important part of my research efforts involves the singularity of the destiny of the drive in the violent sexual actings at the age of adolescence (Roman, 2012, 2014a, 2015a). The focus of my work is to consider that the involvement of the body of the adolescent in a hand-to-hand relation that is imposed on the victim, may be perceived as the beginning of a new scene. This new scene, which is a part of a process of repetition, will try to give meaning to the elements of the traumatic history, in line with the hypothesis that the acting may be considered as an avatar *and* as a rekindling of the work of symbolization.

It is thus in line with these clinical interests around adolescence, the mental reorganizations that characterize it, and the *catastrophes* it confronts us with, that I propose to reevaluate the efficiency of the notion of *catastrophe of symbolization*.

Toward a Definition of Catastrophes of Symbolization

So what are these catastrophes of symbolization? While the term *symbolization* is part of our conceptual heritage in the field of psychoanalysis with, in particular, the proposals for a distinction between primary and secondary symbolization (Roussillon, 1991, 2014), the term *catastrophe* is not self-evident.

The reference that I propose here for the term *catastrophe* certainly goes beyond the common sense of the term *catastrophe*. It is derived from Greek and refers to the idea of *upheaval* and *denouement* (although the semantic dualism of the term *denouement* may be of interest to the clinical concept of catastrophe: *untie the knots* and *find a way out*). For that matter, it should be noted that the pejorative connotation of the term *catastrophe* (associated with destruction) is not necessarily proven (from an etymological point of view, the catastrophe is also a *turn of events*) – although this pejorative connotation currently dominates the use of this term in French.

Furthermore, the term *catastrophe* has, since the works of the renowned mathematician René Thom on the theory of catastrophes, a tinge of another dimension. It has gained an extremely dynamic side as Virole points out:

> The theory of catastrophes by René Thom proposes "an epistemology of the gaze," according to the beautiful expression of Krzystof Pomian, that is posed on forms and that may rise from them to trace back the dynamics from which they are derived through deployment. (Virole, 1992, p. 31)

The theory of catastrophes thus seeks to grasp and model, at the mathematical level, a number of changes as well as the traces of these changes. Once again I will use the proposals of Virole in his *bridging* function between the world of mathematics and the world of psychology:

> According to this second meaning *(that is, the meaning of the theory of catastrophes),* a catastrophe is the disappearance of a stable form. This disappearance leads to the establishment of a new form following a modification

> of the forces that act on the system. (Virole, 1992, p. 31; emphasis is the original text)

It is indeed in line with this accepted meaning that we need to understand the term *catastrophe of symbolization:* as a modality that reflects a reactivation of the processes and that contributes to the work of symbolization in its dual disorganization/reorganization valence. Put differently, the catastrophes of symbolization account for a *turn of events* within the person's mental life, the scripting of which on the projective scene – which might be considered as a new trauma scene – provides information on its effects on the dynamics of that person's mental life.

In the article on catastrophes of symbolization (Roman, 1997a), I do not propose, strictly speaking, a definition of catastrophes of symbolization, but I describe their four main forms of expression (which I presented as "four indicators"), which are illustrated by some fragments of responses to the Rorschach test. These four expressive forms concern the responses in the dynamics of their production; it is indeed a matter – beyond the content of the responses that are considered through their scoring – of reflecting the context of their production. The declensions of catastrophes of symbolization are then as follows:

- A primacy of immediate perception or responses that are related to what is seen or experienced;
- effects of white that affect the binding within the discourse;
- clusters of denial that reflect ruptures in the representative process;
- attacks on the holding and protective shield functions within the transference play.

As I have already mentioned, these different expressive forms are traces of failure of the work of symbolization. Today, I propose to reformulate them around three major areas which, for that matter, deserve to be addressed using the Rorschach test (Roman, 2015b), as well as the thematic tests (CAT, TAT) or play tests (the Scenotest in particular):

- The area of sensory investment in the projective material when producing a response (symmetry, color and shading, and so on), or the area of *elaboration of affect*; here the underlying issue is the *fate* of affect.
- The area of the continuum of the representative process in the elaboration of discourse, bringing together the effects of white and the clusters of denial (which de facto refer to the same process logic), or the area of *construction of the substance of narcissistic continuum*; here the underlying issue is the construction of the scene as a support function.
- The area of the transferential engagement that reveals the quality of the protective shield, or the area of *processing the excitement in the bonding*; here the underlying issue is the plasticity *versus* the porosity of boundaries with the identification of the *transference behaviors* that are particularly pertinent indicators (Freud, 1915/2001).

Psychodynamics of Sexual Violence in Adolescence and the Projective Scene

The presentation of some theoretical–clinical elements as a basis to apprehend, from a psychodynamic perspective, the projective clinical practice in adolescents who are engaged in violent sexual actings – from the catastrophes of symbolization point of view – will provide context for the testing of the trauma issue.

I have supported for several years, in line with the works of Claude Balier (1998) and André Ciavaldini (1999), in particular, the hypothesis that violent sexual actings in adolescence *contribute* to the adolescent process. While these actings out indicate suffering rather than the destiny of infantile sexuality in the adolescent process (Gutton, 1991, 1996), they are also an opportunity to relaunch this process. From there, we can understand that acting out during adolescence allows the opening of a new scene for the infantile traumatic experiences that are remobilized through the pubertal trauma – if one is willing to consider the quest of meaning in adolescent violent behavior.

If we follow the proposals of Ciavaldini (2005) who describes *acting out* as an "uncompleted affect," then we can think that the emergence and/or primacy of the sensory (or the quest for the sensory) within the violent sexual behavior would reflect a current incompletion of the affect. Ravit, Di Rocco, Bécache, and Carka (2013) stress, for that matter, that such acting out mobilizes a "quest for the non-manifested part of the subjective position" and the quest for echoes of "what has been lost in the primary mirror reflection." The sensory is mobilized in this area as the path (one path) to reestablish a symbolization process that is always, repetitively, failing. In this context, "sensory excess" (Ravit, 2010) may be understood as serving an attempt to establish a figuration of trauma.

This figuration requires a scene, another scene that is both a violent sexual behavior scene – as it reflects the involvement of affect against a background of *unawareness* of one's own affects as well as the affects of the other (the victim) – and a clinical encounter scene that is based on the projective device. Indeed, the projective scene may be conceived of as a traumatic repetition scene that is both a *catastrophe scene* and a *turn of events scene*. The excitement that is supported by what is *displayed* in the projective material (Roman, 1998) tests the symbolization potential and invites the adolescent to explore the traces of infancy in its traumatic inscriptions, particularly with the prospect of processing self-seduction that is specific to puberty (Gutton, 1991) and resuming the libidinal subversion through the investment in the new sexualization of the body (Dejours, 2013).

Projective Clinical Approach to the Catastrophes of Symbolization

The presentation of the expressive forms of catastrophes of symbolization will be divided into the three previously defined areas, based on the projective test protocols of adolescents who are accused or convicted of acts of a sexual nature, collected from the EvAdoGroupe's research. This research was directed toward the evaluation of the potential for change in adolescent perpetrators of sexual violence, based on a longitudinal research protocol that includes, inter alia, a proposal of test–retest using the Rorschach and TAT. I have randomly selected the Rorschach and TAT protocols of two male adolescents to illustrate the projective clinical approach to catastrophes of symbolization: Corneille, aged 18, and Charles, aged 17. For each of the three areas of focus, references to the respective Rorschach and TAT protocols of both adolescents will be identified as follows:

- The Rorschach, Corneille: A
- TAT, Corneille: B
- The Rorschach, Charles: C
- TAT, Charles: D

Area of Sensory Investment in the Projective Material

The first area is that of sensory investment in the projective material when producing a response (quasihallucinatory traces, return of what is seen or heard, hallucinated sensations) or the area of elaboration of affect.

A certain number of catastrophes of symbolization figures that reflect the primacy of the perceptual-sensorial investment may be identified through the projective test protocols of both adolescents.

A – Corneille (the Rorschach)

The response was characterized by clinging to symmetry (which proved to be recurrently present throughout the protocol) which may be considered in its subjective self-support function (we could mention the notion of *subjective vertebration*):

Card I: "What am I supposed to say? … a pelvis and the bone … there's still an axis of symmetry in the middle, a mirror would be needed, I'm sure it will be on all the images. You can imagine many things about that… Ummm."

This subjective self-support function unfolds in the context of the involvement of the adolescent in the narcissistic investment:

Card VII (takes the card in his hand): "Well, I must repeat the axis of symmetry. I think I have seen them all, it could be two silhouettes, two heads, it looks like two girls, although, not even… They are looking at each other or I look at what I am in the mirror with the axis of symmetry."

Based on this response, one may question the attempt by Corneille to open and create an intrapsyche and intersubjective space for the composition of affect (Roussillon, 2002).

Emphasis on color in pastel cards through responses in which color takes precedence over the elaboration of form; implicitly, a questioning emerges regarding the origin and substance of the material, a questioning that supports the emergence of affect:

Card VIII: "Well, still the axis of symmetry… These two red spots on the sides could be insects, lizards really, there are legs, insects, a thingy like that. Anyway, it was done with watercolor, you can see it right away, all of them, I think."

Card IX: "Again, the presence of colors and axis of symmetry. Or rather, it looks like two dragons or two seahorses. The presence of orange stands for fire, also white, red, yellow. A blend of warm colors. If you want, plastic or aluminum, plus a green flame, green, blue, purple, anyway, something obviously toxic" (he looks out of the window).

We may note, particularly, with regard to Card IX, the evolution of the visual sensory (the named colors) and kinesthetic sensory (warmth, with *warm colors*) toward the affect (reference to *toxic*) that relies on the identification of the substance *(plastic, aluminum)*.

B – Corneille (TAT)

Confrontation with one of the least figurative TAT cards (Card 11) mobilizes an attempt to construct the stimulus from the clarification of the perceptual-sensory input:

Card 11 (takes the card in his hand): "This, this image reminds me of something, I'm sure I've seen it. Oh well, here, we're outside, at the edge of a castle, there are rock falls, a stock of stones, an opening, a fortress, a wall anyhow."

Note the importance given to the aspects that are related to the construction of spaces (inside–outside, passage, delimitation…), against the background of a recollection of which we may raise the hypothesis of a quasihallucinatory emergence ("This, this image reminds me of something, I'm sure I've seen it").

C – Charles (the Rorschach)

As for the protocol of Charles, it is peppered with responses that reflect the raw perceptual trace that originates from the instinctual emergence, against the background of a perseveration that is focused on weapon responses as a vehicle for aggressive drives:

Card II: "A bullet hole. Anything else? No, we could believe it's a bullet hole, like this line in the middle. That's all."

Card VI: "We could believe it's a bullet hole like this line in the middle. That's all." (enquiry: bullet hole, entry, exit and path of the bullet).

Area of the Representative Process Continuum in the Elaboration of the Discourse

The second area is that of the representative process continuum in the elaboration of the discourse, bringing together the white effects and clusters of denial, or the construction of the substance of narcissistic continuum.

The protocols of the two adolescents who were selected for these illustrations provide the opportunity to understand the figures of catastrophes of symbolization that are marked by ruptures in the representative process.

A – Corneille (the Rorschach)

The construction of the background against the symmetry challenges (weighs down?) the process of figuration:

Card I (takes the card in his hand): "What am I supposed to say? … a pelvis and the bone.… There's still an axis of symmetry in the middle, a mirror would be needed. I'm sure it will be on all the images. You can imagine many things about that.… Ummm."

Resuming verbalization over this first card is necessary here to describe the rupture effects (white effects, clusters of denial). We may indeed note the contrast between the announcement of the imaginary potential of the card ("You can imagine many things about that") and the impossibility for the adolescent to produce additional responses to this card, beyond the anatomic and quasidevitalized response that was previously elaborated ("a pelvis and the bone").

Reference to white seems to harm the representation continuum:

Card II: "It could possibly look like this white space, I don't know if you can picture the Mallaig Tower, well, the main tower is missing. I can't say anything more."

Through this response to Card II about which we can stress the crucial involvement of the central white detail, the impact of this vacancy appears to be twofold from the viewpoint of the continuum of the representative process of Corneille: on the one hand, there is a limitation (even a censorship) of representation ("The Mallaig Tower, well, the main tower is missing"), and on the other, a limitation of the projective engagement ("I can't say…").

The attack and/or disqualification of the human representation is developed in connection with a reference to caricature:

Card III: "Axis of symmetry. It looks like two species of human beings, caricatured, anyway, the red spot in the center certainly looks like a bow tie.... We can go round in circles."

Card III' – retest: "Still the axis of symmetry. It could be a bit like a bow tie there, in the middle, this that is gray appears like two silhouettes, it's a bit imaginary, it's not two men. All this stuff is a bit like those Chinese arts. It looks like nothing. You may wonder what's the use of hanging such a thing at home."

We can measure the place and function of the investment in the sensory, as both a basis – or a reassurance in the representative process – and a reflection of the risk of disqualification of the imaginary world. Furthermore, in the retest, the questioning regarding the interest of exposing such a card ("What's the use of hanging such a thing at home") questions another form of rupture: What is the understanding by the adolescent of the projective testing? What *projection* may be identified in this call on the psychologist regarding the *hanging* of the card *at home*? What risk does the contact with the card reflect from the intimate point of view?

Insistence on the structure of the stimulus takes precedence over representation:

Card IV: "Axis of symmetry. You could almost say it's a giant or something like that with its two big feet at the bottom of the image" (he scratches his head) "spitting out something in the center, this sort of corridor in the image, from top to bottom, vertically."

Reference to the *corridor in the picture* and to the vectorization ("from top to bottom, vertically") tends to overwhelm the potential to construct an image when faced with the stimulus.

Too little representation or too much of the stimulus feeds the risk of discontinuity and mobilizes an active movement when faced with the card:

Card VI: "Only one thing but which doesn't even represent the whole image.... I would like to retouch a bit ... a volcano, the chimney in the center, just a chimney, a chimney passage. Around, it's already too much, it just needs to be precise."

Faced with the intensity of the excitement that is mobilized by the stimulus and the expression of the overwhelming feeling that creates a limitation of the representative potential ("just a chimney"), Corneille attempts to regain control over the stimulus itself ("I would like to retouch a bit").

B – Corneille (TAT)

The quest for the representation support confronts the adolescent with the risk of constructing the form on the background and creates a confusion between the form and the background:

Card 1: "What's this?" (Flips the card) "What's this stuff ... what's this... a book rest? A book itself? A painting? ... I see a man, anyway, a man or rather a boy looking at this object but he's half asleep... What else would you like me to say? It may be a table as he's seated... now what, he's seated."

The confusion between the representation and its support ("...a book rest? A book itself?"), which are considered as interchangeable, reflects the fragility of the basic narcissistic foundations. The inference that contributes to the representation of the object ("It may be a table as he's seated") questions differently the precariousness of the representative agency against the testing of the representation of the absence of representation.

Card 16: "True-false? There could be two stories: One, I can say nothing, it's not a story, cause there's nothing so I'm not going to start philosophizing on nothing, tell things about nothing. It's been snowing lately so it could be a ski trail because it's white. That's all...."

In the proposed narrative for the last card of the TAT test, the adolescent oscillates between the failure of an internal scripting ("one, I can say nothing, it's not a story") and clinging to the current experience ("It's been snowing lately"), reflecting the primacy of the perceptual.

C – Charles (the Rorschach)

The excitement that is triggered by the color and by the stimulus dispersion first disorganizes the ability to produce representations (splitting between *"multitude of things"* and *"I can see nothing"*) and then allows the construction of the stimulus (relying on naming the achromatic color):

Card X: "X is ten. There's a multitude of things there.... I can see absolutely nothing on it. Oh, maybe here ∨ an animal skull ∧ Here, at the front, the grey spot, it looks like the front of a Churchill tank. Yeah, it makes sense."

Here we can note the function of cards flipping as a support in the response production, a support that is reinforced by the reference to an auto-representation of the support function ("Yeah, it makes sense").

D – Charles (TAT)

With the proposed narrative to this TAT card, perceptual inhibition is a perfect example of the *effects of white*:

Card 5: "How many are there?" (takes the card in his hand) "Phew.... I can't see here, I see nothing at all, I'm really blind."

Clinician: "Do you have any idea?"

Charles: "No, I can't see anything here."

Area of Transference Engagement

The third area is that of transference engagement, as a reflection of the quality of the protective shield, or the area of excitement processing within the bond.

This third area particularly reveals the manifestations in the form of transference acting out that pepper the projective production.

A – Corneille (the Rorschach)

Questioning the intervention, involvement, or intent of the clinician about the stimulus production is part of a background of denial of the *established* dimension of the material within the context of a representation fragility:

Card IV (enquiry): "All of it [localization in the center] that's it. I can't say more. Have you noticed the feet?"

It is as if the mark of the clinician on the stimulus could guarantee the reliability of the perceptual experience.

Along the same lines, soliciting the clinician on the artistic trend of the stimulus is an attempt at reassurance within a context of doubts about the representation production (while the proposed response is part of the popular responses to this card):

Card V: "Axis of symmetry. It looks a bit like a bat. These images are modern, which period?"

D – Charles (TAT)

The explicit call on the clinician in a sensory solicitation helps to support the process of representation:

Card 13B: "Don't you have more concrete stuff to show me? Kind of something to catch my eye? It's the story of a kid, it's the story of a kid who has been abandoned by his parents in the desert and who lives out there and fends for himself and dies in this hut when he gets old, well, when he's old" (yawns, restless, moves his legs).

Note the somatic and sensorimotor involvement of Charles in the response production (the somatic expression of affect?).

During retest, acting out the failure experience as a here-and-now resolution also supports the elaboration of the narrative,

Card 13B' – retest (He takes his wallet and pulls out two 100 Swiss franc bills that he carries in his hand): "This is the story of a boy waiting for his dad at the entrance of the house" (some coins fall, he's bending down to pick them up). It fell by itself.... Um.... Waiting for his dad at the entrance of the house and he's late as usual and his dad comes and apologizes and gives him a rattle and there you go everyone is happy."

Lastly, the questioning (the failure?) of the representative potential is expressed at the risk of exhaustion, with a falling back on a strictly sensory approach:

Card 16 (flips the card, then flips it again): "Wow… I'm going to see a lot of white snow, that's it. It doesn't inspire me much I know. White. And if you were to tell a story? Impossible with a white stuff, with white outlines, it's going to be hard, it's going to be difficult. It was actually a trick question. You've worn me out with all these stories, it leaves me with nothing for the last one. No, nothing but white, possibly white-yellow."

Beyond the persecutory emergence, we may note the latent disorganization at the heart of the discourse, which goes along with the loss of form versus background differentiation ("Impossible with a white stuff, with white outlines").

Conclusion

The various proposed illustrations explicitly show both the rich overview of catastrophes of symbolization that are considered to reflect the destiny of trauma, and their dynamic nature. These catastrophes of symbolization or turns of events in the person's mental life bear within them the seeds of reorganization potentials, the fate of which is to be monitored as they emerge in the projective tests, card by card and from one test to the other, beyond what is observed in these very examples of isolated responses or narratives presented within the context of this chapter for illustrative purposes.

The use of the notion of catastrophes of symbolization which, I have to point out, was initially part of a psychosomatic clinical concern, and which is here centered on the testing of the clinical approach to violent sexual behavior in adolescence, demonstrates, if necessary, the continuum of acting issues (Roman & Dumet, 2009), from somatic acting (somatization) to violent acting (auto-directed or hetero-directed). These clinical practices, as is well-known, are marked by a splitting activity regarding parts of the infantile experience that are discarded and/or cut off from subjectivity – a clinical approach of ego splitting, or most probably the ego splitting (Roussillon, 1991) that reflects a failure in the symbolization of early experiences, before language, which are felt and nonsymbolized (or poorly symbolized).

The projective scene may be an opportunity to revive symbolization, a work that is known for not following linear paths: the catastrophes of symbolization are part of these turns of events in a person's mental life that show and reduce the splitting in the activities of the drive, its transformation, and its destiny. In this respect, it is really the path of the drive that can be assessed from the identification of the catastrophes of symbolization in this subtle activity between perceptual traces, affective emergence, and conceptual constructions (Freud, 1896/2001) on which projective productions in their expressive complexity (verbal, textual, mimic-sensorimotor, etc.) can provide a useful insight.

Lastly, this identification also understandably relates – well beyond the clinical practice in children and adolescents – to clinical practice in adults, in the field that is now commonly called narcissistic-identity pathologies (Roussillon, 1991, 2014). This clinical practice proves to be pragmatic for the catastrophes of symbolization, because they reflect the fragility of the elaboration of early traumatic experiences that belong to nonsymbolic binding, in a time prior to language, as evidenced by earlier works on clinical practice in adults (Roman, 2014b).

Acknowledgments

This chapter was originally published in French and is reprinted here in English with permission: Roman, P. (2017). Traces traumatiques et figures projectives des catastrophes de symbolisation. *Bulletin de psychologie, 70*(4), 265–273. © Bulletin de psychologie.

References

Balier, C. (1998). La violence à la lumière des processus adolescents [Violence in the light of adolescent processes]. *Adolescence, 31,* 117–126.

Brelet, F. (1986). *Fantasme et situation projective* [Fantasy and projective situation]. Paris, France: Dunod.

Ciavaldini, A. (1999). *Psychopathologie des agresseurs sexuels* [Psychopathology of sex offenders]. Paris, France: Masson.

Ciavaldini, A. (2005). L'agir: Un affect inachevé [Acting: An unfinished affect]. In J. Boushira & H. Parat (Eds.), *L'affect* (p. 137–162). Paris, France: PUF.

Dejours, C. (2013). L'inné et l'acquis – La cohabitation entre l'infantile (pulsionnel) et le pubertaire (instinctuel) [The innate and the acquired – The cohabitation between the infantile and the pubertal]. *Carnet psy, 6*(173), 37–41. http://doi.org/10.3917/lcp.173.0037

Freud, S. (1896/2001). Letter 52 to Wilhem Fliess. In J. Strachey (Ed. & Trans.), *The standard edition of the complete psychological works of Sigmund Freud* (Vol. 1, pp. 173–280). London, UK: Vintage Classics. (Original work published in 1896)

Freud, S. (1915/2001). Observations on transference-love. In J. Strachey (Ed. & Trans.), *The standard edition of the complete psychological works of Sigmund Freud* (Vol. 12, pp. 157–171). London, UK: Vintage Classics. (Original work published in 1915)

Gutton, P. (1991). *Le pubertaire* [The pubertal]. Paris, France: PUF.

Gutton, P. (1996). *Adolescens* [Adolescence]. Paris, France: PUF. http://doi.org/10.3917/puf.gutto.1996.01

Janin, C. (1996). *Figures et destins du traumatisme* [Figures and fates of trauma]. Paris, France: PUF. http://doi.org/10.3917/puf.janin.1996.01

Ravit, M. (2010). Du traumatisme à la fascination dans la clinique du passage à l'acte [From traumatism to fascination in clinical work with the passage to the act]. *Psychologie clinique et projective, 16,* 29–49. http://doi.org/10.3917/pcp.016.0029

Ravit, M., Di Rocco, V., Bécache, E., & Carka, D. (2013). De l'illusion meurtrie à la désillusion meurtrière [From bruised illusion to murderous disillusion]. *Psychologie clinique et projective, 18,* 167–184. http://doi.org/10.3917/pcp.019.0167

Roman, P. (1997a). Troubles somatiques et catastrophes de symbolisation [Somatic disorders and catastrophes of symbolization]. *Psychologie clinique et projective, 3*(1), 75–87.

Roman, P. (1997b). La méthode projective comme dispositif à symboliser [The projective method as a device to symbolize]. In P. Roman (Ed.), *Projection et symbolisation chez l'enfant* (pp. 37–51). Lyon, France: PUL.

Roman, P. (1998). Pouvoir et pour-voir du clinicien dans le champ judiciaire [Power and scope of the clinician in the judicial field]. *Cahiers de psychologie clinique, 10,* 47–63.

Roman, P. (2012). *Les violences sexuelles à l'adolescence – comprendre, accueillir, prévenir* [Sexual violence in adolescence – understanding, welcoming, preventing]. Paris, France: Elsevier-Masson.

Roman, P. (2014a). Les violences sexuelles dans la famille à l'adolescence et l'épreuve de la différenciation [Sexual violence in the family during adolescence and the challenge of differentiation]. In F. Houssier (Ed.), *Violences dans les liens familiaux* (pp. 69–84). Paris, France: In Press.

Roman, P. (2014b). Violence et psychopathologie: L'agir sexuel violent et la butée de la perversion – Contribution des épreuves projectives [Violence and psychopathology: Violent sexual behavior and perversion – Contribution of projective tests]. In B. Gaillard (Ed.), *La psychologie criminologique* (pp. 99–124). Paris, France: In Press.

Roman, P. (2015a). Les violences sexuelles à l'adolescence et l'épreuve du corps-à-corps: L'illusion d'une sexualité sans tabou? [Sexual violence in adolescence and the trial of hand-to-hand contact: The illusion of a sexuality without taboos?]. *Cahiers de psychologie clinique, 45,* 225–236.

Roman, P. (2015b). *Le Rorschach en clinique de l'enfant et de l'adolescent* [Rorschach in the clinic of the child and teenager]. Paris, France: Dunod.

Roman, P., & Dumet, N. (2009). Des corps en actes: Symbolisation/désymbolisation à l'adolescence [Bodies in action: Symbolization/desymbolization in adolescence]. *Cliniques Méditerranéennes, 79,* 207–227. http://doi.org/10.3917/cm.079.0207

Roussillon, R. (1991). *Paradoxe et situations limites de la psychanalyse* [Paradox and boundaries of psychoanalysis]. Paris, France: PUF. http://doi.org/10.3917/puf.rouss.1991.01

Roussillon, R. (2002). L'homosexualité primaire et le partage de l'affect [Elementary homosexuality and sharing of affect]. In D. Mellier (Ed.), *Vie émotionnelle et souffrance du bébé* (pp. 73–93). Paris, France: Dunod.

Roussillon, R. (2014). *Manuel de psychologie et de psychopathologie clinique générale* [Manual of psychology and general clinical psychopathology]. Paris, France: Elsevier-Masson.

Virole, B. (1992). Morphogénèse des stéréotypies motrices dans l'autisme infantile [Morphogenesis of motor stereotypies in childhood autism]. *Sémiotiques, 3,* 31–62.

Winnicott, D.-W. (1989). La crainte de l'effondrement [The fear of breakdown]. In D.-W. Winnicott (Ed.), *La crainte de l'effondrement et autres textes* (pp. 205–216). Paris, France: Gallimard.

11

From Bipolar Disorder to Melancholia and Mania

The Contribution of Projective Tests in the Study of Manic Depressive Disorder in a 16-Year-Old Girl

Estelle Louët

Marielle was 16 years old, the youngest of three siblings. Her elder sister was protective and pampered her, but her relationship with her brother was more conflict-ridden. The family history revealed a period of maternal depression requiring hospitalization roughly 20 years earlier; in addition, a maternal aunt was treated repeatedly with electroconvulsive therapy. This was the second time that Marielle had been admitted to the hospital unit. Her first hospitalization, a year earlier, was due to the sudden onset of major depression symptoms accompanied by malnutrition, weight loss (7 kg), catatonia (major psychomotor slowing down that rendered her virtually stuporous, waxy flexibility, cataleptic attitudes), and delusions that took the form of Cotard's syndrome: She claimed to have neither hair nor teeth and proclaimed herself "dead"; feelings of guilt emerged in parallel – "I am a criminal". The second hospitalization, during which the psychological assessment was carried out, happened in the aftermath of a manic episode the symptoms of which were as striking as they were worrying, rapidly catching her family's attention. There were psychomotor agitation symptoms including fugues, hypersyntonia (heightened emotional reactivity), and irritability, accompanied by tachypsychia and logorrhea. Marielle also presented with almost total insomnia and anorexia. A complete psychological assessment, including an intellectual efficiency scale (Wechsler Adult Intelligence Scale; WAIS-R) and two projective tests (the

Rorschach and TAT), was proposed to better understand this adolescent's psychic organization.[1]

While taking the tests, Marielle was constantly changing, from one session to another and even from one moment to another. While she could be active and assertive, she could also take on an astonishingly different and regressive stance involving some silliness. In any case, Marielle found it difficult to invest in the test situation, which she essentially accepted in submission to the adult rather than as an opportunity to express her difficulties in a more personal manner. She was unable to pull herself together when she took the tests because she remained preoccupied with personal and relational concerns which encroached upon the test period. Without hesitation and in a rather disorderly manner, she revealed her hatred of her mother, and how strict she was. She perceived this as a restriction on her freedom, and her numerous sexual activities were evoked without embarrassment.

Her overall level could be described as below average, with a better performance on the verbal intelligence quotient, on average (VIQ: 83) than on the performance intelligence quotient (PIQ: 82). However, there were widely dispersed scores within the scales and even within subtests themselves. Even though Marielle was able to function at a minimal level of adaptation and satisfactorily adhere to conformist thought (understanding: 10), the lack of cultural interest and a concentration deficit disorder led to the failure observed in some subtests (information: 5, memory for numbers: 6). With regard to performance, Marielle was penalized by her slowness (Code 4) and her difficulty in adapting to new situations and instructions. She seemed to experience difficulty in organizing, making sense of, and uniting the material.

The Rorschach Test

Overall Clinical Impressions

The restricted production – Marielle's protocol had only 18 replies – contrasts with the numerous remarks uttered during the test period (see the complete protocol in Table 11.1). These remarks showed the resonance to both the perceptive and manifest characteristics of the images and their latent evocations. The multiple comments and precisions thus highlighted great sensitivity that borrowed the affective coloration from the material's more or less sustained colors. While the color black referred to "darkness" and "sorrow," as well as to "horror," pastel colors offered relief associated with liveliness and "niceness," in a contrast that was particularly visible in the choices made at the end of the test, and which strongly questioned the role of splitting mechanisms.

The repeated turning of the cards and the interrupted discourse also revealed Marielle's anxiety, actively counterinvested by the mechanisms of inhibition and

1 Many thanks to Caroline Thompson for proofreading my English text, and for her precious long-time friendship, and to Zoé Andreyev and Sandra Misdrahi.

specific behavior, such as laughter and the manipulation of the cards. The iterative comments about the "bizarre" nature of what she perceived draws our attention to the ways in which this material resonated for Marielle, in particular with its references to the body and its multiple representations. While she obviously participated in the test, the iterative formulations of the unreal nature of her projections revealed the need for reassurance, whereas her capacity to consciously interpret vacillated in an atmosphere that was clearly anxious and depressive.

Thought Processes

Exclusively focused on global responses (G) and detail responses (D), the manner in which the material was interpreted revealed the lack of flexibility in the grasp of knowledge of the world, subjected to the need to incorporate the different aspects of the material into single representations. Perceptual apprehension preferentially occurred on a global (G%: 78%) and simple mode. This overinvestment underlined the need to control the emergence of fantasies that could otherwise undermine the self-representation. This defensive movement was perfectly illustrated in Card V, where two common animal representations, "butterfly" and "bat," ended up being combined into an ultimate global picture which united and merged them into one: "a butterfly-bat." When global responses revealed perceptual elaboration (3 elaborated G), it was, once again, to maintain an active control over thoughts relative to the emergence of fantasies and drives. This was particularly true with red cards (II and III), where combining different ink blots to produce a single response made it possible to avoid directly integrating color into the response and to master the drive's impact. The effort toward perceptual development was thus underpinned by defensive necessities, in this case, rigid control.

Detail responses appeared exclusively in the last card, in a scattered manner to which Marielle was immediately sensitive, as evidenced by her comment: "It is more and more separated, it is always only symmetrical drawings but separated, detached." By interpreting each blot separately, Marielle maintained control over the material whose effectiveness ensured anchoring in reality. The formal approach was invested as a reference to shared and shareable thought (F%: 67, F+%: 83). This reflected that her social skills were never seriously jeopardized by the impact of fantasies brought on by the materiel. Cards II and III, associated with the movement of human figures (K responses), were rather exemplary of the vitality of drives as well as the need to control them. Her mentions of figures referring to an infantile universe – "little guys" – are all attempts to distance the emergence of sexual and aggressive tendencies. These figures can be invested as a bond (Card II) or as an investment of the body, in which the appeal to narcissism or the material's quest for symmetry was evident. In this regard, the reference to "face-to-face" was a perfect example as it underscored the difficult encounter with another person and the conflict it entailed, causing one's self-representation to falter: "The heads are missing.... They're bizarre" (Card II). Face-to-face confrontation was thus a means by which a scene could be frozen, maintaining aggressiveness in a state of potentiality; pausing over an image made it possible to hold off aggression while keeping the object within sight, as in a mirror.

While energy was mobilized to ensure that self-representation and its limitations remained stable, resources could not be freely invested to support the active investment of thought, replaced by the defensive need to control what emerged within the inner world. The drive and fantasy activities reflected by projective upsurges, and the responses that invested movement (2 K, 1 kobC), prevented the exploitation of thoughts whose freedom of expression was hindered.

Conflict Management

Quantitative and qualitative approaches revealed the greater prevalence of the sensory register compared with the kinesthetic approach that was nonetheless present (2 K), reflecting a sensitivity to the environment and its demands, as well as the need to repress the expression of feelings which constantly threatened to overwhelm her (CF kobC). This adolescent addressed affects in a particularly problematic manner, expressed as much in her hypersensitivity as in the difficult connection between affects and representations.

The analysis of the narcissistic level revealed an incomplete self-image, bearing the scars of a fundamental narcissistic castration unable to pave the way for an oedipal symbolic castration. This absence was experienced at the very heart of her being. Marielle's sense of self seemed shaken, awakening feelings of strangeness – or was it foreignness? – and of oddity. The characters are "little guys" (Cards II and III), in reference to the necessarily good men of her childhood, maintaining all identification in an infantile register where the issue of the renunciation of bisexuality need not arise. This absence was mentioned: "The heads are missing" (Card II) – acknowledged but immediately denied – "But one can imagine them." It was the almost conscious dimension of the movement and coexistence of both emptiness and fullness that draws our attention here: The head, like a fetish, was actively viewed in a blank space (central S), a void, thus denying the absence and its effects. The evocation of para-human figures that belong to the imaginary world helps keep any reference to male or female sexual images at a distance. Instead, images of "little guys," "angels," and "giants" awakened Marielle's sense of oddity: "They're weird....," which was undoubtedly summoned by the blurring of the borders between the inner and outer world, fleeting and indistinct borders, except when resorting to projection. The persecutory dimension can be invasive, as evidenced by the focus on the physical features that she interpreted as more or less benevolent: "They're weird, it feels like it makes me...." (Card VII). This persecutory dimension often arises from severe death anxieties linked to the fear of object loss: "Already I don't like the black ones, they're mournful" (multiple choices). Bonds are mobilized in defense against depression. Reciprocity and sameness are summoned, sweeping away all conflict, as evidenced by Card VII: "It looks like two angels of the *same* type looking at each other.... It looks like weird angels. It looks like a scale even." This shift from double to single is incessant and evokes a rapprochement that is as exciting as it is worrying. The objective is to reduce to *one* that which cannot be understood in a dual relationship, a situation that inevitably involves separations and conflicts ("*two* angels of the *same* type ... it looks like angels... It looks like a scale even").

Marielle finds it difficult to accept gender differences. She remains strongly attached to the signs of infantile bisexuality where phallic appropriation ensures the maintenance of a redeeming omnipotence, counterinvesting the impact of any weakness. There is thus a back-and-forth movement between passive regressive and active phallic choices, but she fails to attain a clear feminine identification. The difference between men and women thus disappears in favor of the quest for narcissistic unity that is quite difficult to preserve. Maternal images reflect the precariousness of these images' function as containers, which fail to shield Marielle from destructive drives, insufficiently linked by eroticization. The access to possible conflictualization is thus barred by the relationship with the object, which is marked by a dependence that is as necessary as it is, paradoxically, persecutory (Card VII).

The affective coloration is clearly depressive, leaving little room for any other expression, in particular libidinal. It manifests itself essentially in a sensory dysphoric register which laughter and smiles attempt to counterinvest. Relying on the senses seems necessary to allow access to emotional expression, which, in its absence, remains difficult to define. Sadness can thus emerge, sustained by an indispensable back-and-forth movement between peripheral sensory elements – "dark", "black" – and a thick layer of emotions – "sad" – both supported by the equally essential need to invoke the mechanisms of projection: "It's black it's sad, it's always horrific stuff." These adjustments are indispensable to maintaining an inner/outer border struggling to establish itself in a stable and reliable manner. As a result, in an attempt to reassure herself, Marielle has moments in which she wavers: "It's funny they're all tiny" (Card IV) and "You don't see this out in the streets or maybe at carnivals" (Card IX).

Although there are some libidinal elements, these are oppressed by destructive movements whose sadistic coloration is clear: "It looks like a beast whose skin has been plucked and here is the skin" (Card VI). The animated senses and the use of excitation, which clearly act as antidepressants, counter the prevalence of the theme of death. The fear of being overwhelmed by the emergence of fantasies and drives prompts Marielle to turn to control as a defense mechanism and leads to rigidified functioning and limited exchanges. Fortunately, however, this path allows the expression of sensory and affective sensitivity which more readily express themselves as a shield from regression, "a child's drawing" (Card VIII), as well as through a more labile mood supported by eroticization.

Conclusion of the Rorschach

Marielle's hypersensitivity both to the effects of the environment and to the emergence of her inner world is an essential point of vulnerability in her current psychic functioning, reflecting how fragile the protective shield of her psyche is. The objects she brings up to support an overly fragile self-image also awaken a relationship of dependency that is at once lifesaving and persecutory. Marielle is torn between being too close, with the risk of losing oneself in the other, and being separated, with the risk of persecution. This alternative is set up as a protection against feelings of distress, expressed through death anxieties. In this context where fear of object loss is at the forefront, choosing a neutral identity ensures the maintenance of an infantile omnipotence that keeps sexuality in a bisexual category. While rigid defenses are summoned in an attempt to contain the emergence of fantasies and drives that Marielle fears might overwhelm her, other defensive modalities, such as labile and narcissistic or even projective ones, may be mobilized, offering a healthy range of defense mechanisms.

The Interpretation of the TAT Protocol

Marielle's TAT protocol is unusual, often neglecting the material's latent content (please find the complete protocol in the section Marielle, TAT). It is supplanted by a largely personal vision that, nevertheless, is expressed hurriedly in a narrative that is frequently interrupted. As the test progresses, and as the material becomes less and less figurative, the narrative becomes increasingly longer. The loss of external support mobilizes an active counterinvestment by Marielle, leading her to introduce even more characters into her narratives, filled and animated with multiple fanciful twists.

The narratives reveal a sharp contrast between a rich and somewhat labile production and the difficult formulation of conflict as evidenced by the profusion of *conflict evasion* discourse procedures specific to the C series (see Appendix 3), which now always allow her to contain the emergence of fantasies or projections. This is visible through the temporary grammar mistakes.

The relatively widespread use of labile processes (B series) reflects the intensity of her inner world, which expresses itself in a relational scene invested by libidinal movements. The introduction of characters (B1-2) and the emphasis on the representations of relationships (B1-1) are evidence of an object investment nourished by the massive presence of fantasies and dramatic events. The eroticization of relationships (B3-2) and the expression of affects (B1-3/B2-2) may lead to a potential oedipal conflict. But this does not last, and Marielle rapidly closes up, discovering the defensive shield these labile processes represent. This reflects the insufficient structuring nature of these defenses.

The emergence of lability is often accompanied by rigid processes (Series A), which ensure adequate monitoring of emotional expression and, more broadly, excitation. Temporal and spatial precisions as well as cultural references are often called upon to ensure that when the inner world surfaces, it is controlled. These references enable the occasional expression of conflict in a back-and-forth movement between contradictory psychic movements (A2-4) even though it often comes down to the need to avoid drive overflow.

The conflict avoidance processes of the C series are the most widely represented in Marielle's protocol. They are considered mechanisms of inhibition (CI) expressed through numerous interruptions of speech (CI-1), and are frequently marked by highly perceptible anxiety (CI-3). Moreover, they are often marked by the anonymity of characters and, in most cases, by unspecified motives of conflict (CI-2). Emphasis on the factual with regard to the content of the cards may occasionally be mobilized to support avoidance behavior (CF-2).

The dominance of CN, CL, and CM discourse procedures emphasizes the weaknesses that Marielle must guard against. Narcissistic defences are mobilized in an insistent manner throughout the protocol. They are expressed through the emphasis on self-sufficient positions (CN1) drawn from a narcissistic source, as clearly illustrated by Marielle's expression "so she takes it on herself" (Card 3BM). The figures she identifies with offer very contrasted representations, opposing figures that are haloed and idealized (CN2+) on the one hand, and massively attacked and disqualified, and even fecalized on the other (CN2-): "He looks more like a brute; her, she's beautiful and gentle" (Card 4) and "The other one is very rich, and the other is very poor" (Card 9GF). Idealized and loved or, on the contrary, disqualified and hated, these images suggest support for identification, and reject all compromise and thus all conflict. Other narcissistic processes (CN3, CN4) reveal the need to freeze all drives, by overinvesting boundaries and sensations. Her use of the expression *looks like* perfectly illustrates this movement that shifts investment from within toward the outside – that is, toward appearance. The expression *looks like* supports the uncertainty that is associated not with doubt about thoughts, but, rather, with the consistency of objects whose depth can only, paradoxically, be revealed through the surface: "She doesn't look very happy" (Card 2) is not sadness, and "He looks like a brute" (Card 4) is not brutality! The expression *looking like* is not only a figure of speech, it is the very consistency of the object that is put into doubt. Here, the *appearance* becomes the *being*, and the surface reflects some form of interiority searching for contours. Marielle's singular denials that prevail over the entire content of perception are worth noting: "This image can't be seen" (Card 7GF). A rather peculiar formulation with regard to a card that encourages participants to narrate a potentially conflictual mother–daughter bond, given that the little girl looks away, as a female/maternal figure leans toward her, a book in hand, to tell a story.... This initial remark, which does not significantly impede the young girl's capacity to make associations, condenses, in our opinion, the necessary turn to the perceptual surface which involves *the perceived* – in this case her refusal to gain access to a story and to meaning; Marielle proceeds thus: "It is the *story* of a young girl who dreams of becoming a woman" (Card 7GF). From depth to surface, from the object to image, the drive investment is mainly narcissistic, thus ensuring the triumph of the ego.

The object relations thus reflect a dependency on the object that is both necessary and painful, and sometimes persecutory. Themes of support frequently recur, highlighting the anaclitic attachment to the primary maternal object. This attachment is vital and complex (CM1; Cards 3BM, 11, and 12BG). Dependence on the environment is reflected as much in the content, occasionally taking on a pathetic expression – "They remain attached to each other through the bonds of love" (Card 10) and "Their parents are beside them, the boat is well secured" (Card 12BG) – as in the forms of discourse in which the participant's fantasies take shape. The stories are full of propositions that refer to this necessary support.

The CL processes reveal the vulnerability of borders (CL1) and underline the prevalence of splitting mechanisms (CL4) that are perfectly illustrated by the highly heterogeneous plethora of defense modalities. This splitting ensures the maintenance of a sufficiently effective anchoring, opposing an adaptive force to the overflow of primary projection.

However, the most elaborate defenses fail to manage libidinal and aggressive drives which may erupt abruptly, through fantasies and massive sadistic representations (E2–3) as well as through clearly persecutory projective themes (E2–2) "She's going to take revenge" (Card 5) and "She is under his command" (Card 6GF). The logic behind this discourse can thus be undermined by temporary grammatical mistakes. It can also be weakened by the disorganization of identity and object landmarks and, occasionally, the disorganization of temporal, spatial or logical causality: "She finally realizes that wherever she goes she's not well" (Card 2) and "It's a young couple, they've been married a long time" (Card 4).

While drives struggle to express conflict, relations are called upon to support the self-image that has remained fundamentally flawed. Primary and secondary defenses thus clash, unable to let conflict fully unfold, given the fragile and unstable psychic scene.

The Problematic

Although the interpersonal and intrapsychic conflict can be addressed, the vulnerability of the more elaborate defences prevent it from coping with the very intense expression of drives. Thus, while under the cover of lability, relationships are invested and nourished by drives; they fall outside the logic of complementary desires and thus lack oedipal elaboration. There appears to be little differentiation in relation to parental images, with differences disappearing in favor of a quest for narcissistic unity that is difficult to maintain. The weakness and badness of identity figures seem to be cultivated, albeit in a bond strongly tinged with a destructive and passionate component (Cards 5 and 6GF).

Retaliation is proportionate to the damage suffered, justifying revenge by bypassing what is forbidden: "She'll take revenge, she has a fixed idea in her mind" (Card 5). Violent exchanges and the desire to control and manipulate objects are in opposition to an intolerable experience of dependence, restoring positions of helplessness that are just as unacceptable (Card 7GF). The eroticization of relationships exposes one to the painful risk of being dependent on an object and losing it. Positions of powerlessness and passivity are thus actively counterinvested by vows of omnipotence and a narcissistic withdrawal. This logic prevents the access to the difference of genders and the conflict of desires. While external norms appear to be familiar and reflect social adaptation, they seem to function in an all-or-nothing mode, relying on extremely split references: Sometimes external and imposed, these references can take the form of an archaic superego that is as implacable as it is cruel. The intensity of the hatred of objects fuels grandiose masochistic positions that set the stage for a negativism driven by expiatory vows. The sadomasochist component of the object relationship, perfectly illustrated in the expression of beating fantasies, maintains a relationship of dependence and counterinvestment – all could be lost in a movement that might be summarized thus: "I need the object even if it mistreats me" to "I need the object to mistreat me." In this context, the persecutory drift appears to be part of the struggle against the anxiety associated with object loss (Card 3BM).

Given the absence of sufficient barriers, the intensity of drives, reactivated in this period of adolescence, is expressed massively, revealing a weak relationship between affects and representations. The connection of two drive-related affects – that is, love and hate – is hampered by the problematic manner in which aggressiveness is handled, the intensity of which is revealed in the sadistic fantasies, even when they are turned against the self. Sadistic aggressive impulses, mobilized in the relationship with parental figures, thus return to persecutory themes in the form of superegoistic demands. Hatred leads to a massive rejection of object ties whose dependence, despised, is paid for by attacking these ties and by destructiveness. However, love, enveloped by fusional ties, uncovers the intensity of the fears associated with being captured by an archaic maternal figure. Excitability, very easily set off, reveals how the psyche is overflowed, to the detriment of the activity of representation. Confronting castration anxiety awakens other demons – that is, the demons of fundamental narcissistic inconsistency! When castration fails to achieve a symbolic opening, the wound literally bursts within the body and must be fiercely defended by negating all differences. While the attachment to infantile bisexuality preserves one's membership of the two sexes, the narcissistic phallic appropriation ensures omnipotence by refusing to confront powerlessness. When differences remain, there is a strong opposition expressed through caricatured forms of all-powerful figures that fail to offer satisfactory supports for identification, as their magnificence or mediocrity reveal either their dangerousness or their vulnerability.

Marielle's case reveals borderline functioning in which depression mobilizes extreme defensive positions. The desire for omnipotence and triumph over the object alternates with narcissistic collapse, the intensity and brutality of which raise concerns about potential acting-out through self-aggression. The presence of labile resources nevertheless ensures the existence of a good libidinal component, even though this is currently masked by an intense and destructive sadistic component.

Marielle, Rorschach

Table 11.1 Complete Protocol for the Rorschach Test of 16-Year-Old Patient Marielle

Rorschach Card, Duration of Response, and Protocol		Scoring
Card I 3" 1. It's a dark carnival mask . . . (smiles at the same time); that's all I see (encouragement) < v > This image doesn't inspire me ... the colors ... They're dark. It's black, it's sad, always horrific stuff.	There are no strings to attach it and there are holes for the eyes and holes for the teeth, for the mouth... Maybe a wolf head with holes to put the strings (DdS under D lat.) These are the beast's ears. (?) If I meet this in the street it must be scary at night ... and even during the day. [*Testing the limits:* Maybe a bat ... this aspect (she traces the contours with her fingers) (?) with a bat's eyes].	Gbl FC' Obj → Clob Criticism C' Comment Clob Comment
Card II 10" 2. It's two men stuck to each other. The heads are missing but one can imagine them. It's two weird guys but it's original I find the form a bit like the first one. < v > v It's symmetrical [if you fold] the lines in the middle, it's the same.	Two little guys facing each other. With a hat (red top D) the head (DdS between red and black) the hands joined together, bodies and feet and that I don't know (red bottom D). Perhaps a red heart or the shape of a butterfly. [Additional response: D F+ A] It can be many things, a heart that one draws without paying too much attention except that here it's original. Not the heart of the body it's not like that. [Additional response: D FC Symb.]	G K H Comment Symmetry comment
Card III 8" 3. Looks like two guys again, two guys working out across each other, around a table, and it's always symmetrical.	Two guys around a table, it looks like they want to move the table that they're lowering themselves to get the strength to lift the table. I don't know what this red stuff is maybe... Something, a knot placed on the table (DS table included) [D F+ Obj] (Characters) an arm, also the chest, a bit of the arm maybe folded like this ... I don't know (stretches herself)	G K H Ban Symmetry comment
Card IV 2" 4. That's a giant! (Laughs) a giant seen from below ...	The head, its limbs (lat. top. D), its feet and one therefore sees from below so it's bigger there, and the head is very small. It's a thing from a fantasy world. I wouldn't want to meet this in the street (fear?). No it's funny, they're all tiny (yawns) it's not mobile, it's not true.	G FE (H)

Table 11.1 continued

Rorschach Card, Duration of Response, and Protocol		Scoring
Card V 3" 5. V A butterfly 6. A bat... 7. A butterfly-bat	More like a bat with the head, the antennae-like things, the ... what are these called ... the wings to fly and the hind legs. A butterfly is more beautiful, and it doesn't have wings like that. It looks like a UFO stretching out its arms (laughs) an extraterrestrial. [Additional response: W M H/Obj]	G F+ A Ban G F+ A G F– A/A
Card VI 5" 8. This is an animal skin I don't know ... looks like a beast whose skin has been plucked and here is the skin. 9. V Seen from upside down it looks like a tree, a bit weird but a tree, it has the form, a small bush (laughs).	The head and the body with the legs... it's... one can find that in people... (yawns) A small bush (Top D) and the trunk and the tree's leaves (Bottom D) ... a small bush behind and here's the tree (yawns)	G F+ A Ban D/G F+ Nat
Card VII 5" 10. Seems like two angels looking at each other. They're weird, it feels like it makes me... 11. V and on the other side, a cave, the entrance to a cave, for example.	It looks like weird angels. It even looks like a scale. The wings are missing but there's the head (1st third) the body joined to it (2nd and 3rd third) it looks like a scale even. (WS) As if everything was painted it would be like a cave (yawns, ask for a handkerchief)	G F+ (H)/Obj Dbl/G F+ Nat
Card VIII 5" There's color here for once. 12. < V A child's drawing, I don't know it's hard to tell what it is even if there are colors. 13. It's a guy with a beard and a hat on his head.	Nothing ... I can't tell. With children's drawings, you can't always tell what it is. (W) hair: D lat. pink; hat: D orange pink; eyes: D pink; mouth D blue; beard D gray. (*Testing the limits*: yeah, I don't know much about animals, I can't say... head, body, legs)	Chromatic color comment G CF Art G F– Hd
Card IX 25" 14. < V This looks like a guy, some kind of hair with a head, a kind of body with a coat over it. They are all imaginary guys	The head with the ears (D pink) and his clothing (the rest) you think it resembles a person!... An imaginary guy one doesn't meet in the street or maybe at the carnival! (Laughs and yawns at the same time) or a big teddy bear! But one which doesn't smile. [Add.: W F– A]	→ Shock D/G F+ (H)

Table 11.1 continued

Rorschach Card, Duration of Response, and Protocol		Scoring
Card X 16" It is increasingly separated, they are only drawings, always symmetrical but separated, detached, but nevertheless meet.	It's more complex, there's more to notice when it's separate	Comment. Symmetry comment
15. The marine stuff looks like crabs and	Kaki	D F+ A
16. The blue stuff like blue flakes or	(D blue lat.) Flakes but it's white in general so blue...	D CF Frag
17. Fireworks stuff.		D kobC Ex
18. There are two bugs looking at each other ...	Black crabs (Top D gray) Pliers there (laughs and makes a gesture on the image) (Median green D). [Additional response: D F+ Obj]	D FC' A Ban

Notes. To code Rorschach responses, we used the French School method (Rausch de Traubenberg & Chabert), which is significantly different from the Exner or R-PAS coding process (Anzieu, Chabert, & Louet, 2017; Chabert, 1983). A = whole animal; Art = Art; Ban = common response; CF = color form response; D = common detail response; Dbl = white space (common detail response); Ex = explosion; F = form; FE = vista-form response shading dimension; FC' = form-achromatic color response; Frag = fragment; G = whole space; Gbl = space response (whole space); H = whole human; Hd = human detail; (H) = whole human (fictional or mythological); K = human movement response; Kob = inanimate movement response; Nat = nature; Obj = object.

They are only drawings! And how should I take them? I can spread them out. I don't like the black ones, they're spooky. I don't like those drawings. (At the same time she chooses three pastel-colored cards)

I don't like any of them. I can choose the ugliest in any case, two ugly ones: Cards V and VII.

Choice +: colored or black? I can choose black ones no? Cards X and IX.

Choice –: Card V represents a bat; bats are ugly. It's scary if you meet them in a cave precisely. (Takes Card VII) This is a cave, the entrance to a cave. It has a black tunnel and bats can be found inside, unpleasant things for example, a tunnel as black as death.

Choice +: Card X because it is animated. It's colorful. It's nice. Except for the dark things here like crabs (D gray sup).

Card IX: Looks like a teddy bear but it's not smiling; if it'd had a smile I would have liked it! (?) Unpretentious.

Table 11.2 Psychogram

R=18	G 14	G% 78%	F 10 (8+; 2-)	A 6	A% 33%
T=15	(1 Gbl, 2 D/G)			(1 A/A)	
			K 2	H 2	H% 16–33%
F% 56%	D 4	D% 22%	FE 1	Hd 1	
F+% 82%			FC' 2	(H) 2	
			CF 2	(H)/Obj. 1	
				Obj. 1	
T.A.: G D Dbl Dd			kobC 1	Nat. 2	
Erlebnistypus (TRI): 2K/4 ∑C					
Complementary Formula: 1k/0.5 ∑E				Fgt 1	
RC% 7/18=39%				Ex 1	
				Art 1	

Notes. ^ = right position; v = upside-down position; < = left lateral position; > = right lateral position; A/A = two animals responses added together; A = whole animal; Art = Art; Ban = common response; CF = color form response; D = common detail response; Dbl = white space (common detail response); D/G = whole space starting from common detail response; Ex = explosion; F = form; FC' = form-achromatic color response; Fgt = fragment; FE = vista-form response shading dimension; G = whole space; Gbl = space response (whole space); (H) = whole human (fictional or mythological); H = whole human; Hd = human detail; K = human movement response; Kob = inanimate movement response; Nat = nature; Obj = object; R = responses; RC% = The ratio of the number of answer, given to cards VIII IX X in regard to the total of responses; TRI = The ratio between human movement responses and color responses.

Marielle, TAT

Card 1

Fifteen seconds: "It's a young boy who was going to school and who's going back home because it's time to go home. He has a violin lesson but he doesn't want his teacher to come give him his lesson so he's wondering how he will break the violin. ... and he thinks that if he does he'll surely be punished so he decides to daydream until his teacher arrives."

Card 2

Thirty seconds: It's the story of a woman who's traveling, a student, and then she goes to different countries and she finally realizes that wherever she goes she's not well. So she decides to return to her native country because she misses her family." (Stretches, yawns) "I don't know, I don't like doing this." (Image?) "The student, she must surely have seen scenes she would not have liked to see if she had known that it was like that. ... The woman in the foreground doesn't look very happy."

Card 3BM

Twelve seconds: "One can imagine lots of stuff!" (Subaggressive) "It's the story of a woman who has just been beaten by her husband because her husband drinks too much and she has no family. Except her husband. So she takes it on herself and is always crying and hoping for better days." (Stretches)

Card 4

Twenty-five seconds: "It's the story of a couple who have been married for a long time. This couple is young but they have been married for a long time. He's rather, he looks more like a 'brute'!" (Smiles) "Her, she's beautiful and gentle. ... He's always calling for a fight against everyone ... and she only wants peace. ... She always tries to prevent him from getting angry, to keep him calm but … he only does what he feels like and even with her by his side, he is determined to leave."

Card 5

Thirty seconds: "I am not inspired.…" (Encouragement from clinician) "I don't know, it's the story of a lady who enters a room her husband had locked ... and she sees that it was he who had hidden all the objects she had lost in this room ... that's why she decides to do the same thing. ... She's going to take revenge she has a fixed idea in her head, she closes the door behind her as if she hadn't found out, but will make him suffer to know why he did that! I don't know much, I don't like doing this."

Card 6GF

Twenty-three seconds: "It's the story of a woman who is angry with her husband every second, every minute of every day because she is under his orders. Man is King for him. So she has to do what he wants. ... He wants his wife to do whatever he wants. She's under his orders. It is thanks to him that she can buy everything, all her clothes, all that she has, she must be grateful. And yet she tells herself that ... that she should never have married this man, that she should have stayed with her parents, that she should have become a nun, I don't know."

Card 7GF

Twenty-five seconds: "This image isn't clear. ... It's the story of a girl who dreams of becoming a woman but everybody treats her like a little girl and she's fed up, she tells herself that one day she will leave her house and that she will do whatever she wants. She tells herself that she has to play the game of adults, that is, to do everything that they tell her to do, but later when she'll be big, she will no longer play with her dolls for sure. She'll be in her own house, no one will bother her, she will run her life as she sees fit and not according to what others want."

Card 9GF

Twenty-five seconds: "It's the story of two women who are jealous of each other. Because one has a lover, and the other doesn't, but the other one is very rich and the other one is very poor." (Stretches) "But ... I don't know what to say for this image. ... Can you read back what I said? ... Yes there's one who has a man, who intends to marry him but only she can't because she's very poor and her father doesn't want to. ... I'm sick of it, I don't know what to say about it."

Card 10

Ten seconds: "It's the story of a couple who got married very quickly. ... They had many children. They had much joy, much pain. They had it all. They had nothing. They had everything, but they lost it all, even their children, but they are together and since they are believers, they remain attached to each other through the bonds of love, the bonds of marriage."

Card 11

< ∧ "How should I take this?…" ∧ "There's nothing to be seen!… What's this thing?" (Black) "It's the story of an ant that travelled everywhere, well everywhere, that travelled a lot on its little feet and found itself here in a cave while before it was under the sun with its friends the ants, someone put it there, most likely a little girl, or a child, a child, who undoubtedly played with it and who before killing it put it in a cave hoping that it wouldn't die and that it would leave on its feet. So this ant will die painfully, slowly, without its friends the ants because a little girl wanted to play with it, and since she is a little girl she wasn't careful ... yeah ... because what's a little ant in her life, she who is innocent. So the little ant dies as the little girl will one day die."

Card 12BG

∨ "Is it like this? No, like this." ∧ (20 seconds). "It's the story of young children who go for a boat ride. There are two of them in the boat. They're young. They must be about 5, 6 years old, their parents are beside them. Their parents are talking, and they're playing in their boat. The boat is well secured. The parents are no longer paying attention to their children because they are talking about their future house, and the children are no longer paying attention to their parents since they are playing quietly without their parents. But the boat, which had nevertheless been securely tethered, gets detached, but the children leave and the parents talk. The boat goes further and further away. The children are playing so much that they are no longer paying attention to anything. They are having so much fun and the boat keeps drifting. The parents are so engrossed in their discussion that they return without seeing that the children are no longer in the boat and that the boat is no longer in the small, even the large brook of the vast property they have rented. All of a sudden the children stop playing because they're hungry. They look around. They see nothing or if they see, they no longer see their parents, they only see nature. They are lost and as they have played a lot and are tired they fall asleep in the boat and the boat continues drifting."

Card 13B

Fifteen seconds: "It's the story of a little boy who is on a beach with his parents and his one-year-old sister. He's three years old. ... He's already big. ... His parents only look after his little sister. He's noticed. So he decides to make himself a cabin, a big, big cabin with his friends, and he succeeds and they succeed. The cabin seems large but in fact it is small but it's nice there when he's sad. ... He's noticed that he is no longer the child that used to be taken care of before, that he was less considered because he had grown up. He thinks and tells himself what a beautiful life. He is only 3 years old, but he is very intelligent for his age; it's true that he doesn't speak well but he understands a lot of things grown-ups don't see. So he decides to take his little sister to his cabin and to stay hidden in there with her. That way, his parents, if they find their child ... will take their child in their arms and will kiss them both, because the parents love their children even if the children don't understand it."

Card 13MF

Twenty seconds: "It's the story of a young man who got married to a young woman who was 10 years younger than him, knowing that he's 30, and who both decided to settle down on the top floor of a building. But one day when he was out, someone came during the night and killed his wife, and when he came back he saw his wife in her bed, but she was dead and he agonized, cried, and regretted having left his wife alone, at night. ..."

Card 19

Thirty seconds: "It's the story of a family, a big family. They're at least ten, ten children and two parents obviously. They are very cheerful, very happy. They live a very happy life. All together. Everything is perfect. They're happy, very happy together. ... But one night it snows so much, there's so much wind, it rains so hard that they're stuck in their cottage and can no longer go out anymore. So everyone begins to pray because they are a family of believers, but they pray in vain because they remain stuck under the snow, rain and wind. There is no longer any communication, the telephone is no longer working, nothing works anymore, no TV, nothing. The children are all scared. They are between 1 and 20 years old. The parents and children decide to stay in the same room to keep warm because even the heating isn't working anymore. They have no food left. They are still stuck in their cottage. They are all tired, exhausted. So they all fall asleep ... and one day the last-born, the 1-year-old, wakes up and shouts to her brothers and sisters and parents that the ball is there. She's talking about the sun, because the snow has melted and they can finally come out. Yet she's only 1 year old and has very little time."

Card 16

(Laughs) "I don't feel like it." (Encouragement from clinician). "There was once a family that lived in Rocquencourt [town in France], a family with three children. The first child had left because she got married at the age of 23, the second child is still with his parents, yet he's 20 years old, and there is a third child. She's in hospital against her will, despite the fact that she has never smoked drugs or cigarettes like her brother, that she's never been raped like some of her friends, that nothing has ever been done to her and that she wants to leave, but nobody wants to let her out, but she'll succeed because she wants to live her life, irrespective of whether it will be short or long."

Acknowledgments

This chapter was originally published in French and is reprinted here in English with permission: Louët, E. (2011). Du diagnostic de trouble bipolaire à la problématique mélancolique et maniaque chez une adolescente. In C. Chabert & C. Azoulay (Eds.), *12 études en clinique projective: Approche psychanalytique* (pp. 143–163). Malakoff, France: Dunod Editions. © Dunod Editions.

References

Anzieu, D., Chabert, C., & Louët, E. (2017). *Les méthodes projectives* [The projective methods]. Paris, France: PUF.

Chabert, C. (1983). *Le Rorschach en clinique adulte. Interprétation psychanalytique* [The Rorschach Test in adults: A psychoanalytical interpretation]. Paris, France: Dunod.

Additional Suggested Reading

Chabert, C. (2018). *Psychanalyse et méthodes projectives* [Psychoanalysis and projective methods]. Paris, France: Dunod.

Chabert, C., & Louët, E. (2013). Troubles bipolaires et manie-mélancolie: Continuité ou rupture? [Bipolar troubles and manic depression: Continuity or a split-off?]. *Psychologie clinique et projective, 19,* 11–54. http://doi.org/10.3917/pcp.019.0011

Chabert, C., Louët, E., & Camps, F. D. (2017). *Les dépressions extrêmes: Approche psychanalytique et projective* [Severe depressions: Psychoanalytical and projective approach]. Paris, France: Dunod.

Consoli, A., Brunelle, J., Bodeau, N., Louët, E., & Cohen, D. (2014). Diagnostic transition towards schizophrenia in adolescents with severe bipolar disorder type I: An 8-year follow-up study. *Schizophrenia Research, 159*(2-3), 284–291. http://doi.org/10.1016/j.schres.2014.08.010

Louët, E., & Azoulay, C. (2016). *Schizophrénie et paranoïa: Etude psychanalytique en clinique projective* [Schizophrenia and paranoia: Psychoanalytical study in the projective field]. Paris, France: Dunod.

Louët, E., Consoli, A., & Cohen, D. (2010). Psychodynamic-oriented psychological assessment predicts evolution to schizophrenia at 8-year follow-up in adolescents hospitalized for a manic/mixed episode: Interest of an overall subjective rating. *Journal of Physiology, 104*(5), 257–262. http://doi.org/10.1016/j.jphysparis.2010.08.004

Rausch de Traubenberg, N. (1970). *La pratique du Rorschach* [The practice of the Rorschach Test]. Paris, France: PUF.

12

Psychosomatic Economy

A Notion Cherished by Rosine Debray

Marie-Christine Pheulpin

"By their very definition, it is individuals, rather than diseases, who are psychosomatic!" (Rosine Debray regularly addressed these words to her students). In June 1986, I went to the Institute of Psychology located at Serpente Street in the Paris VI district. I was familiar with the "house." This is where I had undertaken my psychology studies and had been trained in projective techniques. Yet on that particular day, I was rather apprehensive, as I went to keep my appointment with Prof. Rosine Debray. I had run into her from time to time and was thus aware of the classy style of this blonde, tall lady whose hair was always impeccably styled and whose gray-blue eyes were almost metallic. I was essentially familiar with two articles she had written with Vica Shentoub as they were on the required reading list for all projective psychology students: "Theoretical Foundations of the TAT Process" (Shentoub & Debray, 1970–1971) and "How to Deal With Excessive Phantasmic Richness? Interpretation of an Unusual TAT Protocol" (Shentoub & Debray, 1978–1979). I also knew that she had an interest in somatic pathologies, diabetes in particular, and that she was a strong and passionate advocate of a theoretical model that, thanks to her, was beginning to gain acceptance at the University.

As a young clinical psychologist, I had therefore come to express my interest in enrolling in the course for a *diplôme d'études approfondies* (DEA; master of advanced studies, which is a 1-year degree that precedes entry to a PhD program) and maybe in a PhD program as well. Under the supervision of Prof. Jacqueline Lanouzière, my postgraduate studies, which had revolved around adult patients hospitalized with serious, and even extremely serious, asthma, had piqued my curiosity. Indeed, I had observed that, on the one hand, these patients frequently distanced themselves from the other, and on the other hand, they had a fragile psychic state: Was this pattern consistent? More specifically, could this have been detected before it degenerated? We had a brief and productive meeting: I was to send her a written project and start reading Pierre Marty's books. Back then, I did not know the extent to which this first meeting would influence my training. Enrolled in the DEA–doctorate program, I soon began a course at the Psychosomatic Institute of Pierre Marty (IPSO Pierre Marty) where theoretical seminars and televised consultations of adults with Marty, and mothers and babies with Debray, deeply influenced the clinical psychologist I would later become.

As part of a wide and comprehensive research dynamic that was globally underpinned by the original hypothesis of the Psychosomatic School of Paris – in other words, that there is a correlation between deficient mental functioning and the possible development of somatoform disorders – part of my studies were founded on the concepts of psychosomatic organization and disorganization. These concepts necessarily include the concepts of psychosomatic economy and mentalization which are clinically tested in a more innovative way using projective tests (Pheulpin, 1993, 2001, 2013; Pheulpin, Baudin, & Bruguière, 2017).

I will therefore analyze the contribution of projective methodology to the study of these two concepts. Specifically, I will assess the qualities of the preconscious on which the quality of mentalization ultimately depends.

Somatic Expression and Projective Methodology: An Original Approach

Assessing the psychic functioning of patients admitted to hospital, in order to provide them with more appropriate care is always a delicate process, because they are inevitably enduring a state of crisis. Since the appearance of the book *L'investigation psychosomatique: sept observations cliniques* (Psychosomatic Investigation: Seven Clinical Observations; Marty, de M'Uzan, & David, 1963), it has become common practice to consider both the mental and somatic aspects of patients' psychosomatic economy. This requires clinical psychologists to go beyond simply listening to the content of a patient's discourse and, much like in classical psychoanalytical assessment, be attentive to the patient's associations, silences, tensions, and efforts to overcome difficulties and cope with the psychologist's attention. The quality of the relationship between patients and clinical psychologists consistently involves transference and countertransference dynamics. Patients' comments about their symptoms and their ability to give feedback about their childhood enable therapists to assess their structural organizations and identify the main common particularities and characteristics. "This triple assessment – structural, habitual, current – should enable therapists to access patients' best level of functioning as well as the state at which may occur regression at the origin of and/or secondary to somatic disorganization" (Debray, 1996, p. 38).

This triple assessment, however, is not always easily applicable. Specialized in projective methods and in the TAT in particular (Debray, 1973), Debray thus initiated a method that combined interviews and projective tests in her studies with insulin-dependent diabetes patients (Debray, 1980, 1983).

At her instigation and under her guidance, some researchers drew on this theory and methodology and ventured into the in-depth analysis of psychic functioning in medical settings where both patients and practitioners – caught between a sense of urgency and patients' chronic states – were reluctant to listen to a hypothesis about the unconscious. Brigitte Hammer thus focused on women diagnosed with breast cancer, Fabienne Seron on patients who had received kidney transplants, and Doris Vasconcellos on patients with HIV/AIDS. For my part, I studied patients urgently hospitalized and suffering from acute severe asthma. Catherine Lestang conducted research on disabled patients, and Marie-Frédérique Bacqué explored how the failure to undergo complete grief work was manifested in the body. In line with Debray's studies, and undoubtedly building on Nina Rausch de Traubenberg's first study on the psyche–soma connection in patients with congenital heart disease, which she presented in her thesis defense in 1965, a broad field of research emerged (Rausch de Traubenberg, 1965). This field has remained prolific to date, driven by the regular studies undertaken or led by the members of the projective psychology French School.

In this theoretical and clinical context, it is now an accepted fact that projective tests are precious tools capable of helping explain the different adjustments involved in the regulation of a person's global psychosomatic economy (Pheulpin, Baudin, & Bruguière, 2017). Moreover, they make it possible to assess a person's singular resources and, naturally, those associated with their mental functioning in particular. Above and beyond the polemics surrounding diagnosis is thus the issue of prognosis which leads to the assessment of the therapeutic measures which would be best for a given patient.

The Projective Situation and Economic Perspective

By disrupting the then-established relational modalities, the introduction of projective material at the heart of the clinical encounter was well suited to the assessment of the global psychosomatic functioning of patients: How will patients accept this change that forces them to disinvest in the dual container/supportive relationship in which they have been engaged, and invest in a new and strange (look, imagine, speak) modality in which the test object acts as a "third party"?

Beyond the change in the relationship, the singularity of the projective situation encourages patients to speak about themselves *via* latent evocations. The concrete, ambiguous, but nonneutral objects proposed provoke unceasing excitement that patients must address. Throughout the psychological assessment, the clinical psychologist must thus observe the means through which patients express themselves, when, and the extent to which energy flows in the different sectors of activity: Is mental activity involved? Are sensory and motor activities involved? Is it a question of temperament or somatics? The focus on free-associative expression from one clinical approach to another, from one test to another, from one card to another, and from one response to another places the economic perspective at the core from the outset.

However, while they pave the way for great expression, projective tests essentially structure psychic activity. Owing to the connections made possible by the preconscious, it is possible to reflect on the drives mobilized by the excitement the situation provokes. To this end, affective energy should be neither too strong nor too weak. Moreover, it should be evenly spread between unconscious representations and processes, on the one hand, and between conscious functions, on the other. Such investment can be revealed from the initial interpretations of protocols that focus on the involvement of emotions and fantasies, as well as on the verbalization quality. Debray emphasized this in her TAT discourse analysis grid developed in 1989 and revised in 1996, in which she defined the first impression of the overall protocol as follows: "It's about responding to the following question: 'Is there detectable psychic activity involving tolerance to intrapsychic anxiety, depression and intrapsychic and interpersonal conflicts?'" (Debray, 1997, p. 27).

To make it easier to identify, the question can be broken down thus: Are these protocols restricted? Do they merely propose weak content with few or no connections? This is what seems to suggested by the narrative response to Card 1 given after a patient had been staring at the card for a 20-s latency period: "A boy looking at the material, dunno ... looking at how it's made ... that's all." In this example, the approach appears to be essentially descriptive and minimal. If we refer to Freud's first topography, the approach relates to the perception–consciousness system; it highlights the difficulties associated with figuration and weak associations as well as a clearly fragile psychic foundation and psychic space. Indeed, is not the person looking at the material also my patient? Much like the boundaries between the external and internal space, those between the interpreter and the interpreted are porous and uncertain. There remains, however, a sense of curiosity for the object, an act underpinned by life.

Are these protocols somewhat similar to those discussed above, but fraught with the emergence of primary processes? In any event, this is what a different narrative in response to the TAT Card 1 seems to suggest: "It is a child with his violin. One eye is open, and the other closed. He's mulling over his violin. He's also pouting, seems like it ... because here it's the brain that's working. ..."

"One eye is open, and the other closed" highlights the perception of a rare detail. It is almost a false perception which takes on a special meaning for the person even if, for us, it remains rather imperceptible. This narrative demonstrates the lively nature of unconscious contents. When these contents are put into words, they partly reveal a certain flow between the unconscious and preconscious systems, on the one hand, and on the other, a certain mobilization of mental processes that the person seems to directly integrate in an unsettling manner: "It's the brain that's working."

Or do these protocols lead to the production of detailed responses in resonance with the cards' latent evocations and in which patients express their fantasies, which are more or less in line with mental defense mechanisms? This is what yet another different narrative to TAT Card 1 seems to suggest: "For me, it's a little boy whose father was a violinist, and this father died leaving the violin to his son ... and it symbolizes the career this child will follow, because his father had the same career. It's somewhat about continuity." This context reveals substantial mental activity, notably with regard to how depression develops. Indeed, its development is no longer based on the perception of external objects alone, but on their investment as well.

While the projective situation undeniably enables an initial analysis of mental functioning from an economic perspective, projective tests make it possible to understand all of the different aspects of this functioning.

The Quality of Mental Functioning and Its Prognosis

According to the Psychosomatic School of Paris, psychic activity protects the body or supports reorganization when somatization sets in. If we accept this view, then the analysis of *mentalization* is of the utmost importance; this analysis provides the foundation for all psychosomatic investigations. While *mentalization* is a key concept in Marty's theory (1976, 1980), it is a difficult concept that has not always been fully understood and has often met with disapproval. I believe the criticism frequently leveled against this concept is partly linked to the terms used to describe the structural organization of the psychosomatic classification (well-mentalized, uncertainly mentalized, poorly mentalized). This criticism had led to repeated attempts to find new definitions.

In a relatively recent article, Claude Smadja noted that Michel Fain had once humorously suggested "made in psyche" while stressing its specificity: A *made in psyche* "based on treating the drive energy derived from the soma in an original manner, thus giving rise to emergent figures, i.e., mental representations" (Smadja, 2010, p. 12). Drawing on Fain's definition, Smadja defined mentalization as follows:

> Mentalization can be defined as a continuous process in which the drive is transformed resulting in different figures of psychic expression. These transformations involve the structure of the psychic apparatus (unconscious, preconscious and conscious system), of psychic functioning (primary and secondary functioning), and above all, representation dynamics. In essence, mentalization is a continuous process of drive transformation equivalent to objectalization. (Smadja, 2010, p. 12)

A great practitioner of these methods, Debray proposed a definition of metapsychology grounded in clinical psychology as early as 1997:

> Today mentalization is a debatable term because it is much too elliptical and excessively condensed. It actually stands for the purely human ability which constitutes the psychic apparatus – I must insist – the ability to tolerate and

> negotiate, and to manage anxiety, depression and interpersonal and intrapsychic conflicts. It is well known that the development of the psychic apparatus, and thus of this purely human ability to tolerate anxiety, varies from one individual to another and even within the same individual at different moments of his/her life. (Debray, 1997, p. 24)

This discourse partly reveals Debray's perception of the assessment of psychic functioning as an indispensable first step. We are struck, however, by her passionate defense of the nonexistence of a typical psychic apparatus and evolution, dynamics inherent to life itself. Psychosomatic economy and its constant modulations thus reject fixed and schematic classifications. It particularly rejects useless classifications to which the psychosomatic model is much too often reduced. From this perspective, projective tests are thus significant tools, because they allow a sophisticated assessment of mentalization and all its aspects.

By constituting the psychic withdrawal necessary for mentalization, the preconscious – that is, the key feature of the theory and of psychosomatics – determines the quality of mental operations. Marty identified three axes of mentalization: *thickness, fluidity,* and *permanence.*

As a metaphor related to space, *thickness* refers to the number of layers of representation formed over the years. A first approach might focus on a quantitative analysis: Rorschach productivity and/or abundance or poverty in the TAT. This approach, however, is insufficient and must be completed through a qualitative analysis of the representations. This is especially true given that the persons assessed are often in a state of crisis that translates into tension – that is, into a parody of their usual mode of functioning. When it comes to the mental state, fragile functioning may appear as stupefaction and evoke major depression. In this form of depression that is characterized by decreased vital energy and silence on the psychic scene, mental functions – which may include oneiric life – can appear to be erased. Normal functioning rich in primary processes may be overwhelmed by these same processes. Other fields of activity (behavior, character, investment of the reality, and facts) may also display – often in a manner inversely proportional to the mental activity – similar movements of exacerbation or abrasion of usual manifestations. There is therefore a need for a meticulous analysis of the quality of responses.

The Rorschach is a significant test because it first encourages unbinding and then forces the participant to engage in the process of binding in order to create meaningful figures. An analysis that takes into account strong indicators from the different approaches to understanding and from determinants and contents is thus essential.

Regarding the different approaches to understanding, it is obvious that focusing on the structural quality of G as well as on all other approaches to understanding is of utmost importance. If we take Catherine Chabert's definition of an elaborate G (one that "demonstrates the structural organization of engrams by combining different parts of a task; this combination needs to be done by the subject"; Chabert, 1983, p. 99) and extend it to D, Dd, and Dbl, all operant and nonoperant movements that take on an organizing role essentially demonstrate the lively nature of the psyche. This in itself is an important pointer among seriously ill patients.

Much like the structural quality of the approaches to understanding, analyzing M responses is equally valuable. When the compromise between perception and projection remains harmonious, it

> is the perfect prototype of the transitional product. The greatest paradox is that images belong both to perceptive reality and to illusion. While accessing the transitional world demonstrates an individual's potential for creativity and his/her mentalization capabilities, M responses may also represent the same potential and capabilities. Sufficient M responses may thus represent an interesting factor in diagnosis, allowing [us] to differentiate between psychic organizations with adequate mentalization capacities from the organizations in which representations and the mental scene are weak. (Chabert, 1983, p. 138)

As with the creative dimension reflected by the elaborate approach to understanding and by M responses, the affective dimension may also play a role in the *thickness* of thought. This may particularly be reflected by sensory determinants insofar as the responses they characterize do not exclusively involve perceptive behavior, clearly revealing the need for the simultaneous analysis of contents. This is the only condition that enables an analysis from an economic perspective to situate affects with respect to representations; the notion of "small quantities" or the "right distance" – that is, excluding extreme absence or invasion – is at the very heart of the thought process. Regarding affective expression, there is still a need to focus on identifying how depression is expressed. Depression attests to some form of mental activity involving positive symptomatology, involving symptoms that can be seen or heard, an argument that sheds light on the hypothesis of essential depression.

The creative and affective dimensions can thus make it possible to provide more elaborate responses, in varying degrees and to a greater or lesser extent. To some extent, Erlebnistypus (a concept developed by Rorschach to determine the personality type) reflects this richness by accounting for the dual organization of drives – that is, comprising representations and affects.

Lastly, among the most relevant Rorschach indicators used to assess the thickness of the preconscious, the presence of symbolic content reflects consistent mental activity by introducing "mechanisms such as figuration, displacement and condensation" (Chabert, 1987, p. 17) and by respecting the double injunction that the instructions impose on patients.

Instructions along the same lines make it possible to assess the thickness of thought when using the TAT. Once again, the instructions "Look at a picture card then tell a story about it" require participants to bind the conscious and unconscious arrangements which mobilize the latent content of images in one and the same movement. "The 'representations-affects' structure which, by definition, is unorganized like everything else governed by primary processes, may or may not be understood on a preconscious-conscious level in order to be symbolized through language" (Shentoub et al., 1990, p. 29).

Fluidity is a dynamic factor within the preconscious and reflects the movement between different layers of representation – that is, the movement across layers. In this context, the TAT is a highly valuable test. Indeed, the TAT focuses on narrating, and it emphasizes the binding process. Narratives thus reflect different levels of mental functioning and reveal the shift from one level to another.

The first interpretation of the protocol enables a brief assessment of the quality of mental activity: Is it laborious? Easy? Unchanging? Irregular? If so, to what extent? Yet again, simply analyzing this initial approach is far from sufficient. To evaluate intrapsychic circulation, a meticulous analysis of discourse procedures and how they progress seems imperative. I believe that this approach is close to the notion of legibility which introduces *thickness* and *fluidity,* two components that come together and mutually reinforce each other through effective binding:

Legibility is synonymous with the process of binding when:

- Narratives are invented;
- The implemented procedures are flexible, varied, and sufficiently robust to help in narrative construction;
- The affects associated with the representations seem to be modulated by stimulus variation;
- Phantasmic resonance is associated with the latent evocations of the images. (Shentoub et al., 1990, p. 132; Note: *Phantasmic resonance* refers to when the conscious or unconscious fantasy implicitly expressed by one member of a group leads to the formation of the fantasy among the other members of the group. This metaphoric occurrence turns the initial fantasy into the central concern of the group for a varying period of time.)

Borrowed from André Green (1973), who used the writing metaphor to explain how an analysis session progressed, the notion of legibility has been somewhat abandoned in recent years. Although it no longer appears in the new TAT interpretation manual (Brelet-Foulard & Chabert, 2003), I am convinced that this notion is still relevant.

Between narratives plagued by the weight of essential depression and florid narratives containing the added advantage of pleasure, the pleasure to tell, to create, to show, and so on, fluidity varies widely from one protocol to another. It cannot, however, be assimilated into the narrative style, which can be easy, rich, and even seductive, as opposed to the intrapsychic circulation, which remains highly limited. This fluidity is thus shallow and hardly nurtured by unconscious life. As a result, it cannot adequately permeate psychoanalytic structures. Moreover, where permeability exists, it undoubtedly involves inhibition, which is the expression of unconscious defenses and which, almost paradoxically, alters the formal quality of the narrative.

By introducing the notion of temporality, *permanence* reflects the stability or irregularity of the functional quality of the preconscious. This third characteristic of the preconscious can be assessed by focusing on the changes in the quality of mental activity as the protocols are presented. Do mental mechanisms stand the test of time? Knowing, however, that discontinuity – that is, changes in the quality of thought (abstract, diffluent, operative, etc.) affects us all, what really matters is the resumption of mental functioning at its best. Is this always possible, or do mental mechanisms crumble as they gradually lose their functional value? Do they abruptly yield and let what may be defined as mental blanks – that is, elements associated with essential depression – take center stage?

The notion of *permanence* thus appears to be closely associated with life and death. It has both a diagnostic (quality of mentalization) and a prognostic value. Given this diagnostic and prognostic value, an analysis of TAT Card 16 is fundamental: What can be said of mental functioning when no image is presented at the end of the psychological assessment? Put differently, to which behavior and manifestations does Card 16 give rise? Which of these are the most consistent and the most intense? I began to reflect on these powerful questions following an experience that still perturbs me to this day. When presented with the blank card, one of my patients made only one gesture: She grasped my upper arm and held onto me. Once again, albeit in an extreme manner, Card 16 revealed the intensity of essential depression: There were no more words; only "nothing" or a "blank" was left. For other patients, Card 16 gave a glimpse of psychic life. It revealed that creativity was possible, even though it could not always be expressed through a story as the given instructions required. It demonstrated nevertheless that mobilizable resources existed. While Card 16 may sometimes appear to propose a shortcut to a patient's mental functioning – the content of the "narrative," the quality of mentalization – that experience taught me the extent to which projective tools can reveal possible mental activity that psychosomatic consultation is not always able to detect. It appears as though the expression of potential resources for a "more psychic tomorrow" could emerge from today's projective situation. This tomorrow may be just around the corner if we provide the necessary resources to help patients along this path.

A broad scope of research around the notion of psychosomatic economy has now developed at the crossroads of projective methodology and psychosomatic therapy. This notion concerns all individuals without exception. Psychic activity that is determined by the functional quality of the preconscious is undeniably involved in this economy.

The preconscious may be described as a space or an area in which the psyche undergoes transition. It can also de defined in terms of *regressive thickness* – that is, in terms of its ability to contain and stimulate both regredient and progredient psychic oscillations. When questioned in the light of psychosomatic economy and its infinite modulations, people's ability to "play" paves the way for new research avenues such as tolerance to regression as a determinant factor that may help alleviate disorganizing "splits."

Subsequently, building on the studies of patients with corporeal symptomatology, some clinical psychologists are currently analyzing how the oscillations between passive and active positions may provide indicators for the psychic treatment of somatic precariousness (this mainly involves the team of projective psychologists from the University Paris 13, who have worked alongside their colleagues from the University of Istanbul. This undoubtedly provides an opportunity to build on Debray's studies on the challenges of accessing the passive position (Debray, 1992, 1999), as she described them following her clinical observations of mothers and their babies. These involved observing the psychosomatic economy of the babies for whom the consultation was sought, and naturally, that of the mother–baby dyad and even of the father–mother–baby triad (Belot & Debray, 2008).

Rosine might be gone, but she continues to make us think. For this, many of us remain deeply grateful.

Acknowledgments

This chapter was originally published in French and is reprinted here in English with permission: Pheulpin, M. (2014). L'économie psychosomatique, une notion chère à Rosine Debray. *Psychologie clinique et projective, 20*(1), 167–180. https://doi.org/10.3917/pcp.020.0167 © Erès Editions.

References

Belot, R.-A., & Debray, R. (2008). *La psychosomatique du bébé* [The psychosomatics of the baby]. Paris, France: PUF.

Brelet-Foulard, F., & Chabert, C. (2003). *Nouveau manuel du TAT: Approche psychanalytique* [New manual of the TAT: Psychoanalytical approach]. Paris, France: Dunod.

Chabert, C. (1983). *Le Rorschach en clinique adulte: Interprétation psychanalytique* [Rorschach test in clinical psychology of the adult: Psychoanalytical interpretation]. Paris, France: Dunod.

Chabert, C. (1987). *La psychopathologie à l'épreuve du Rorschach* [Psychopathology and Rorschach Test]. Paris, France: Dunod.

Debray, R. (1973). *L'interprétation psychanalytique du TAT: Contribution à une théorie des critères diagnostiques* [The psychoanalytical interpretation of the TAT: Contribution to a theory of the diagnostic criteria] (Unpublished doctoral dissertation). University Paris Descartes, Paris, France.

Debray, R. (1980). *L'organisation mentale des diabétiques insulino-dépendants: Recherche sur l'économie psychosomatique* [The mental organization of the insulin-dependent diabetics: Research on the psychosomatic economy] (Unpublished doctoral dissertation). René Descartes University, Paris, France.

Debray, R. (1983). *L'équilibre psychosomatique: Organisation mentale des diabétiques* [The psychosomatic balance: Mental organization of the diabetics]. Paris, France: Dunod.

Debray, R. (1992). Aléas de l'accès à la position passive ou les vicissitudes de la pulsion d'emprise [Uncertainties of the access to the passive position or the vicissitudes of the drive of influence]. *Revue française de psychanalyse, 56*(5), 1441–1444.

Debray, R. (1996). *Clinique de l'expression somatique: Psychanalyse des liens psyché-soma*. [Clinical study of somatic expression: Psychoanalysis of the links psyche–soma]. Lausanne, Switzerland: Delachaux et Niestlé.

Debray, R. (1997). TAT et économie psychosomatique: Un bilan actuel [TAT and psychosomatic economy: A current involvement]. *Psychologie clinique et projective, 3,* 19–37.

Debray, R. (1999). Aléas de l'accès à la position passive [Uncertainties of the access to the passive position]. *Revue française de psychanalyse, 63*(5), 1785–1788. http://doi.org/10.3917/rfp.g1999.63n3.1785

Green, A. (1973). *Le discours vivant* [The lively speech]. Paris, France: PUF.

Marty, P. (1976). *Les mouvements individuels de vie et de mort: Essai d'économie psychosomatique* [The individual movements of life and death: Essay on psychosomatic economy] (Vol. 1). Paris, France: Payot.

Marty, P. (1980). *L'ordre psychosomatique: Les mouvements individuels de vie et de mort. Essai d'économie psychosomatique* [The psychosomatic order: The individual movements of life and death: Essay on psychosomatic economy] (Vol. 2). Paris, France: Payot.

Marty, P., de M'Uzan, M., & David, C. (1963). *L'investigation psychosomatique: Sept observations cliniques* [The psychosomatic investigation: Seven clinical observations]. Paris, France: PUF.

Pheulpin, M.-C. (1993). *Asthmologie: Un regard de psychologue clinicienne* [Research on asthma: The look of a psychologist clinician] (Unpublished doctoral dissertation). University Paris Descartes, Paris, France.

Pheulpin, M.-C. (2001). L'investigation psychosomatique approfondie: Intérêts diagnostique et pronostique des épreuves projectives [The in-depth psychosomatic investigation: Diagnostic and prognostic relevance of projective methods]. In E. Ferragut (Ed.), *Psychopathologie de la douleur. Évaluation, thérapies, prévention* (pp. 93–104). Paris, France: Masson.

Pheulpin, M.-C. (2013). *Adultes en détresse: De l'expérience du corps à la scène psychique* [Adults in distress: From the experience of the body to the psychic scene] (Unpublished thesis for habilitation to supervise research). University Paris Descartes, Paris, France.

Pheulpin, M.-C., Baudin, M., & Bruguière, P. (2017). *Clinique des états du corps: Approche psychanalytique et projective* [Clinical study of conditions of the human body: Psychoanalytical and projective approach]. Paris, France: Dunod.

Rausch de Traubenberg, N. (1965). *Implications psychologiques des cardiopathies congénitales: Effet des interventions correctrices* [Psychological implications of congenital heart diseases: Effect of the corrective interventions] (Unpublished doctoral dissertation). University of Paris, Paris, France.

Shentoub, V., & Debray, R. (1970–1971). Fondements théoriques du processus-TAT. [Theoretical fundamentals of the TAT process]. *Bulletin de psychologie, 24*(292/12-15), 897–903.

Shentoub, V., & Debray, R. (1978–1979). Que faire d'une excessive richesse fantasmatique ? Interprétation d'un protocole inhabituel de TAT [How to deal with excessive phantasmic richness? Interpretation of an unusual TAT protocol]. *Bulletin de psychologie, 32*(339/3-7), 309–322.

Shentoub, V., et al. (1990). *Manuel d'utilisation du TAT: Approche psychanalytique* [Manual of the TAT: Psychoanalytical approach]. Paris, France: Dunod.

Smadja, C. (2010). Introduction au concept d'économie psychosomatique [Introduction in the concept of psychosomatic economy]. *Revue française de psychosomatique, 1*(37), 9–15. http://doi.org/10.3917/rfps.037.0009

13

Mentalization and Projective Methods

Training and Research in Psychoanalysis-Oriented Clinical Psychology, Using the TAT Scoring Grid Developed by Rosine Debray

Marie-Frédérique Bacqué

From Psychodiagnosis to Clinical Research

Both the TAT and the Rorschach are projective methods that are used worldwide. They enable a diagnosis of the mental organization of an individual with, particularly in France, psychoanalysis-oriented training and interpretation. However, far from being confined to this global approach, the TAT provides very specific information on the mentalization nature of the person, as defined by Rosine Debray, "a mental work involving tolerance to intra-psychic anxiety, depression, intra-psychic and interpersonal conflicts." Debray did not settle for developing, together with Vica Shentoub and the research team in projective psychology of University Paris 5 (today Université de Paris), new and more appropriate scoring grids for studies on mentalization (Debray, 1987, revised in 1996), which was a concept from the Psychosomatic School of Paris. She used those grids for training psychologists in psychoanalytic clinical practice. Along the same lines, the TAT scoring grid was highly relevant to other collected materials in the framework of research: When clinical interviews are transcribed and analyzed as in texts from the TAT protocol, they provide an equally efficient study of mentalization. For psychoanalytic clinical practice, imaginative abilities that are stimulated by the latent content of the cards, knowledge of defense processes, assessment of possibilities to identify ego functions, and legibility of discourse are valid and reliable pointers, both in preliminary diagnostic and prognostic interviews and in the analytic therapy that would ensue. In psychoanalytic research, the TAT scoring method enables a diagnosis of the mentalization capacity of patients, which may be confronted with the validation attempts of neuroscience in the case of empathy deficit and social cognition deficit in autistic or schizophrenic patients.

Psychoanalytic Interpretation of Projective Methods: A Link Between Psychology and Psychoanalysis

Debray was fully committed as a psychologist and psychoanalyst. She always accepted her "two jobs" along with two others: teacher and researcher. As a psychologist, she had a passion for projective methods and did not hesitate to support the psychoanalytic approach of administration and interpretation when influential psychoanalysts in key university positions were opposed to it. As a psychoanalyst, she always supported projective methods, although she was initially dedicated to psychosomatic clinical practice, as well as to psychology of somatic patients and to psychosomatic balance in adults, as she was thinking that the first balance in life was that of the mother–baby dyad.

Today, the psychoanalytic approach using projective methods is the main specialty of the Laboratory of Clinical Psychology and Psychopathology in the Psychology Institute of University Paris 5 (now University Paris Descartes). But before gaining its international reputation, there was a struggle between those who supported confining projective methods to cognitive processes and those who viewed tests as part of applied psychoanalysis. This disagreement arose from the idea that tests should be reserved for psychoanalysts, and they should not be passed on to nonanalyzing psychologists. In 1983, the first seminal work of Catherine Chabert was in favor of training in psychoanalytic clinical practice for psychologists who do not necessarily have experience as psychoanalysts, but who are, however, able to use Freudian metapsychology in the interpretation of projective procedures (Chabert, 1983).

Debray precisely recognized (Debray, 2002) that she lived in the golden age of psychoanalysis in France. She was, then, fully committed to the psychoanalytic interpretation of projective procedures. On her retirement, she felt some bitterness in the history of the psychoanalytic movement to which she belonged, which was no longer institutionally rewarding or gratifying enough in her view. She turned her strong interest in human relations to her loved ones and to the future of her students and patients.

Passion for the Projective Methods Shared By Vica Shentoub and Rosine Debray

The outstanding relationship between Rosine Debray and Vica Shentoub was based on a shared passion for the projective methods. Their joint achievements abounded between 1969 and 1978, then Debray published on her own, from her postgraduate thesis (Debray, 1973), which was specifically on the psychoanalytic interpretation of the TAT, to her dissertation for a doctorate of state on mental organization in diabetic patients (Debray, 1983). Initially, Shentoub was undoubtedly the main force behind their joint efforts, due to her personality, her Anglo-Saxon and French culture, her experiences in World War II, her shared view with her husband Salem Shentoub (from 1953) regarding the TAT tool, and lastly, her capacity to fight a multifront adversity: Some academics and analysts were not keen on the mix of views that would turn a tool with an analytic instruction into an approach to making a diagnosis of the substantive mental organization of an individual and of their current defenses.

Debray was my thesis director from 1986 to 1989. As a student in clinical psychology, I met her through her teachings on psychology of somatic patients, on projective methods, and particularly on the Rey Complex Figure Test. Then as a teacher–researcher myself, I met her on a regular basis through her teaching for the DESS (equivalent to the current master's degree) in clinical psychology, her direction of the educational psychology diploma program, and within the framework of the psychosomatic approach to young and older patients. At IPSO (Instiut de Psychosomatique at the time) where her mother–baby consultations took place, I would see her at her seminars, while I was receiving training in working with adults and children. When a group of young psychoanalysts went to Armenia (originally in the Soviet Union) within the context of the IPSO–Médecins du Monde (Doctors of the World) association, I was able, together with my colleagues Malika Merzougui and Claire Lamblin, to consult with her on a regular basis regarding our activities there (Bacqué, 1990). On the day of my *viva voce*, she suggested that I had interesting-enough additional experience to publish in the *Journal de psychanalyse de l'enfant*. Although I was a senior lecturer in Lille University, I continued meeting with her on a regular basis; I attended thesis examination committees, conferences, and informal meetings, in which we discussed analytical practice and analytical schools.

Personality of Rosine Debray

First, to paraphrase Marie NDiaye, Rosine Debray was a "powerful woman" (Ndiaye, 2009). This was visible in her size and her athletic proportions, her orderly blond hair, her way of watching and concentrating on a patient, and initially remaining in a "smiling" silence that displayed her enjoyment in thinking. An encounter with this woman, who was generally dressed in orange-yellow pantsuits, triggered a tonic alertness that stimulated interaction. At the doctorate level, interactions were always productive, even when a colleague would express herself, because Debray had an infectious passion for listening to others. One could really perceive and find oneself reproducing the intensity of her attentiveness. All of her doctoral students were well suited to do so; there was a good atmosphere in the alternate Saturday morning meetings, when we shared our progress. From a common identification with the professor, the senior practitioner, the professional guide, I retain a sense of enjoyment in psychoanalytic practice and research. Later, I learned to free myself from student inhibitions to develop a relationship in which admiration would no longer get in the way of creativity. We freely and more profoundly discussed psychoanalysis. We often spoke about the challenges in reconciling a "free" or responsible practice, although in constant learning with institutional requirements. The language of Debray was adorned with words that I believe revealed her major work themes and personality. What topics would often come up in conversations with her?

- Dynamism (process, vigorous, lively, mental reanimation);
- Regulation (balance, progression, regression, mentalization);
- Explosive conjunction (excitement, conflicts, discharge, astonishment);
- Phantasmic richness (fantasy, florid, gift, brilliant).

The selection of this vocabulary was not based on random occurrences; It really represented the author and her thoughts.

Dynamics of Mental Organization

In the way she appeared, Debray embodied dynamism. Her physical aspect, her vigilant listening, and her deepest desire to be an analyst consistently showed her personal application of her theses. What could be more demonstrative than this ability to meet others in their absolute originality with such ethical fairness that encouraged transference, a unique transference for each person?

Needless to say, for Debray, instinctual movements underlie relationships, whereas mental stagnancy and immobility lead to a growing morbidity in life. We often discussed this with regard to the interpretation of M responses in the Rorschach and lability in the TAT. Debray believed that the eroticization of a relationship should be appreciated as a "lively" quality demonstrating potential libidinal investments. Problems begin when these investments face anxiety, depression, or desire for fusional absorption.

The well-known title of her 1987 book *The Rebelling Babies/Mothers* reveals a permanent remodeling of the dyad, based on the organizations of the two protagonists, but more importantly, based on the introduction of the analyst as a third party. Debray deeply connected with the twosome who sometimes consulted her only once. She instilled a natural exchange while listening to the mother and keeping an eye on the baby. As the ear of the mother and the attention of the baby, she verbalized the interpretation to the mother and the baby. For example, Anne who had experienced primary insomnia at 15 months: "Mom's eyes are closed when mom is sleeping, and Anne wants mom to keep her eyes open to take care of her" (Debray, 1987, p. 58). For Alban – almost 3 years old – who repeated the words of his father, Rosine recast his words: "You say mental shock, very good ..." (2001, p. 95).

From First Clinical Impressions to the Study of Mentalization: A Real-Life Training for Clinical Psychologists

I have always thought that such clinical practice, which combines precise listening, a good therapeutic alliance, and accurate interpretation, is in total continuity with the study of projective methods – particularly, with what Debray added to the TAT scoring grids, involving overall clinical impressions of a protocol.

In 1986, then in 1989 (revised in 1996 and introduced by Catherine Azoulay in 2002 with the other TAT grids; Azoulay, 2002), a very targeted analysis of the processes used was preceded by a great deal of emphasis on the subjective and thus transferential impressions of the clinician. This was totally new. The first clinicians were discreet about their transferential feelings. It was indeed the psychoanalyst expressing herself in Debray. This preliminary work had already enabled the establishment of hypotheses on mental functioning, which could be subsequently validated or invalidated by the methodical scoring of discourse processes. Transference running during the test was directly probed in the part titled clinical feelings and revealed to the consciousness of the clinician (Lisbeth von Benedek was severely critical of this in her 1989 thesis: The majority of encountered analysts keep a syncretic vision of their countertransference; Von Benedek, 1989). Moreover, the mentalization abilities were also assessed by the clinician, because this involved responding to the question, is there any identifiable mental work in connection with tolerance to intra-psychic anxiety, with depression and with intra-psychic and inter-personal conflicts?

The participation of Debray in the elaboration of the TAT scoring grid explicitly outlined the link between the resulting text in the TAT and the therapeutic interpretation in analytical psychotherapy, perhaps in the treatment.

TAT is actually a tool which was developed by Murray in 1935 and which was initially used in industrial psychology. This tool, which Vica and Salem Shentoub and subsequently Debray transformed, is a typical psychoanalytic tool: It is constantly "at work," elaborating, and takes into account the different transferences (patient/clinician/patient, patient/TAT, clinician/TAT), enables a diagnosis that is most closely related to the mental functioning of the patient, and lastly, assesses mentalization resources for a possible psychotherapeutic change.

In Debray's scoring grid, the revisited dynamic viewpoint was against a "cross-section" of the psyche. The TAT-created narrative was no longer just "considered as a mainly cognitive product indicating neutralized energy and mature affects within a perspective where adaptation to reality is decisive, along with the '*self-serving regression*' which enables a controlled imaginary activity" (Shentoub & Debray, 1970–1971). Yet, beyond the diagnostic, all TAT-created narratives enable a prognostic of therapeutic resources within a person.

Thus, beyond the diagnostic purpose, the second TAT dynamic contribution that was raised through the scoring grid that Debray developed was aimed at training clinicians in analytical psychotherapy, perhaps in psychoanalysis. By raising in-depth questions about their first impressions, clinicians gradually developed self-confidence and learned to permanently question their diagnoses and their prognoses. This reached the point where the TAT scoring grid that Debray elaborated became a model that could be exported to the Rorschach analysis, to clinical research interviews, and to psychologists' training. From my perspective, the approach of Debray to projective methods was so fully in line with what Michael Balint called "training-cum-research" (Balint, 1957) – involving groups working on cases – that projective methods would be to clinical psychologists what Balint's training-cum-research groups were to general practitioners.

Regulation of Mental Functioning

The personal attitude of Debray perfectly represented her vision of preconscious permanent functioning, according to the first topic of Freud. One of the greatest contributions of the TAT is the detection of the ability to filter attacks on the self in cases of internal or interpersonal conflict. Each TAT card reactivates a universal conflict in participants asked to tell a story. Rigidity, lability, inhibition, behavioral acting-out, or inability to cope with excessive fantasy, are to be grouped as frequent or exceptional modalities of mental functioning. Debray viewed this process from a structured psychopathological perspective that was related to the contribution of psychosomatics: Defensive modalities may be either organized as phobic reactions (to objects with a known symbolic) or eroticized, leading to a failed repression. They may even need compulsive repetitions, or may even lead to the construction of neoreality. In these cases, such an organization joins that of neuroses or frank psychoses.

Yet when defenses are not organized, a dilution decreases their efficiency and lets anxiety invade the person. The person may lose control of reality by putting up the same invariable and dim defenses to internal and external phenomena. Reality may also be literally taken for what it is: Actions and facts take the place of the imaginary, filling the thinking apparatus. The case of depression, a polysemic term as if there were a depression symptom and a depression personality, is entirely typical of this variability.

This is why Debray mainly focused on the mentalization of depression. Essential depression is a depression that is not mentalized, leading to a hemorrhage of word representations that are cut off from affects, the affects being only expressed on the behavioral and somatic levels. Grieving first love objects is the root of mentalization (Bacqué, 2008). In my thesis on the failure to grieve, it was striking how the ability to mentalize was a clear advantage when those who were confronted with serious illness were able to find resources through object investment of the loved ones, or in a release through sublimation activities. However, difficulty in developing affects of guilt, of autodepreciation, and of anything falling within the depressive symptomatology went hand in hand with a defensive weakness, leading to moments of massive anxiety or mental void that projective methods could detect (Bacqué, 1992). I could definitely see how regular psychiatric scales of depression and anxiety (like the Zigmond and Snaith or Hamilton scales) did not absolutely take into account the absence of defense.

Only projective methods, and particularly the scoring grid for the TAT of Debray, were able to recognize that the absence of defenses and symptoms did not certify the quality of the mental functioning of a patient, but rather what Americans would call alexithymia (De Tychey et al., 2010) – that is, the inability to identify and put words to the subjective experience within oneself.

In the assessment of the organization of defenses, Debray introduced the psychosomatic classification of Pierre Marty (1990). Indeed, regulation leads to balance although discontinuity in mental functioning is a lifetime rule. However, although Debray mentioned this point, she stressed that it is the overflowing of the psychic apparatus that leads patients to serious, perhaps lethal, disorganizations (Debray, 1991).

"Explosive Conjunctions"

Debray often used the expression *explosive conjunctions*. This refers to a series of factors that could at any moment tip the psychosomatic balance into a "threatening" crisis for the patient. These crises that evoke *decompensation,* a concept of Bergeret, were visible with the TAT cards, which from my perspective were the most psychosomatic cards – that is, the cards that led to regression. Cards 11, 16, and 19 were particularly anticipated for our case studies: How can patients use their deepest resources, the earliest resources of their mental development, to build a narrative from blurred, disturbing, empty, or almost empty, contents. This was when scenarios of mediocre legibility appeared with rough representations, in which depression surfaced in a vacuum aspiration form instead of a sadness or self-incrimination form.

The explosive conjunction showed the fragility of mentalization. However, behind the weak linking of object representations and words, it was also the availability of these representations that seemed to be blocked by events, leading the mental functioning to pay dearly for its absence of fluidity. The reminder of any previous nonelaborated conflicts through confrontation with TAT cards pointed to the occurrence of such explosive conjunctions, due to a lack of mentalization. Similarly, for certain cards (particularly for Card 16), the impossibility of answering the instruction revealed the absence of mental resources when facing the explosive conjunction.

This was one of my thesis conclusions in 1989 (Bacqué, 1989). The major issue of mental etiology of somatic disorders needed to be reexamined. Stating that cancer, asthma, or diabetes is psyche-borne was far more than controversial. Numerous articles from the Chicago School and from psychosomatics practitioners in the 1950s needed to be questioned. As a matter of fact, all of these studies on the personality of somatic disorders were retrospective, and they only demonstrated the mental effects of the disease. Thus, one of my thesis conclusions dealt with the effects of the crisis, as an explosive storm in the body of leukemia patients, on their psyche (Bacqué, 1989). Not all patients reacted the same way; although well-mentalized patients could perceive the destructive effects of the threat of death associated with illness and treatments, their libidinal investment capacities were a significant support for their narcissistic injury. In her book *Epistle to Those Who Somatize*, Debray took up the issue of patients who were unconsciously calling to a loved one, a doctor, or a therapist for help through a somatic symptom (Debray, 2001). Counterintuitively, she argued, "Far from paring the somatic expression to a simple fragility, a deficiency or even a deficit, which may however be the case, it may be a richness that enables immediate discharge of excess excitement, subsequently supporting re-organization" (Debray, 2001, p. 33). In contrast, others considered narcissistic injury an irreversible damage with no somatic, behavioral, or mental escape; during the TAT session, they were still unable to rely on the material bonding, and even less could they create the relationship when it was missing from the manifest content in the card.

Protective Phantasmic Richness

A distinguishing feature of the manifest content in the TAT is that it allows patients to think of it a priori as an out-of-date set of images to comment on. However, just after thinking this (or expressing it as a criticism of the material or the situation), the depth of the task becomes obvious to the participant. Identifying with the character in Card 1 (a boy who is caught up in a more or less intense inner reflection in front of an adult object) is not all there is to it, because the time dimension in this card (symbolically perceptible through different plans in the drawing and through the dream-like atmosphere in which the boy is "floating") calls for a clear response with respect to this boy. Regression is not simple, particularly with this first card.

An ordinary description that could lead to a sense of absurdity may then be taken over by a dive into an imaginary world. However, available representations must meet latent affects from the oedipal conflict. While fantasies surface in one form or another, the ability to spontaneously link them with an energy that is slaked with the pleasure of building a coherent content (to "round the story out" as Vica Shentoub would say) will enable its author to follow the "not so puerile" instruction ("tell a story from this card" often brings youth activities to mind).

The possible *excessive phantasmic richness* illustrated the use of an overflowing imagination (Shentoub & Debray, 1978). Christophe Dejours (quoted by De Tychey et al., 1991) distinguished himself among certain psychosomatic practitioners by stating that mentalization is "an activity that is regulated by the self, since it necessarily involves a neurotic mental functioning that reflects the ability to mobilize fantasies and to process the solicited drives while staying in touch with the external reality" (De Tychey et al., 1991, p. 48). This contribution shows that delusional productions in which primary processes hinder legibility cannot qualify as mentalization. A familiar example is the obvious irregular mentalization in our oneiric productions. Sensorial nightmare productions are even less mentalized, and fully dismantled links between affects and representations awaken the sleeper. However, in certain dreams, the lack of mentalization may lead to unconscious reorganizations that enable recreation of new associations of ideas.

Bergeret took up this issue, considering that mentalization is "the mental use of imagination," but this does not mean that it is a resolved issue with respect to the latest mentalization approaches. Fonagy (1991) stated that "thinking about thinking" relates mentalization to a metacognition aptitude, whereas Lecours and Bouchard defined mentalization as a mental elaboration process: "We propose to explain mentalization in reference to a general category of mental operations including representation and symbolization, particularly leading to transformation and elaboration of instinctual experiences into mental phenomena and increasingly organized structures" (Lecours & Bouchard, 1997, p. 858). In their opinion, mentalization is essential for modulation and tolerance of affects, serving as a veritable "immune system of the psyche." This idea is reinforced by the fact that mentalization is not an all-or-none phenomenon but rather "a continuous process, a permanent transformation of mental contents through multiplication and organization of representations" (Lecours & Bouchard, 1997, p. 858).

Is Mentalization But a Thought?

Debray would not have appreciated the way the concept of *mentalization* is evolving. While the Freudian definition (without Freud giving it this name) had numerous applications in theoretical and clinical psychoanalysis (De Tychey et al., 2000), it was taken up by the neurosciences with impoverishing criteria: making it a conscious process of social cognition along the lines of the mind theory.

Although new theoretical approaches stemmed from psychoanalysts (Peter Fonagy is a psychoanalysis professor at the Freud Memorial and head of the department of Health Clinical Psychology at University College London), they define mentalization from a conscious perspective. Mentalization emerges from intersubjectivity: "The Self develops through self-perception, thinking and feeling in the mind of another person" (Fonagy, 1991). Thus, "mentalizing depends on being mentalized" (which we subscribe to, with respect to the development of babies), and it primarily relates to a conscious phenomenon ("self-awareness is necessary to self-regulation, mentalizing is seeing yourself from the outside and others from the inside"; Fonagy, 1991). As Allen, Fonagy, and Bateman (2008) pointed out, mentalization refers to both empathy and insight, it could be based on the function of mirror neurons, being very irregular in those with borderline personality disorder and mainly lacking in patients with autism.

In his numerous publications, Fonagy developed *mentalization-based treatment* (MBT) to increase the capacity for mentalization in order to improve the regulation of affects and interpersonal relationships of patients with borderline personality disorder. However, what about daydreaming, free associations, and more precisely, the preconscious function of mentalization ahead of consciousness that enables the junction between affects and representations? Debray, like most psychosomatics practitioners would certainly be surprised if it were possible to learn mentalization through psychoeducation. When comparing the teachings of all of the clinically trained projective practitioners at the University Paris Descartes (today Université de Paris), we are convinced that mental functioning develops continuously through the ebb and flow of mentalization. Analytical psychotherapy enables a progressive deconstruction of certain pathogenic processes in a context within which transference can be established thanks to the faith of patients in the therapist (Cannone et al., 2012). It is in the course of such mental work that mentalization can deploy all of its dimensions (thickness of representation layers, availability and fluidity of their circulation, and permanent filtering of emotions and affects).

Conclusion

In this short overview, one might conclude that psychoanalytical theory enabled Freud (1915/2001, 1926/2001) and the majority of psychoanalysts to finely describe the clinical processes of mentalization. In the context of the theory of anxiety, the first and second topics of Freud established a model for how some people could or could not transform the energy of the psyche into thought or somatic or motor expression. Just as psychoanalytic instruction is based on free associations, the possibility of *saying what it could be* with the Rorschach and of *telling a story* with the TAT enabled, in a more restricted framework (the test period), the collection of personal evocations of a predetermined theme. Thus, projective methods serve as a preferred "container" of imaginative productions, which are representative of the mentalization possibilities of the person. From 1978, Debray added factual processes into the scoring grid to show that mental clinging to the manifest content in a card demonstrates a representation weakness or a locked expression, this being for emotional reasons. She pursued her contributions for educational and research purposes. By adding a preamble regarding "the first, overall impression of the protocol" to the 1989 scoring grid, she enabled young clinicians to develop both confidence in their diagnostic skills and self-knowledge through the investigation of their countertransference toward patients and the testing situation.

By adding the *assessment of mental functioning modalities*, which enables listing the *dominant defensive modalities* and proposing a *hypothesis on structural organization,* she enabled clinicians to take an in-depth look into a major concept of psychoanalysis-oriented psychopathology – that is, the concept of mentalization. While we note that the notion of mentalization that Debray developed does not correspond to the one that has seemed to prevail internationally since 2000, we consider that the unconscious aspects of mentalization are the ones that psychoanalytical work will reveal, ahead of mentalization, which becomes more or less conscious in the course of, or after, analysis.

Debray fundamentally studied the psychosomatic balance of an individual over the course of their life. Her unitary approach even extended to the mother–baby dyad, then to the father–mother–baby triad. Using the TAT, in collaboration with the team at University Paris 5, she developed a psychoanalytic method to observe psychopathological functioning when dealing with universal conflicts. Her scoring grid, which she completed based on that of Vica Shentoub, enabled a great deal of research on mentalization, but further, it could become a diagnostic and prognostic tool when included in the clinical practice of preliminary interviews and psychoanalytical psychotherapies.

Acknowledgments

This chapter was originally published in French and is reprinted here in English with permission: Bacqué, M. (2014). Méthodes projectives et mentalisation: formation et recherche en psychologie clinique psychanalytique avec la fiche de dépouillement du tat de Rosine Debray. *Psychologie clinique et projective, 20*(1), 181–197. https://doi.org/10.3917/pcp.020.0181 © Erès Editions.

References

Allen, J. G., Fonagy, P., & Bateman, A. W. (2008). *Mentalizing in clinical practice.* Arlington, VA: American Psychiatric Publishing.

Azoulay, C. (2002). La feuille de dépouillement du TAT: Des origines à nos jours [The TAT scoring grid: From its beginnings until the present]. *Psychologie clinique et projective, 8,* 21–59. http://doi.org/10.3917/pcp.008.0021

Bacqué, M.-F. (1989). *Perte d'objet et lutte anti-dépressive: Inscription dans le corps de la faillite du travail de deuil* [Object loss and antidepressive struggle: An inclusion in the body of the failure of mourning grief] (Unpublished doctoral dissertation under the direction of Prof. R. Debray). University Paris Descartes, Paris, France.

Bacqué, M.-F. (1990). L'enfant arménien: Capacités de réorganisation à la suite de pertes multiples [The Armenian child: Mental reorganization following multiple losses]. *Journal de la psychanalyse de l'enfant, 9,* 165–176.

Bacqué, M.-F. (1992). Mentalisation de la dépression au Rorschach et au TAT: Comparaison dans le cadre d'une maladie somatique grave et d'un épisode dépressif majeur [Mentalization of depression in Rorschach and in TAT: Comparison between serious somatic disease and major depressive episode]. *Bulletin de la Société du Rorschach et des méthodes projectives de langue française, 36,* 77–92. http://doi.org/10.3406/clini.1992.1002

Bacqué, M.-F. (2008). Des séparations aux deuils, place de l'aptitude à la séparation comme organisateur psychique [From separating to grief, place of the separating ability as a psychic organizer]. *Dialogue, 180,* 23–38. http://doi.org/10.3917/dia.180.0023

Balint, M. (1957). *The doctor, his patient and the illness*. London, UK: Pitman.

Cannone, P., Grimaldi, M.-A., Bert, A.-L., & Bacqué, M.-F. (2012). Proposition d'une méthode d'évaluation de l'entretien psycho-dynamique: Analyse approfondie d'une étude de cas en oncologie [Proposal of an assessment method of the psychodynamic interview: detailed analysis of a case study in oncology]. *L'evolution psychiatrique, 77*(3), 418–432. http://doi.org/10.1016/j.evopsy.2012.03.003

Chabert, C. (1983). *Le Rorschach en clinique adulte: Interprétation psychanalytique* [The Rorschach Test in clinical work with adults: Psychoanalytic interpretation]. Paris, France: Dunod.

Debray, R. (1973). *L'interprétation psychanalytique du TAT. Contribution à une théorie des critères diagnostiques* [The psychoanalytical interpretation of the TAT. Contribution to a theory of the diagnostic criteria] (Unpublished doctoral dissertation). Université Paris Descartes, Paris, France.

Debray, R. (1983). *L'équilibre psychosomatique: organisation mentale des diabétiques* [The psychosomatic balance: The mental organization of diabetics]. Paris, France: Dunod.

Debray, R. (1987). *Bébés/mères en révolte* [The rebelling babies/mothers]. Paris, France: Paidos/Le Centurion.

Debray, R. (1991). Réflexions actuelles sur le développement psychique des bébés et le point de vue psychosomatique [Current reflections on babies psychological development and the psychosomatic vision]. *Revue française de psychosomatique, 5,* 27–37.

Debray, R. (2001). *Épître à ceux qui somatisent* [Epistle to those who somatize]. Paris, France: PUF. http://doi.org/10.3917/puf.bonn.2001.01

Debray, R. (2002). Témoignage: Mes années 70 avec Vica. [Testimony: My 70s with Vica]. *Psychologie clinique et projective, 8,* 11–19. http://doi.org/10.3917/pcp.008.0011

de Tychey, C., Diwo, R., & Dollander, M. (2000). La mentalisation: Approche théorique et clinique projective à travers le test de Rorschach [Mentalization: Theoretical and clinical approach in Rorschach Test]. *Bulletin de psychologie, 448,* 469–480.

de Tychey, C., Garnier, S., Lighezzolo, J., Claudon, P., & Rebourg-Roesler, C. (2010). An accumulation of negative life events and the construction of alexithymia: A longitudinal approach. *Journal of Personality Assessment, 92*(3), 189–206. http://doi.org/10.1080/00223891003670125

de Tychey, C., Rebourg, C., & Vivot, M. (1991). Étude comparée des conceptions de l'imaginaire et de la mentalisation: Réflexions sur leur opérationnalisation au test de Rorschach [Comparative study of the conception of the imaginary world and of the mentalization: Reflection on their operationalization in Rorschach Test]. *Bulletin de la Société du Rorschach et des méthodes projectives de langue française, 35,* 45–66. http://doi.org/10.3406/clini.1991.958

Fonagy, P. (1991). Thinking about thinking: Some clinical and theoretical considerations in the treatment of a borderline patient. *International Journal of Psychoanalysis, 72,* 639–656.

Freud, S. (1915/2001). Papers on metapsychology. In J. Strachey (Ed. & Trans.), *The standard edition of the complete psychological works of Sigmund Freud* (Vol. 14, pp. 105–259). London, UK: Vintage Classics. (Original work published in 1915)

Freud, S. (1926/2001). Inhibitions, symptoms and anxiety. In J. Strachey (Ed. & Trans.), *The standard edition of the complete psychological works of Sigmund Freud* (Vol. 20, pp. 75–174). London, UK: Vintage Classics. (Original work published in 1926)

Lecours, S., & Bouchard, M.A. (1997). Dimensions of mentalisation: Outlining levels of psychic transformation. *International Journal of Psychoanalysis, 78,* 855–875.

Marty, P. (1990). *La psychosomatique de l'adulte* [Psychosomatic of adult]. Paris, France: PUF.

Ndiaye, M. (2009). *Trois femmes puissantes* [Three strong women]. Paris, France: Gallimard.

Shentoub, V., & Debray, R. (1970–1971). Fondements théoriques du processus TAT [Theoretical fundamentals of the TAT process]. *Bulletin de psychologie, 24*(292/12-15), 897–903.

Shentoub, V., & Debray, R. (1978–1979). Que faire d'une excessive richesse fantasmatique? Interprétation d'un protocole inhabituel de TAT [How to deal with excessive phantasmic richness? Interpretation of an unusual TAT protocol]. *Bulletin de psychologie, 32*(339/3-7), 309–322.

Von Benedek, L. (1989). *Le travail mental du psychanalyste* [Mental work of psychoanalyst]. Paris, France: Éditions Universitaires.

14

Changing While Remaining the Same

Self-Representation Confronted With Aging

Benoît Verdon

Freud (1905a/2001) very early on expressed clear pessimism regarding the appropriateness of starting psychoanalysis for people over 50 years of age, because of the lack of plasticity of their mental processes, among other reasons. In 1928, his resistance became even more blatant. Then aged 72 himself, he wrote to Jones: "The young and the old now appear to me as most opposed as regards what the human mental life is capable of. Any understanding between these two age groups is to be dismissed" (Schur, 1975, p. 482). When reading that one could easily be led to conclude that nothing in old age echoes one's former mental life, and that nothing in one's childhood experience is likely to provide any significant remobilization for the experiences inherent to this so-called period of involution. Moreover, when comparing aging and psychosis, Ferenczi stressed that

> when aging, man has a tendency to withdraw the emanations of the libido from the object of his love and to concentrate on his own self the decreasing libidinal interest he still has. Elderly people become narcissistic – in the same way as children – and lose much interest in family and in social events. ... The symptoms of aging may be compared to a rock that emerges when a gulf, cut out from the sea and no longer watered by any river, dries out. (Ferenczi, 1921/1974, pp. 150–151)

This belief in the uniform degeneration of mental functions with increasing age was also fostered by the first conclusions of the research work in projective psychology. Rorschach himself hardly ever proposed to apply his test to elderly adults. Of the four elderly cases presented in *Psychodiagnostic,* only one deals with an 80-year-old woman "mentally well preserved," and the other three are examples of the use of the test in elderly people suffering from brain disorders. Therefore, from this unique protocol, which Rorschach himself admits to having analyzed without prior knowledge of the patient's age, since it had been collected by someone else, his diagnosis proposal was that of "latent or stable schizophrenia." Faced with this contrast between clinical practice and projective assessment, he states simply "that similar cases have reinforced [his] opinion that almost quite identical results are obtained in normal elderly subjects" (Rorschach, 1920/1967, p. 154). Thus, he retained a few signs that supposedly characterize elderly subjects: prevalence of formal responses, and among those, of vague or inappropriate ones, a poor integration of colors and movements, and a prevalence of "animal" responses over more original contents.

In the decades that followed, several studies were carried out to collect information on the effect of age on the Rorschach factors, and they almost uniformly determined a deficiency in cognitive functions, an inability to make full use of one's inner resources, an inconsistency in affective reactivity, a difficulty in establishing relationships with others, and the importance of anxiety and depression. These results, which are in accordance with Rorschach's conclusions, relied on highlighting similar changes in the quantitative data of the summary scores, all of which enhanced the idea of a general degeneration of the mental life in "normal" elderly adults. However, Poitrenaud and Moreaux (1975) and Panek, Wagner, and Kennedy-Zwergel (1983) as well as Hayslip and Lowman (1986) insist that most of these works do not provide truly pertinent information on normal aging. Rather, very often they were carried out among elderly people living in geriatric institutions, and no cognitive assessment was conducted, the sociocultural environment was not taken into consideration, and sometimes the color discrimination ability of these elderly was not checked. Yet, Eisdorfer (1963) showed that the richness of the protocols (as assessed by the number of responses and M responses) collected from 242 adults, aged between 60 and 94 and living at home, seemed to depend more on intellectual level than on age. Several contemporary studies (see also Ames, Metraux, Learned Rodell, & Walker, 1995; Baudin, 2005; Reichlin, 1984; Shimonaka & Nakazato, 1991; Valente-Torre, 1993; Verdon, 2012) have made it possible to moderate the idea of a general degeneration of mental functioning: Using the Exner method, Ferreira Novo and Silva (2002), Mattlar, Carlsson, Forsander, Karppi, and Helenius (1992), Mattlar, Knuts, and Virtanen (1985), and Vázquez and Osuna (2002) demonstrated that the quantitative differences between the protocols of young or elderly adults were in the end not significant.

There were also changes in psychoanalytic practice and theory. Abraham (1920/1973), Bergler (1947), Fenichel (1945), Gitelson (1948/1973), and Jones (1948/1969) soon adopted more moderate viewpoints than Freud's and Ferenczi's. Since the end of the 1970s, mostly in France, Canada, and the US, communications and written analytical papers have written on this matter (Abraham, Kocher, & Goda, 1980; Andreoli & Quartier, 1976; Assoun, 1983; Balbo, 1980, 1982; Balier, 1976, 1979, 1982; Bergeret, 1982; Bianchi, 1978, 1980a, 1980b,

1982a, 1982b, 1983a, 1983b, 1985, 1987, 1989, 1999; Charazac, 1983, 1989, 1998a, 1998b, 2001, 2002, 2005, 2008, 2010; Clerk, 1995; Dedieu-Anglade, 1981; Gagey, 1983, 1989; Guillaumin, 1982; Herfray, 1984; Janin, 1982; Le Gouès, 1984, 1991, 2000; Péruchon, 1987, 1993, 1999; Pollock, 1982; Quinodoz, 1987, 1994, 1997; Simeone, 1988; Verdon, 2003, 2004a, 2004b, 2007a, 2007b, 2011a; Villa, 2010; Wertheimer, 1982). These works have mainly dealt with narcissistic wounds and the predominance of castration anxiety, regression processes, tensions between the ego and the ideal ego, the revival of oedipal conflicts, investment by reliance on the object, and so on. Everyone agrees how important it is not to turn a demographic group into a clinical entity: Each individual age according to their own mental resources and fragilities.

Aging: A Challenge to Narcissism

Aging is a fundamentally difficult experience. Seeing one's body change and become weaker, while facing the social (retirement) and cognitive (memory) consequences of getting older requires us, on the mental level, to deal with loss so as to be able to represent ourselves as changed, as different from before, without suffering from narcissistic wounds that are too violent. Indeed, this a genuine paradox: How to change while remaining the same? How to give up and bring to a close a former state of being, while maintaining one's trophic narcissistic and object cathexes?

By reflecting on the complex links between the body and the psyche, and on the complex dialectics of narcissistic and object cathexes, psychoanalytic theory has conceptualized the libido as "the dynamic manifestation of the sexual instinct in mental life" (Freud, 1922/2001, p. 244). This pertains to the transformation of the somatic sexual tension and its psychological elaboration; it is open to distribution and displacement; it has varied purposes, sources, and objects; and it plays a major role in supporting relational and identifying cathexes (Freud, 1905b/2001; Laplanche & Pontalis, 1967). Although sexual arousal is of course obtained by stimulating the erogenous zones, it is also reached through bodily experiences that are remote from the sexual activity itself (inner or peripheral feelings) and "from ideas – that is, from memory traces – therefore also by the path of deferred action" (Freud, 1897/2001, p. 269).

The issue of the fate of the libido remains in fact visible in the quality and diversity of one's self-representation, which is closely linked to the relationship with the object. And, as Pontalis puts it, if some ruins offer an overpowering picture of desolation such as those of "a bombed-out, disaster-stricken city, ... a dilapidated district, emptied of its inhabitants, ... or an abandoned construction site" (Pontalis, 1997, p. 126–127), other ruins can engender a sweet melancholy and nostalgia, such as those of a monument whose nobleness is enhanced by "not being what it once was, by having lost, over time, its function and 'raison d'être' and by being still standing, still displaying what made it be" (Pontalis, 1997, p. 126–127). Thus, going through the aging process appears as a psychological experience in which self-representation is particularly challenged by the issue of change: Castration, passivity, flexibility of masculine and feminine identifications, but also porosity of the limits caused by intense narcissistic fragilities, are all likely to become psychological issues of major importance.

The Rorschach Test and Self-Representation: Method

In addition to quantitative research, this chapter describes the diversity of the challenge of self-representation due to aging through the Rorschach Test. The Rorschach is indeed a valuable tool for such an investigation, because it tests the limits both through the diversity of the structural configuration of its cards (compact or scattered, full or hollow, sometimes bilateral) and their sensory configurations (prevalence of black, gray, and white, presence of red or soft colors). In a study by Ishihara (1976), 110 protocols were collected among 50- to 90-year-old men or women, either ordinary people or nonpsychiatric outpatients, all of whom underwent both a medical and a neuropsychological examination to ensure they did not display any cognitive disorder. Also their ability to discriminate colors was checked (Ishihara, 1976).

The method used in the research presented here to understand the representation of the self and the diversity of its forms is a qualitative method that thoroughly studies each protocol (dynamics of the test administration and succession of answers, quality of the discourse, quality of each provided response in reference to the specific symbolism of each card). We paid particular attention to the structural and thematic dimension of the responses – namely, to the formal quality of the form and of the M responses, to the contents, to the human contents, of course (in particular to the popular response to Card III), to the linked sexual identifications, but also to the anatomical responses as well as to the symbolic contents that testified to a possible change in the representation of the body (animal, object, plant), and to the responses given to Card V, whose compact construction often allows a unitary representation of the body. The stability, the integrity (or nonintegrity), the livelihood (or not) of the responses was thoroughly investigated. The various contents sometimes carry sexual symbols through their receptive or penetrating, castrated or phallic functions; sometimes they focus on protective and differentiating qualities (responses related to "the skin" such as clothes, furs, coats of arms, carapaces, whose lack of resistance is at times violently denounced), and sometimes they testify to major weaknesses in the integrity of the unity of representation of the body (defective body, shadow, corpse, human representation with elements of the animal or vegetable kingdom). Those diverse contents are likely to carry information on the quality, diversity, and specificity of the problems linked to individuation and sexual identifications involved in the mental work of self-representation (Boizou, Chabert, Rausch de Traubenberg, 1978; Chabert, 1983, 1987; Rausch de Traubenberg & Sanglade, 1984; Sanglade, 1983).

With the help of a few examples of card processing, gathered in the author's clinical practice and research, we wish to illustrate how interesting the Rorschach

Test is in accounting for the potential richness of the mental work of representation, to show how narcissistic and object cathexes can remain mobilized despite aging – and to try to grasp the bearable or unbearable dimension of going through this change: limited loss as regards castration, or more drastic collapse of the narcissistic foundations.

Result

First of all, we notice that the compact construction of the Card V often provides a unitary and stable representation of the body, neutral or narcissistically invested:

Woman, 58: "A big butterfly that flies above flowers to take their nectar."

Woman, 63: "I can see a bird spreading its wings."

Woman, 72: "A bat, or a bird, a bird with a beak ... A bird with a long beak."

Woman, 91: "It's definitely a bat! It's a nice drawing, elegant, but it's not a sympathetic animal."

Man, 65: "Of course, a bat or a screech-owl or those types of animals and I don't see anything else. It's well done; it's really a bat. For something which is a matter of chance, it's always surprising."

Man, 71: "A man who is hang-gliding, who watches with interest the scenery passing by."

Man, 76: "The first idea – it's a butterfly, you have the butterfly's antenna and the tip of ... not its feet. ... There's a little ball the pollen can touch and hang on."

Man, 82: "Oh the beautiful long-eared bat, its wings, its little feet behind! A long-eared bat."

But for some participants, the compact construction of the card is not sufficient to provide support for their narcissistic fragilities, which can be spotted by the accent put on the erosion of representations: The participant struggles to provide a form clearly differentiated from the back, and we can then notice numerous depressed, morbid, or even ruined body representations (again, for Card V):

Woman, 54: "That is the back of a rabbit someone is carving before sautéing it in a saucepan ... or a crushed snail."

Woman, 64: "A bat that is tired, its wings hanging low."

Woman, 68: "I don't know, I see two animals lying down, sick or dead, I don't know. I do not see them sleeping. Considering their position, they are sick or dead."

Woman, 77: "It's definitely the bat. Maybe a ... No ... a swatted ant ... not a mouse, a cicada or something like that, swatted" (thumps the card with her fist).

Man, 53: "Always an anatomical part, a bit deformed. The bottom of the pelvis. There is a strange mixture between the bone part and the flesh part."

Man, 61: "A brace of rabbits, a hunting trophy. It's sad. The rabbit's legs ... It's not exactly like that. It's black, it's not ... there are two rabbits but there is just one head, it's incoherent."

Man, 76: "The bat. The domineering nastiness. Darkness, death, destruction."

On the other hand, the attention paid to the disruption of the human body in the popular response to Card III by several elderly subjects may appear as striking. Although, on this card, on the perceptive level, the integrity of the human body is not obvious, a priori it does not prevent one from picturing whole men or women. But it is also well known that the splitting up, devitalization, and hybridization of human representations can reveal potential narcissistic weaknesses known to be particularly worrying in young adults with identity disorders (Chabert, 1987; Emmanuelli & Azoulay, 2009; Rorschach, 1920/1967; Schafer, 1960). Yet, in the protocols of elderly people without any psychotic functioning (but neurotic, borderline, or narcissistic functioning), it is possible to find responses to this card such as (Card III):

Woman, 62: "It makes me think of the skeleton, of the iliac bone, of the hips. Do you want something else? ... Two birds in their nest, on their nest, but it is too symmetrical. It makes me think more of hips. Oh, I never thought that a woman's hips would make you write so much!" (she laughs).

Woman, 68: "It looks like two small animals, it's more alive than the rest. Here, legs, but I don't see what two legs would do here, standing by themselves. Two objects facing each other, two small beings facing each other and telling each other stories. But the legs are cut off."

Woman, 75: "Oh, that's very cute, a dance associated with a dream ... yes, associated with a dream because there's no ... in what I call a character, there's no continuity. It's sort of weird. Part of it is imaginary, it's sort of a dream since the characters are split in two parts."

Woman, 77: "African dancers. Well, they're skeletons of course."

Woman, 79: "Two contorted bodies, a little like those we now see in modern art. But I don't see what this red stuff in the middle is. Maybe it's a decoration. It could be lungs. Two somewhat fabulous small characters whose bottoms would have been deliberately cut off from the legs in order to strike the imagination."

Woman, 80: "So these are two women fighting over a gold ingot, a bag full of provisions. 'That's mine' – 'No, it's mine.' During the fight they lost their hats. A cartoonist has drawn the scene and split them in halves. We can also say that in their bag there's a leaking bottle. It makes a small running spot."

Woman, 82: "This looks like Josephine Baker ... I really don't see what the red spot can be. Will you tell me afterward? I really see two dancers; here, they have 'un truc en plumes' [a feathered something] and here it is their legs, cut knee-high."

Woman, 85: "Two guys in a position in which their bottoms are splitting up from their legs ... because here it's cut off. They're not stable at all."

Woman, 91: "Two butlers, or two waiters ... or two ... two bowing actors. It could be theater dogs, artist dogs. The head could be a dog's head."

Man, 70: "The Cro-Magnon man, ergots rather than feet; they are beginning to stand up, to become stable. These are man's ancestors."

Man, 73: "There are two characters, their arms are folded, and their lower part is only sketched. They are truncated characters. There are two branches, two parts of branches. And then the red spots, it could be a blood spot."

Man, 78: "These are shoes, legs with shoes at the end. We're getting close to characters ... the heads ... they're more animal than human. ... The symmetry is very striking, although it is not total. I can't say much more. Two characters, human and nonhuman at the same time, let's say stylized, with a paw that retracts in the back and a weird leg. In fact it is the branch of a tree that ends with a shoe."

Although a certain sensitivity undoubtedly highlights the absence of unity of the body representation, it is important to note that most of these responses remain very much alive: Under the cover of art, humor, or the imaginary, the M responses remain active within scenarios endowed with an often obvious libidinous dimension. In other responses, self-representation appears in the form of a transfer onto "botanical" or "object" contents. In some protocols, often those of participants who present a neurotic personality structure, such responses remain occasional, subdued, and alive; but in others, who present a borderline or narcissistic personality structure, they appear to be recurrent, even morbid, thus betraying an intense narcissistic wound:

Woman, 57: Card I: "A pansy eaten by many slugs, snails ... Many parts are missing. You have to imagine colored spots in the middle; the leaves are very incomplete. We have problems with slugs in the garden and they have eaten all the pansies. Something eaten by moths, an old book eaten by moths or by paper-worms. Normally they'd rather eat in the middle, but so what. A book with a whole between two pages. The paper-worms have eaten it in the middle and the slugs all around."

Woman, 58: Card IV: "An ancient shriveled parchment that rolls and rolls up."

Card VIII: "A tattered, all torn up boat sail."

Woman, 63: Card IV: "A ragged coat, as if falling in tatters, you see. It is fraying from all sides, the sleeves are a little ..."

Card I: "Bits of scrap iron. Somewhat like when iron is rusted. The iron falls off."

Woman, 75: Card II: "It's a flower that is losing it leaves, almost at the end of its ... that is almost fading. Something faded. A flower that says: 'I'm giving up, I no longer exist,' like an orchid, a flower that I hate because I always see a feminine sex in it ... a uterus. I'm going to have a surprise when you tell me what it is."

Woman, 75: Card X: "It could be a flower, a kind of orchid. Personally, I don't like orchids very much; there is something evil in them. ... It's probably because I know they grow on rotting ground. Something delicate and fragile, although a little distressing, in spite of the rather optimistic colors. Something a little tragic, a little ... A flower that is rotting a little, that is withering ... and, at the same time it is rather fragile. It makes me think of flowers, flowers that do not last very long, delicate and fragile flowers that make you dream but that are ... in fact, that don't last, that have something ephemeral."

Woman, 78: Card IV: "A sort of tower ... There are small crenels. There are stones that are falling. You can see the tower is in ruins."

Card VI: "A ruin with a tower. A tower that is beginning to fall to pieces."

Man, 71: Card IV: "Two old boots. Because of the shape at the bottom and of the lace at the top. Old, worn out shoes, with crooked, folded sides. They cracked, they are torn."

Man, 74: Card VII: "Pieces of rusted sheet iron, like old cars in a dump. Cushions, stuff not very ... plastic, rotting or torn out plastic foam."

Man, 76: Card VI: "Rags. A scarecrow. Poverty. Garbage. Miserable rags. An impression of something torn, discolored. When there are rags, there is a scarecrow then dirt, and finally rubbish and garbage."

In many protocols, reaching the body representation is directly linked to the animal or human content. Once again, if none of the protocols makes it possible to presume serious identity disorders compatible with a psychotic functioning, the predominance of responses linked to the body highlights the narcissistic fragility, which is partly due to the challenge of aging and partly to more structural narcissistic fragilities.

Yet, some responses illustrate castration problems, dealing with a neurotic personality structure (the whole protocol interpretation leads to that conclusion):

Woman, 58: Card I: "A candle-moth. It is a little damaged, there's dust or else the scales of its wings are peeling off."

Woman, 63: Card I: "A brain, a very damaged brain cross-section. There are spaces that could represent ventricle sections, small tubercles here, holes."

Card VII: "It still reminds me of anatomic cross-sections of the spinal cord or of the brain, something like that. It's been damaged when cutting."

Man, 72: Card II: "A hemorrhage. Totally destroyed kidneys and bladder. When I say hemorrhage, it is because it makes me think of blood, of something liquid. It's a hemorrhage at the level of the kidneys, or the bladder, I don't know how to put it; my children studied medicine, not me."

Man, 79: Card X: "Vaguely resembles a frog, with appendices ... an injured frog maybe, losing its ... The hind legs are unfolding, the tongue is stretching out to catch an insect but it may be wounded."

Other responses emphasize more the lack of consistency and the diffuseness of the limits. These protocols turn out to be overloaded with very damaged self-representations, where the limits appear unable to remain containing, protective, or differentiating, and unable to guarantee any inner vitality. Such protocols, particularly collected in older but not yet very old adults, illustrate the narcissistic fragility mobilized independently of the outside reality of the old age reached. We find them more frequently in the protocols of participants with borderline or narcissistic personality structure:

Woman, 54: Card VI: "The depiction of an artist, but an artist whose skin is spread on either side of the backbone and whose skin has been kept as a hunting trophy. It's a cutaway drawing. The head is here; it's the identity flag."

Woman, 63: Card X: "A small piece of backbone, it does not look like much. It could be a human body opened onto the void, onto nothingness, a little. A human body that split open."

Woman, 66: Card I: "It's a poor butterfly, it's in trouble. It's a ... It's a butterfly that has gone through a tornado, and it's going to die very soon. It used to be a very beautiful butterfly. I don't like its small legs: they're too short. ... It's a butterfly that has been beaten up. It's an extraterrestrial butterfly coming from Mars. and it is distorted, like E.T. But it still remains a butterfly. It's come back on earth and it's too bad. It's falling into small pieces. It's black. It's sad. Poor butterfly [*she smiles*]: This will be my conclusion."

Card IV: "Here, I have nothing more to say. It's an animal whose name I have forgotten ... An ugly and distorted anteater trying to frighten someone. It is misshapen and ugly. It is misshapen. It has a big tail and big feet. It's trying to be frightening. It's the frog that tries to inflate itself to the size of an ox. It's ugly, mean, sad. ... Sad to be so ugly. It's ugly. It's shapeless. It's disturbing. Gosh, how ugly this thing is! It's the future. ... It's grief."

Woman, 67: Card II: "The shadows of two rabbits. It's two shadows; I don't picture two rabbits like that. ... Although there are red spots that really are on the rabbit. ... On shadows, I don't really know."

Card VIII: "Figures of bears."

Man, 53: Card X: "The same topic again; bits of human bodies. Again, the same notion of symmetry. Still the feeling it is part of the pelvic bone, but after a postmortem. It makes me think of the cutaway drawing of cars that are presented in specialized magazines, each part displayed in the natural organizational order."

Conclusion

As we can see, responses vary and reveal how much growing old neither standardizes nor impoverishes mental process and problems. Nevertheless, the interpretative value of these varied outcomes of the Rorschach protocols needs to be improved according to age, sex, the associative dynamics of the projective process, and the toll of the mental functioning process. More than sex or age, it seems that the previous personality organization plays an important part in the challenge imposed on and/or proposed to the self-representation when growing old. If neurotic organizations sometimes produce damaged representations, we can still observe that the impact leads them to minor disorganization, and better capacities for self-protection, displacement, and symbolization, impairing one part but not, or only rarely, the whole. The study of the same Rorschach factors reveals how growing old can emphasize identity fragilities (linked to differentiation and individuation problematics) for borderline and narcissistic organizations.

One can only wish for further research in that direction since a better understanding of the resources and weaknesses mobilized in mental aging will result in better patient care. Therefore, research that compares such nonpatient data with psychiatric patient data (Clow & Allen, 2002) would be very interesting. Clearly, in a clinical setting, only the analysis of a full protocol can allow us to apprehend the diversity or self-representation of a single subject, that person's fragilities and resources, and their place within the dynamics of mental functioning (Verdon, 2004c, 2011b; Verdon & Duplant, 2006).

The mental apparatus tries to face the feeling of loss and incompleteness, the inevitability of finitude, and the disenchantment of things unfinished. And in many aging adults, the libido that supports their self-investment can still be mobilized. Mental functioning is not wholly weakened, just as the ability to represent oneself as changed is not necessarily branded as a narcissistic collapse. Undoubtedly, for some aging adults, the late narcissistic conflict turns out to be violent, and engenders morbid and depressive deidealization. But for others, representing oneself as incomplete, less powerful, and less confident does not prevent giving responses whose symbolic sexual quality remains of high quality, as well as giving authentically libidinous object M responses that remind us that the physical reality cannot be thought out without the mental reality. This is one of the purposes of our clinical work: to enhance the conviction, very fragile in many aging adults, that life is possible even if you are not complete, and that you can have some value even if you are not fulfilled.

Acknowledgments

This chapter appeared in a similar form in the *Rorschachiana*: Verdon, B. (2011). Changing while remaining the same: Self-representation confronted with aging. *Rorschachiana, 33,* 145–168. https://doi.org/10.1027/1192-5604/a000033

References

Abraham, G., Kocher, P., & Goda, G. (1980). Psychoanalysis and aging. *The International Review of Psycho-Analysis, 7,* 147–155.

Abraham, K. (1973). Le pronostic du traitement psychanalytique chez les sujets d'un certain âge [The prognosis of psychoanalytic treatment in elderly subjects]. In K. Abraham (Ed.), *Essais théoriques – Œuvres complètes* (pp. 92–96). Paris, France: Payot. (Original work published 1920)

Ames, L. B., Metraux, R., Learned Rodell, J., & Walker, R. (1995). *Rorschach responses in old age*. Northvale, NJ: Aronson.

Andreoli, A., & Quartier, F. (1976). Repli et régression névrotique chez le vieillard [Withdrawal and neurotic regression in old people]. *L'Information Psychiatrique, 52,* 1155–1165.

Assoun, P. L. (1983). Le vieillissement saisi par la psychanalyse [Aging: A psychoanalytic view]. *Communications «Le continent gris», 37,* 167–179.

Balbo, G. (1980). Introduction d'un concept psychanalytique du vieillissement [Introduction to a psychoanalytic concept of aging]. *Proceedings of the first Congress of the*

International Association of Psychoanalytic Gerontology (pp. 52–71). Paris, France: Sopedim.
Balbo, G. (1982). Introduction d'un concept psychanalytique du vieillissement (suite et fin) [Introduction to a psychoanalytic concept of aging (Continuation and conclusion)]. *Proceedings of the second Congress of the International Association of Psychoanalytic Gerontology* (pp. 11–18). Paris, France: Sopedim.
Balier, C. (1976). Troubles névrotiques de la sénescence [Neurotic troubles of senescence]. In *Encyclopédie médico-chirurgicale* (37-530-A-30, pp. 29–36).
Balier, C. (1979). Pour une théorie narcissique du vieillissement [For a narcissistic theory of aging]. *L'information psychiatrique, 55,* 635–645.
Balier, C. (1982). Des changements de l'économie libidinale au cours du vieillissement [On the changes in the libidinal economy through aging]. In J. Guillaumin & H. Reboul (Eds.), *Le temps et la vie, les dynamismes du vieillissement* (pp. 63–69). Lyon, France: Chronique sociale.
Baudin, M. (2005). Vieillir au féminin [Feminine aging]. *Psychologie clinique et projective, 11,* 277–288. http://doi.org/10.3917/pcp.011.0277
Bergeret, J. (1982). La deuxième crise d'adolescence: Sénescence et identité [The second adolescence crisis: Senescence and identity]. In J. Guillaumin & H. Reboul (Eds.), *Le temps et la vie, les dynamismes du vieillissement* (pp. 71–78). Lyon, France: Chronique sociale.
Bergler, E. (1947). Elderly neurotics. *Diseases of the Nervous System, 8,* 35–36.
Bianchi, H. (1978). Figures de l'infigurable [Figuring the unfigurable]. *Psychanalyse à l'université, 3,* 525–532.
Bianchi, H. (1980a). Travail du vieillir et «travail du trépas» [Adjusting to old age and death]. *Psychanalyse à l'université, 5,* 613–619.
Bianchi, H. (1980b). Vieillir après Freud [Growing old after Freud]. *Proceedings of the first Congress of the International Association of Psychoanalytic Gerontology* (pp. 1–25). Paris, France: Sopedim.
Bianchi, H. (1982a). La question du sens, question clinique? [Is meaning a clinical issue?]. *Proceedings of the second Congress of the International Association of Psychoanalytic Gerontology* (pp. 137–146). Paris, France: Sopedim.
Bianchi, H. (1982b). Deuil du moi et fantasme du moment de la mort [Ego mourning and time of death fantasy]. *Revue de Médecine Psychosomatique, 24*(1), 33–47.
Bianchi, H. (1983a). Narcissisme et identité à l'épreuve du temps [Narcissism and identity over time]. In I. Simeone & G. Abraham (Eds.), *Introduction à la psychogériatrie* (pp. 47–51). Paris, France: SIMEP.
Bianchi, H. (1983b). Brèves remarques sur la réactivation de la problématique œdipienne à la fin de la vie [Brief remarks on the revival of the oedipal conflict at the end of life]. *Dialogue, 79,* 27–32.
Bianchi, H. (1985). Entre deuil et déni, dynamique du sujet âgé face à la situation de perte [Between mourning and denial, the dynamics of the elderly with regard to the loss situation]. *Psychologie médicale, 17,* 1145–1147.
Bianchi, H. (1987). *Le moi et le temps: Psychanalyse du temps et du vieillissement* [The ego and time: Psychoanalysis of time and aging]. Paris, France: Dunod.
Bianchi, H. (1989). *La question du vieillissement: Perspectives psychanalytiques* [The question of aging: Psychoanalytical perspectives]. Paris, France: Dunod.
Bianchi, H. (1999). Psychodynamique du vieillissement [Psychodynamics of aging]. In J. M Léger, J.P. Clément, & J. Wertheimer (Eds.), *Psychiatrie du sujet âgé* (pp. 46–55). Paris, France: Flammarion.
Boizou, M.F., Chabert, C., & Rausch de Traubenberg, N. (1978). Représentation de soi. Identité, identification au Rorschach chez l'enfant et l'adulte [Self-representation.

identity, identification on the Rorschach in children and adults]. *Bulletin de psychologie, 32*(339), 271–277.

Chabert, C. (1983). *Le Rorschach en clinique adulte: Interprétation psychanalytique* [The Rorschach Test in clinical work with adults: Psychoanalytic interpretation]. Paris, France: Dunod.

Chabert, C. (1987). *La psychopathologie à l'épreuve du Rorschach* [Psychopathology and the Rorschach Test]. Paris, France: Dunod.

Charazac, P. M. (1983). Tabou du vieillard et fantasme du renversement de l'ordre des générations [Old people's taboos and the phantasy of the reversal of generations]. *L'evolution psychiatrique, 48,* 1027–1039.

Charazac, P. M. (1989). Les processus de symbiose et de séparation dans la famille du vieillard [Symbiosis and separation processes in families of the elderly]. *L'evolution psychiatrique, 54,* 373–386.

Charazac, P. M. (1998a). Psychopathologie de la dépendance du sujet âgé [Psychopathology of the elderly subject's dependency]. *La revue de gériatrie, 23,* 717–722.

Charazac, P. M. (1998b). *Psychothérapie du patient âgé et de sa famille* [Psychotherapy of the old patient and the patient's family]. Paris, France: Dunod.

Charazac, P. M. (2001). Psychothérapie du sujet âgé [Psychotherapy of the old subject]. In *Encyclopédie médico-chirurgicale* (37-540-C-50).

Charazac, P. M. (2002). Le dernier conflit d'Œdipe [The last oedipal conflict]. *Psychiatrie française, 2,* 86–95.

Charazac, P. M. (2005). *Comprendre la crise de la vieillesse* [Understanding the crisis of aging]. Paris, France: Dunod.

Charazac, P. M. (2008). Les dynamiques psychiques du grand âge [The mental dynamics in advanced old age]. *Psychologie et neuropsychiatrie du vieillissement, 6*(2), 91–96.

Charazac, P. M. (2010). L'objet du manque dans le travail analytique avec les patients âgés [The object of lack in analytical work with elderly patients]. *Revue française de psychanalyse, 74,* 129–140. http://doi.org/10.3917/rfp.741.0129

Clerk, G. (1995). Psychanalyse et vieillesse [Psychoanalysis and aging]. *Revue canadienne de psychanalyse, 3,* 71–86.

Clow, H. E., & Allen, E. B. (2002). Psychiatric aspects of mental competency in the aging. *Journal of the American Geriatric Society, 50,* 1879–1883. http://doi.org/10.1046/j.1532-5415.2002.50520.x

Dedieu-Anglade, G. (1981). Psychothérapie des troubles psychonévrotiques au cours du vieillissement [Psychotherapy of psychoneurotic troubles in aging]. In *Encyclopédie médico-chirurgicale* (37-541-A-10).

Eisdorfer, C. (1963). Rorschach performance and intellectual functioning in the aged. *Journal of Gerontology, 18,* 358–363. http://doi.org/10.1093/geronj/18.4.358

Emmanuelli, M., & Azoulay, C. (2009). *Pratique des épreuves projectives à l'adolescence: Approche psychanalytique* [Using projective techniques with adolescents: Psychoanalytical approach]. Paris, France: Dunod.

Fenichel, O. (1945). *La théorie psychanalytique des névroses* [Psychoanalytical theory of neurosis]. Paris, France: PUF.

Ferenczi, S. (1974). Pour comprendre les psychonévroses du retour d'âge [A contribution to the understanding of the psychoneuroses of the age of involution]. In *Œuvres complètes, Psychanalyse III (1919–1926)* (pp. 150–155). Paris, France: Payot. (Original work published in 1921)

Ferreira Novo, R., & Silva, D. (2002, September). *The expression of the late adulthood in the Rorschach: Singularity of the personality or age specificity?* Communication at the XVII International Congress of Rorschach and other Projective Methods, Rome, Italy.

Freud, S. (1897/2001). Letter 75 to Wilhem Fliess. In J. Strachey (Ed. & Trans.), *The standard edition of the complete psychological works of Sigmund Freud* (Vol. 1, pp. 173–280). London, UK: Vintage Classics. (Original work published in 1897)

Freud, S. (1905a/2001). On psychotherapy. In J. Strachey (Ed. & Trans.), *The Standard Edition of the Complete Psychological Works of Sigmund Freud* (Vol. 7, pp. 255–268). London, UK: Vintage Classics. (Original work published 1905)

Freud, S. (1905b/2001). Three essays on the theory of sexuality. In J. Strachey (Ed. & Trans.), *The standard edition of the complete psychological works of Sigmund Freud* (Vol. 7, pp. 123–245). London, UK: Vintage Classics. (Original work published in 1905)

Freud, S. (1922/2001). Psycho-analysis. In J. Strachey (Ed. & Trans.), *The standard edition of the complete psychological works of Sigmund Freud* (Vol. 18, pp. 233–259). London, UK: Vintage Classics. (Original work published in 1922)

Gagey, J. (1983). Le vieillard, objet paradoxal de la psychanalyse [The old man: A paradoxical object for psychoanalysis]. *Chronos, 1,* 1–7.

Gagey, J. (1989). Raisonner psychanalytiquement le vieillir? [Aging in terms of psychoanalysis?]. In H. Bianchi (Ed.), *La question du vieillissement. Perspectives psychanalytiques* (pp. 7–32). Paris, France: Dunod.

Gitelson, M. (1973). *Psychoanalysis: Science and profession.* New York, NY: International Universities Press. (Original work published in 1948)

Guillaumin, J. (1982). Le temps et l'âge. Réflexions psychanalytiques sur le vieillir [Time and age. Psychoanalytical reflections on aging]. In J. Guillaumin & H. Reboul (Eds.), *Le temps et la vie: Les dynamismes du vieillissement* (pp. 133–143). Lyon, France: Chronique sociale.

Hayslip, B., & Lowman, R. L. (1986). The clinical use of projective techniques with the aged: A critical review and synthesis. *Clinical Gerontologist, 5,* 63–93. http://doi.org/10.1300/J018v05n01_04

Herfray, C. (1984). Vieillissement: Identité, deuil et castration [Aging: Identity, mourning and castration]. *Bulletin de psychologie, 38,* 523–531.

Ishihara, S. (1976). *Ishihara's tests for color-blindness.* Tokyo, Japan: Kankhara Shuppan.

Janin, C. (1982). A propos de la psychopathologie du troisième âge: Quelques hypothèses psychodynamiques [About the psychopathology of aging: A few psychodynamic hypotheses]. In J. Guillaumin & H. Reboul (Eds.), *Le temps et la vie: Les dynamismes du vieillissement* (pp. 129–132). Lyon, France: Chronique sociale.

Jones, E. (1969). Le fantasme du renversement de l'ordre des générations [The phantasy of the reversal of generations]. In *Théorie et pratique de la psychanalyse* (pp. 372–377). Paris, France: Payot. (Original work published in 1948)

Laplanche, J., & Pontalis, J. B. (1967). *Vocabulaire de la psychanalyse* [The language of psychoanalysis]. Paris, France: PUF.

Le Gouès, G. (1984). Aspects de la vie mentale tardive [Aspects of the late mental life]. *Revue française de psychanalyse, 48,* 1259–1272.

Le Gouès, G. (1991). *Le psychanalyste et le vieillard* [The psychoanalyst and the old man]. Paris, France: PUF.

Le Gouès, G. (2000). *L'âge et le principe de plaisir* [Age and the pleasure principle]. Paris, France: Dunod.

Mattlar, C. E., Carlsson, A., Forsander, C., Karppi, S.-L., & Helenius, H. (1992). Rorschach and old age: Personality characteristics for a group of physically fit 80-year-old men. *British Journal of Projective Psychology, 37*(2), 41–51.

Mattlar, C. E., Knuts, L. R., & Virtanen, E. (1985). Personality structure on the Rorschach for a group of healthy 71-year-old females and males. *Projective Psychology, 30,* 3–6.

Panek, P.E., Wagner, E.E., & Kennedy-Zwergel, K. (1983). A review of projective test findings with older adults. *Journal of Personality Assessment, 47,* 562–582. http://doi.org/10.1207/s15327752jpa4706_1

Péruchon, M. (1987). Valeur fonctionnelle des images parentales dans le vieillissement normal et pathologique [Functional value of the parent images in normal and pathological aging]. *Psychologie médicale, 19,* 1251–1253.

Péruchon, M. (1993). Travail de deuil du moi chez le sujet âgé [Ego mourning process in the old subject]. *Gérontologie, 87,* 13–15.

Péruchon, M. (1999). Régression et/ou désorganization au regard de la sénescence [Regression and/or disorganization with regard to senescence]. *Psychiatrie française, 2,* 126–133.

Poitrenaud, J., & Moreaux, C. (1975). Réponses données au test de Rorschach par un groupe de sujets âgés, cliniquement normaux: Analyse quantitative des protocoles en fonction de l'âge [Responses to the Rorschach Test in a group of clinically normal elderly subjects: Quantitative study according to age]. *Revue de psychologie appliquée, 25,* 267–284.

Pollock, G.H. (1982). On aging and psychopathology. *The International Journal of Psychoanalysis, 63,* 275–281.

Pontalis, J.B. (1997). *Ce temps qui ne passe pas* [The time that does not pass]. Paris, France: Gallimard.

Quinodoz, D. (1987). Psychothérapies des personnes âgées [Psychotherapy of old people]. *Psychothérapies, 7,* 151–158.

Quinodoz, D. (1994). Le travail de vieillir [The aging process]. *L'information psychiatrique, 70,* 319–328.

Quinodoz, D. (1997). Psychanalyse des personnes âgées et fantasme d'éternité [Old people's psychoanalysis and the fantasy of eternity]. *Revue française de psychanalyse, 61,* 1881–1889.

Rausch de Traubenberg, N., & Sanglade, A. (1984). Représentation de soi et relation d'objet au Rorschach: Grille de représentation de soi [Self-representation and object-relationship on the Rorschach Test: Scale of self-representation]. *Revue de psychologie appliquée, 34*(1), 41–57.

Reichlin, R.E. (1984). Current perspectives on Rorschach performance among older adults. *Journal of Personality Assessment, 48,* 71–81. http://doi.org/10.1207/s15327752jpa4801_12

Rorschach, H. (1967). *Psychodiagnostic* (4th ed.). Paris, France: PUF. (Original work published 1920)

Sanglade, A. (1983). Image du corps et image de soi au Rorschach [Bodily image and self-representation on the Rorschach Test]. *Psychologie Française, 28,* 104–111.

Schafer, R. (1960). Bodies in schizophrenic Rorschach responses. *Journal of Projective Techniques and Personality Assessments, 24,* 267–281. http://doi.org/10.1080/08853126.1960.10380969

Schur, M. (1975). *La mort dans la vie de Freud* [Death in the life of Freud]. Paris, France: Gallimard.

Shimonaka, Y., & Nakazato, K. (1991). Aging and terminal changes in Rorschach responses among the Japanese elderly. *Journal of Personality Assessment, 57*(1), 10–18. http://doi.org/10.1207/s15327752jpa5701_2

Simeone, I. (1988). Aspects psychodynamiques du vieillissement [Psychodynamic aspects of aging]. *Gérontologie et société, 46,* 8–20.

Valente-Torre, L. (1993). Au bout de la vie: Le test de Rorschach appliqué à des sujets nonagénaires non détériorés [At the end of life: Rorschach Test given to ninety-year-old not impaired subjects]. *Bulletin de la Société du Rorschach et des méthodes projectives de langue française, 37,* 195–204. http://doi.org/10.3406/clini.1993.1651

Vázquez, N., & Osuna, M. (2002, September). *Entendiendo los diferentes procesos de envejecimiento a través de los indices de Rorschach* [Understanding the different aging processes through the Rorschach Test]. Communication presented at the XVIIInternational Congress of Rorschach and Projective Methods, Rome, Italy.

Verdon, B. (2003). Le paradigme de la névrose à l'épreuve du temps: Remarques à propos de la question de la névrose actuelle [The paradigm of neurosis with regard to time: Remarks on the actual neurosis]. *Champ psychosomatique, 30,* 83–100. http://doi.org/10.3917/cpsy.030.0083

Verdon, B. (2004a). Traitement narcissique de la perte dans la névrose: Observations dans la clinique projective de la femme vieillissante [Narcissistic treatment of loss in neurosis: Observations in projective clinical work with aging women]. *Psychologie clinique et projective, 10,* 315–337. http://doi.org/10.3917/pcp.010.0315

Verdon, B. (2004b). Souffrance névrotique chez le sujet vieillissant [Neurotic suffering in aging subjects]. *Cahiers de psychologie clinique, 23*(2), 35–57. http://doi.org/10.3917/cpc.023.035

Verdon, B. (2004c). Psychopathologie d'une clinique de la perte: La plainte mnésique [Psychopathology of loss: The memory complaint]. In M. Emmanuelli (Ed.), *L'examen psychologique: Situations, méthodes, études de cas* (pp. 483–499). Paris, France: Dunod.

Verdon, B. (2007a). Diversité psychopathologique dans la clinique de la plainte mnésique de l'adulte vieillissant [Psychopathological diversity of memory complaints among aging adults]. *Psychologie et neuropsychiatrie du vieillissement, 5,* 209–223.

Verdon, B. (2007b). Actualité du sexuel chez l'adulte âgé: Réflexions à partir de la clinique projective [The current sexual reality of the elderly adult: Reflections based on clinical practice with projective tests]. *Bulletin de psychologie, 60*(490), 309–321. http://doi.org/10.3917/bupsy.490.0309

Verdon, B. (2011a). The case of thematic tests adapted to older adults: On the importance of differentiating latent and manifest contents in projective tests. *Rorschachiana, 32,* 46–71. http://doi.org/10.1027/1192-5604/a000015

Verdon, B. (2011b). Un fonctionnement psychique marqué par l'exigence narcissique à l'épreuve du vieillissement [Mental functioning characterized by narcissistic requirement confronted with aging]. In C. Chabert & C. Azoulay (Eds.), *12 études en clinique projective. Approche psychanalytique* (pp. 249–276). Paris, France: Dunod.

Verdon, B. (2012). *Clinique et psychopathologie du vieillissement: Apport des épreuves projectives* [Clinical work and psychopathology of aging: Contribution of projective methods]. Paris, France: Dunod.

Verdon, B., & Duplant, N. (2006). Masochisme et angoisse de perte de l'objet: Figure de la psychopathologie de la plainte mnésique [Masochism and object-loss anxiety: A figure of psychopathology in the memory complaint]. *Psychologie clinique et projective, 12,* 119–154. http://doi.org/10.3917/pcp.012.0119

Villa, F. (2010). *La puissance du vieillir* [The force to grow old]. Paris, France: PUF. http://doi.org/10.3917/puf.vill.2010.01

Wertheimer, J. (1982). Les mécanismes de permanence: Le temps, support d'une hypothèse psychodynamique du vieillissement psychologique [Permanence mechanisms: Time as a support for a psychodynamic hypothesis of psychological aging]. *Proceedings of the second Congress of the International Association of Psychoanalytic Gerontology* (pp. 41–52). Paris, France: Sopedim.

Appendices

Appendix 1: Evaluation of Psychic Functioning Using a Schema of Interpretation of Projective Data

The Rorschach Test

I – Clinical Analysis of the Projective Situation and Administrating the Test

- The dynamic of the test situation: clinical impressions, emotional tone, relation to the clinician, verbalization, specific reactivity toward the cards, behavioral manifestations.
- Characteristics of the verbal responses: scoring of the responses, establishment of the psychogram, comparison with normative data, assembling relevant factors: congruence or contradiction.

→ *Formulation of clinical hypotheses*

II – Thought Processes

- Modalities of investment of external reality: simple W, F%, F+% (extended formulas if F% < norms), analysis of F-, H%, A%; qualitative aspect and symbolic dimension of the contents, number and quality of popular responses.
- Modalities of investment of thought activity: quality of the elaboration of the modes of apprehension: W, D, etc., input of M, symbolization, mobilization of diverse registers (variety of modes of apprehension, determinants, contents).

→ *First step: Articulation of the interface between the modalities of investment of thought activity and external reality*

III – Treatment of Conflicts

1. Narcissistic axis:

1-1 – Self-representation – *Identity:* Quality of primary identifications and narcissistic foundations: Integrity of human representations, degree of reality or of life (quality of F, M, H, Hd, At …); Integrity of animal representations, degree of reality or life (quality of F, m, A, Ad, At …); Card V and unitary cards; boundaries between inside and outside: F%, F+%, contents, etc.

1-2 – Self-representation – *Identification:* Characteristics of secondary (sexual) identification movements: Analysis of the H, M, symbolic feminine and masculine contents, cards with sexual symbolism (IV, VI, VII), Cards II and II, etc.

→ *Quality of the investment of self-representation and narcissism*

2. Object axis:

2-1 – Representations of relations: Analysis of the M, m, Bilateral cards (II, III, VII), Cards I, VII, and IX (link to maternal imago).

2-2 – Treatment of affects: analysis of sensory responses, reactivity toward the red, black, gray, and pastel cards, choice test, RC% (% of responses given for the pastel cards).

→ *Quality of the investment of object-representations and object-relations*

3. Defensive organization:

- Rigidity, lability, inhibition: modalities, efficiency
- Neurotic register, borderline register, psychotic register

→ *Second step: Quality of the investment of representations of relations and affects (prevalence of representations or affects – relationship between affects and representations – nature of the anxiety and defensive organization – nature of the conflict)*

IV – Synthesis: Psychological Issues

Articulation conflict/defenses → Psychological issues (oedipal, object loss or narcissistic, identity)

Thematic Apperception Test (TAT)

I – Clinical Analysis of the Projective Situation and Administrating the Test

Impressions, mood, relation to the clinician, characteristics of the narrative, the dynamic of the test situation, specific reactivity toward the picture cards, behavioral manifestations (agitation and/or restlessness, gestures, requests made of the clinician, etc.)

II – First Step

Scoring each discourse using the TAT Analysis Grid. *Extracting* the psychological problematics for each picture card, linked to the latent solicitations.

III – Second Step

Grouping procedures of discourse and defensive organization:

A – Prevalent procedures and defense mechanisms (SCORE +, ++, or +++ according to the frequency and the economic influence)

A: Rigidity
A1: Reference to external reality
A2: Cathexis of internal reality
A3: Obsessive-type procedures

B: Lability
B1: Cathexis of relationship
B2: Dramatization
B3: Hysterical-type procedures

C: Conflict evasion
CF: Overcathexis of external reality
CI: Inhibition
CN: Narcissistic cathexis
CL: Instability of borders
CM: Antidepressive procedures

E: Primary processes emergence
E1: Perceptual distortion
E2: Massivity of projection
E3: Disorganization of identificatory and object landmarks
E4: Impairment of speech

B – Evaluation of Defensive Organisation
- Rigidity, lability, inhibition: modalities, efficiency
- Neurotic register, borderline register, psychotic register

III – Synthesis: Psychological Problematics

Articulation conflicts and defenses → (oedipal, object loss, identity)
→ Synthesis Rorschach and TAT
Evaluation of psychic functioning

Appendix 2: Latent Solicitations of TAT Picture Cards

Card 1: This card seeks to identify helplessness associated with castration anxiety, with different destinies depending on the quality of identifications. Solitude and narcissistic injury associated with immaturity are likely to establish a more or less elaborated fear of loss.

Card 2: This card refers to the father–mother–child oedipal triangle and puts the oedipal organization to the test as well as its more or less structuring character following its decline. Taboo and the renouncement of oedipal love that it requires can also be experienced as an impossible separation from original objects.

Card 3BM: This card solicits the participant's ability to associate affect (sadness) with a representation of object loss. The capacity for mourning (renouncing and shifting investments), guilt, reversibility of depressive affects, and the scaffolding of future desires are put to the test as well.

Card 4: This card refers to the instinctual ambivalence in a couple's relationship: It shows a third party (war, rival, another woman, etc.) that in an oedipal context determines the ultimate departure of the male character. Beyond conflict and heartache, latent demands also refer to separation anxiety and abandonment.

Card 5: Faced with this penetrating and staring feminine and maternal image, the guilt associated with sexual curiosity and with primal scene fantasies is revived. This image can also generate more archaic movements associated with the fear of losing the object's love (narcissistic, depressive, or persecutory aspect).

Card 6BM: The mother–son relationship within a sad context is sought here. Demand is organized around a parricidal fantasy and puts to the test the recognition of the incest taboo; it can also revive the terms of the mother–son relationship, closely associated with the fear of losing her love.

Card 7BM: This card refers to the ambivalent relationship with the father: rivalry or libidinal bond. It can also bring about the phantasmic association of separation and remoteness.

Card 8BM: This card refers to an aggressive scene where grown men confront an adolescent, taking active and passive positions. Parricidal desire, guilt, castration anxiety, and ambivalence are mobilized. Destructive valence can revive fantasies of deadly attacks and the concomitant fear of loss.

Card 6GF: This card refers to a heterosexual relationship with a conflict between desire and defense and summons the fantasies of passive seduction. Object loss may underlie the oedipal relationship with the father (difficult renunciation, scaffolding) or the mother (fear of losing her love in rivalry with the father).

Card 7GF: This card seeks the identification movements from girl to mother which authorize – or not – the accession to the position of woman or mother. Conflict can also be coupled with the revitalization of ambivalence in the mother–child relationship.

Card 9GF: In an oedipal context, rivalry between the two women revolves around a third party, a beloved man. However, aggression can be mobilized when attacking the other leads to her disappearance.

Card 10: This card seeks the possibility of associating tenderness and sexual desire. The threat of separation either remains hidden or is clearly expressed.

Card 11: This card induces significant regressive movements, highlighting singular pregenital issues, typically referred to as archaic maternal imago.

Card 13B: This card seeks to evaluate the ability to be alone, by reviving the feelings of loneliness of the child abandoned by the parental couple in a precarious environment.

Card 13MF: The expression of the couple's sexuality and aggression is sought. Like any card likely to seek deadly fantasies, the issue of abandon and destruction can be revived.

Card 19: This card reactivates any archaic depressive and/or persecutory issues.

Card 16: This card refers to how the participant structures internal and external objects and how they organize their relations to them.

The original French version is in F. Brelet-Foulard & C. Chabert, 2003, *Nouveau manuel du TAT: Approche psychanalytique* [New TAT manual: Psychoanalytic approach]. Paris, France: Dunod.

Appendix 3: TAT Scoring Grid

Series A: Rigidity	Series B: Lability	Series C: Conflict evasion	Series E: Primary processes emergence
A1: Reference to external reality A1-1 Description with attachment to details with or without justification of interpretation. A1-2 Precision: temporal-spatial-numerical. A1-3 Social, commonsense, and moral references. A1-4 Literary, cultural references.	*B1: Cathexis of relationship* B1-1 Emphasis on interpersonal relationships, engaging in conversation. B1-2 Introduction of characters not present in the image. B1-3 Expressions of affects.	*CF: Overcathexis of external reality* CF-1 Emphasis on the everyday, the factual, on doing – flattened reference to external reality. CF-2 Circumstantial affects, references to external norms.	*E1: Perceptual distortion* E1-1 Manifest object scotomization. E1-2 Perception of rare or bizarre details with or without arbitrary justification. E1-3 Sensory perceptions – false perceptions. E1-4 Perception of deteriorated objects or of sick, malformed characters.
A2: Cathexis of internal reality A2-1 Recourse to fiction or dream. A2-2 Intellectualization. A2-3 Negation. A2-4 Emphasis on intrapersonal conflicts – alternating between drive expression and defense.	*B2: Dramatization* B2-1 Direct use of expression; exclamations; personal comments – theatrics; story with surprising developments. B2-2 Strong or exaggerated affects. B2-3 Contrasted representations and/or affects – alternating between contradictory wishes. B2-4 Representations of actions associated or not with emotional states of fear, fear of disaster, frenzy, etc.	*CI: Inhibition* CI-1 General tendency to restriction (long latency time and/or important silences in the narration, need to ask questions, tendency to failure; failure). CI-2 Motives of conflicts not specified, banalization, anonymity of characters. CI-3 Anxiety-provoking elements followed or preceded by a pause in speech.	*E2: Massivity of projection* E2-1 Inadequacy of the theme to the stimulus – perseveration – fabulation outside the image – hermetic symbolism. E2-2 Evocation of the bad object, persecutory theme, arbitrary search for intention of the image and/or physiognomies or attitudes – idealization of megalomaniac type. E2-3 Expressions of massive affects and/or representations – blunt expressions connected to a sexual or aggressive theme.
A3: Obsessive-type procedures A3-1 Doubting: verbal precautions, hesitation between different interpretations, rumination. A3-2 Undoing. A3-3 Reaction formation. A3-4 Isolation between representations or between representation and affect – minimized affect.	*B3: Hysterical-type procedures* B3-1 Putting affects to the fore in the service of repression of representations. B3-2 Erotization of relationships, transparent symbolism, narcissistic details with seductive value. B3-3 Lability of identifications.	*CN: Narcissistic cathexis* CN-1 Emphasis on the subjective experience – personal references. CN-2 Narcissistic details – idealization of the self and/or object represent. (+ or – valence). CN-3 Picture-making – title-affect – posture signifying affects.	*E3: Disorganization of identificatory and object landmarks* E3-1 Confusion of identities – clashing of roles.

Series A: Rigidity	Series B: Lability	Series C: Conflict evasion	Series E: Primary processes emergence
		CN-4 Insistence on borders and contours and on sensory qualities. CN-5 Mirror relations. *CL: Instability of borders* CL-1 Porosity of boundaries (between narrator and subject of the story; between inside and outside; etc.). CL-2 Using the percept and/or the sensorial for support. CL-3 Heterogeneity of functioning modes (internal/external; perceptual/symbolic; concrete/abstract...). CL-4 Splitting. *CM: Antidepressive procedures* CM-1 Emphasis on the anaclitic function of the object (+ or – valence) – appeal to the clinician. CM-2 Hyperinstability of identifications. CM-3 Pirouettes, winking, irony, humor.	E3-2 Instability of objects. E3-3 Temporal, spatial or logical causality disorganization. *E4: Impairment of Speech* E4-1 Syntactic disturbances – verbal cracks. E4-2 Indetermination, fuzzy speech. E4-3 Short associations. E4-4 Associations by contiguity, by consonance, nonsense, etc.

Note. Created by the Clinical Psychology, Psychopathology, Psychoanalysis Laboratory (PCPP), Institute of Psychology, Université de Paris, 71 Avenue Edouard Vaillant, 92100 Boulogne-Billancourt, France.

Peer Commentaries

This compendium is a remarkable synthesis by leading figures of the French School of psychoanalytic projective methods in personality assessment. This skillfully edited and magnificently translated book provides the English-speaking world with access to the rich and vibrant tradition of the French School. It pays fitting tribute to the legacy, mentorship, and contributions of Nina Rausch de Traubenberg, Rosine Debray, and Vica Shentoub, and contains scholarly and creative contributions on theory, methods, and clinical applications with rich case studies, as well as topics such as mentalization, representation, somatic disorders, trauma, and bipolar disorders. This volume is essential reading for advanced students, clinicians, and researchers who want to expand their knowledge on the French School of projective techniques and methods. I literally could not put this book down!

Howard D. Lerner, PhD, Assistant Clinical Professor of Psychology, Department of Psychiatry, University of Michigan Faculty, Michigan Psychoanalytic Institute, Ann Arbor, MI, USA

This precious book shines a bright and searching light on the power of the French School's approach in psychoanalytical theory! As a professor, psychoanalyst, and projective tests expert, I highly recommend this must-have book to mental health professionals, clinicians, and test specialists. It highlights key concepts of personality, such as narcissism and self-representation, and also includes valuable psychoanalytic interpretations of projective tests such as the Rorschach and TAT and their use both in a diagnostic setting and as metacognitive tools in clinical psychology and psychopathology research.

Tevfika İkiz, Psychoanalyst, Professor of Psychology at Istanbul University, Turkey, and President of the Turkish Society of the Rorschach and Projective Methods